Vermont
Off the Beaten Path®

"Follow this guide to a sixteen-sided church, a 55-mile road laid out by George Washington, and scores of other odd sights."

> —Martin Rapp, *Travel & Leisure*

"Shaw's Vermont is a worthy entry in the quirky 'Off the Beaten Path' series of travel guides."

> —Brian Burns, *Southbridge Evening News* (Mass.)

Help Us Keep This Guide Up to Date

Every effort has been made by the editors and the publisher to make this guide as accurate and useful as possible. However, many things can change after a guide is published—establishments close, phone numbers change, facilities come under new management, and so forth.

We would love to hear from you concerning your experiences with this guide and how you feel it could be made better and kept up to date. While we may not be able to respond directly to your comments and suggestions, we'll take them to heart, and we'll also make certain to share them with the editors. Please send your comments and suggestions to the following address:

The Globe Pequot Press
Reader Response/Editorial Department
P.O. Box 480
Guilford, CT 06437

Or you may e-mail us at:
editorial@globe-pequot.com

Thanks for your input, and happy travels!

OFF THE BEATEN PATH® SERIES

Vermont

FIFTH EDITION

by Lisa Shaw

Revised by
Barbara Radcliffe Rogers
and Stillman Rogers

The Globe Pequot Press

Guilford, Connecticut

Illustrations by Carole Drong
Text design by Laura Augustine
Maps created by Equator Graphics © The Globe Pequot Press

ISSN 1533-8037
ISBN 0-7627-2428-5

Manufactured in the United States of America
Fifth Edition/First Printing

For Jack Cook (1926–1992)
Who's going to jump into
cellar holes with me now?

—Lisa Shaw

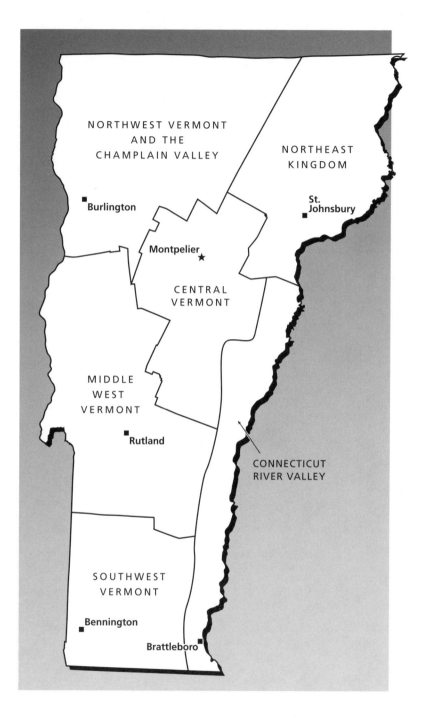

NORTHWEST VERMONT
AND THE
CHAMPLAIN VALLEY

NORTHEAST
KINGDOM

■ Burlington

St.
Johnsbury ■

Montpelier ★

CENTRAL
VERMONT

MIDDLE
WEST
VERMONT

■ Rutland

CONNECTICUT
RIVER VALLEY

SOUTHWEST
VERMONT

■ Bennington

Brattleboro ■

Contents

Introduction

Vermont is as much a state of mind as it is a place. To the rest of the country, the Green Mountain State signifies a back-to-basics attitude that is becoming an all-too-rare commodity in America today. To the people who live in Vermont, this attitude is held on to fiercely, because they are well aware that it is one of the last bastions of peaceful rural life, of our roots. That's why tourism is a leading industry in the state.

This attitude is at the bottom of one of the hottest debates to embroil the state in years: to zone or not to zone. Those Vermonters who are in favor of limiting development and establishing specific criteria about what residents can and can't do with their land want the pastoral Vermont landscape to stay the same for future generations. Those Vermonters who oppose zoning tend to have great pride in their ancestors, that they were able to create this state from nothing more than rocks, thin soil, and sweat. They say, "My family fought for it, I own it, and it's mine to do with as I wish, and don't you trust that I, an eighth-generation Vermonter, know what's best for the state?"

What these factions have in common is a desire to hold on to the old way of life, a view shared by natives and visitors alike. Both sides are afraid to lose what they already have. They're lobbying for the same thing, only they don't realize it.

After all, what can you say about a state that for fourteen years was its own independent republic—from 1777 until 1791—before it reluctantly gave in and became the fourteenth state in the young United States? It is with zeal that some Vermonters today display their Republic of Vermont license plates on the front of their cars.

Just about everything that can be said about Vermont has been said—then quoted ad infinitum. No other state has been so discussed, directed, observed, recorded, and sentimentalized. The myth that hangs over Vermont is far larger than the state itself, but all the words writ and spoken do reflect the inescapable fact that Vermont is unlike any other place. There is a lot here to see, to absorb, and to think about, and if it is the kind of place everyone would like to think of as home, that makes the myth more understandable.

Many people have wanted a part of the state; before it became a republic and was then granted statehood, everyone from New Hampshire to Massachusetts and New York State fought over the largely uninhabitable land that even back then contained a special but hard-to-pinpoint aura.

Because Vermont relies so heavily on tourism these days, even in truly isolated pockets of the state it's difficult to find attractions that are specifically geared toward locals, unless you count feed and grain stores.

There's a saying in Vermont that goes, "You're not considered a native until your family has lived here for eight generations." Given the great exodus from the state during several periods in its 200-year history, those eighth-generationers are not easy to find. Many of Vermont's hill towns lost half their populations during the great westward expansion. Even now some Vermont towns have smaller populations than they did in 1840. In 1850, 154 towns in the state had more than 1,000 people; by 1960, that figure had fallen to 94.

Others more benignly adapt the eight-generation rule to, "You're considered a Vermonter if you've lived here for twenty years"—mostly said by newcomers, or "flatlanders," as they're called up here. Vermonters regard visitors with a half-squinted eye: On the one hand, they realize the economic value tourism brings to the state; on the other hand, some of them wish the state could return to its pre–Revolutionary War days, when there were no such things as electricity and running water. In fact, a large number of Vermonters do indeed live this way, and they can't understand why anyone would want to live in a city.

But many visitors can't imagine what it would be like to live in an area where there's no Chinese takeout right around the corner, though in some areas, like Burlington, Brattleboro, and Montpelier, it's common-place to live among such diversity.

Vermont, though, is still Vermont, a definition that takes into consideration all development and natural resources of present and past, from ski areas to wildlife management areas, from malls to historic monuments. If a trip to the Green Mountain State allows the visitor to appreciate his or her own heritage, as well as that of the state's sights and attractions, then it is a trip worth taking.

Basic Travel Information

Visitors come to Vermont throughout the year; however, some months and seasons are more beautiful—and thus more crowded—than others. Foliage season—usually the last two weeks of September and the first two weeks of October—is Vermont at its best and most crowded. Rooms at inns and hotels, despite sharply increased "foliage rates," typically fill up six months in advance, so it's best to make reservations early.

The last two weeks of October in Vermont are generally just as gorgeous. And while many places and shops will have closed up for the season, there are still lots of attractions to explore. You'll find no traffic; unhurried, friendly service; and some of the maples and oak trees still radiant with their color. Best of all, the weather is perfect: sunny, warm Indian summer days interspersed with cool, crisp nights accompanied by the smell of woodsmoke.

In summer Vermont is lush, green, and fragrant. During the winter, the Presidents' Day holiday usually finds the ski areas throughout the state at their busiest; try visiting the week after instead. Some of the roads that are always closed in winter and spring are marked on good road maps, and others are closed temporarily if they're simply impassable. In spring many tourist-oriented businesses shut down from March through mid-April, during the notorious "mud season" and before the first buds appear on the trees; small bridges can be closed during the thaw due to high water.

Vermonters are Yankee to the core, and they simply can't see any reason to waste all those condo and hotel rooms, restaurants, shops, and recreation facilities at the foot of their ski slopes after the snow melts. Nearly all have become year-round recreation resorts, with guests paddling happily in the ponds that provide snowmaking water, riding the lifts for mountaintop views or hiking trail access, and teeing off where cross-country skiers glide in the winter. Everyone wins, especially visitors looking for a base that includes activities for days when they don't feel like touring the countryside. Just as in winter, these resort complexes offer package deals. They may include golf, guided hikes, nature programs, meals, day camp, and water sports.

Seasonal attractions in small towns throughout Vermont include sugar-on-snow festivals in spring and Fourth of July celebrations and parades in summer. Winter features ski races and Christmas fairs and bazaars. By the way, sugar-on-snow, if you've never tried it, is a natural type of snow cone. Paper cups are heaped with snow and drizzled with freshly made maple syrup, usually the first of the season. The tradition is to follow a mouthful of sugar-on-snow with a big bite of a sour pickle to balance the sticky sweetness.

Although this book will lead you to a number of lodgings in a variety of price ranges and styles, if you are traveling from afar and need to make a number of reservations, or if you find that many of the smaller places we've suggested are filled, there is a service you should know about. **DestINNations New England** can make your reservations for a long

Reservations at State Parks

Reservations for camping can be made any time after January 2 of the same year. Returning campers tie up their favorite sites as early as possible. The parks generally open about May 1. Minimum stays for park reservations vary from two to four days.

For general information on the parks call (800) VERMONT, or contact Vermont State Parks at 103 South Main Street, Waterbury 05671-0601; www.vtstateparks.com. Toll-free preseason registrations can be

made from January 2 to mid-May, 9:00 A.M. to 4:00 P.M. weekdays (except holidays) by calling (800) 299–3071 (southeast parks); (800) 658–1622 (southwest parks); (800) 252–2363 (northwest parks), or (800) 658–6934 (northeast parks).

For reservations after mid-May, call the park where you want to stay. A season pass car sticker costs $75, good for frequent park goers, allowing up to eight people to use park facilities on each visit. Call (800) 241–3655 or write to the above address.

weekend in Vermont or for a trip of several weeks covering all six New England states and help you plan an itinerary as well. Call them at (800) 333–4667, or see their Web site at www.destinnation.com. Their detailed brochure shows all the inns and B&Bs they represent, with complete descriptions.

Tourist Information

Ask for a copy of the *Vermont Traveler's Guidebook* and the *Vermont Winter Guide,* as well as a state highway map, available free from The Vermont Chamber of Commerce, P.O. Box 37, Montpelier 05601; (802) 223–3443; www.vtchamber.com. For more information, contact the Vermont Department of Tourism and Marketing, 6 Baldwin Street, Montpelier 05633; (802) 828–3233. The Web site and toll-free number are pretty easy to remember: www.1-800-vermont.com. Clever, these Vermonters. Welcome centers are located on interstate highways 91 (Massachusetts border), 89 (Canadian border), and 93 (New Hampshire border), and on Vermont 4-A at the New York border, with a complete selection of brochures for each area.

The Vermont Crafts Council, P.O. Box 938, Montpelier 05601; (802) 223–3380; www.vermontcrafts.com, has a booklet listing craft shops, events, and "open studio" tours. Ski information is available from the state tourist office and from Vermont Ski Areas Association, P.O. Box 368, Montpelier 05601; (802) 223–2439; www.skivermont.com. To learn about Vermont-made products of all kinds, from food to crafts, visit www.marketvermont.com.

Northwest Vermont and the Champlain Valley

The northwest corner of the Green Mountain State is set apart by its geography and relative isolation. Even though the trek north logically should have meant that the area would be settled later than its southern counterparts, access to Lake Champlain as a major thoroughfare and trade route allowed settlement to occur relatively early in the state's history. Burlington, for instance, was chartered in 1763, and Swanton, the northernmost town on the lake, was chartered that same year. Settlement, whether by one family or most of the population of a town from Connecticut or Massachusetts, could take longer, but the settlement of towns and villages on Vermont's northwestern shore took place about the same time as that of towns on the state's southwestern border.

Due to its high concentration of businesses—one of IBM's satellite offices is located here—the population is also among the richest in the state. Of the state's top fifteen towns with the highest per capita income, eleven are located in the Champlain Valley.

Today northwest Vermont and the Champlain Valley hold the greatest density of population in the state, partly because of the region's diversity and greater number of attractions and partly because of the warmer climate there, due to the meteorological influences of Lake Champlain. Growing seasons are longer, and temperatures during summer are warmer than in other parts of the state.

Burlington

Burlington, a.k.a the Queen City and the state's most populous town, is just about as cosmopolitan as it gets in Vermont, so much so, in fact, that people in other parts of the state sometimes say that Burlington is not part of Vermont. With five colleges in the area and frontage on

Northwest Vermont
and the Champlain Valley

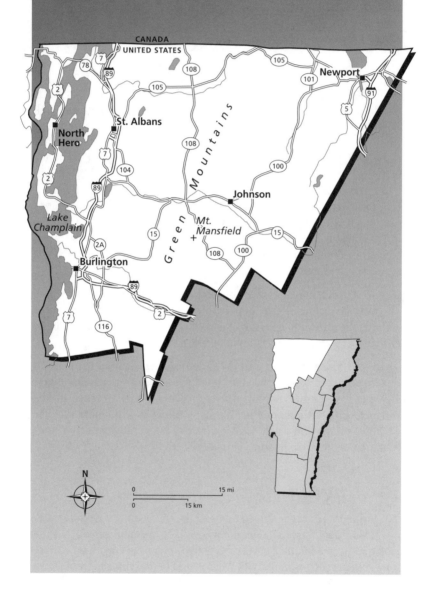

NORTHWEST VERMONT AND THE CHAMPLAIN VALLEY

AUTHORS' TOP HIGHLIGHTS

Lake Champlain
Maritime Museum

Montgomery County's
covered bridges

Royal Lipizzan Stallions

Sterling Falls Gorge

Smugglers Notch

Lake Champlain—not to mention a population of close to 40,000 in Burlington alone—the Champlain Valley is where many rural Vermonters in search of a dose of urban activity go before they head back to the countryside.

Burlington is a great city to walk around in. It's small enough for slow walkers to manage yet offers plenty of sights and shops and eateries so that the adventurous need not get bored. From the waterfront, walk a few blocks up the hill on Main Street and visit **Mirabelle's,** a bright, airy cafe with chintz tablecloths and seat covers, and food and drink to match, à la afternoon tea. At least ten different kinds of teas are available, and they come in pots both large and small. Sandwiches, scones, pastries, croissants, and miniature walnut pastries called ruggies—after the pastry rugelach—are there to go with the tea.

Mirabelle's has an unusual drink, at least for Vermont: hot white cocoa. White cocoa powder stirred into steamed milk tastes like a white chocolate Easter bunny. Choose from a great selection of rich cakes and tarts, chocolate truffle cake, and create-your-own deli sandwiches on sourdough or rye bread or a baguette. Mirabelle's also offers its version of a ploughman's lunch: a variety of cheeses, breads, salads, fruit, and dessert for $5.95. It's perfect for a picnic.

Mirabelle's, 198 Main Street, Burlington 05401; (802) 658–3074, is open from 7:00 A.M. to 6:00 P.M. Monday through Friday and from 8:00 A.M. to 6:00 P.M. on Saturday.

Chocaholics may want to skip lunch entirely and visit **Lake Champlain Chocolates,** where more than one hundred varieties of chocolate truffles await them. Lake Champlain Chocolates, 750 Pine Street, Burlington 05401; (802) 864–1807 or (800) 465–5909; www.lakechamplainchocolate.com, is open Monday through Saturday from 9:30 A.M. to 6:00 P.M. and Sunday from noon until 5:00 P.M. Cheese lovers will want to head for **Cheese Outlet Fresh Market** for the wide variety of cheese, much of which is made in Vermont. In fact, this is a good place to fit up a picnic, drawing from the good selection of wines, over eighty beers, several kinds of olives, pâtés, fruit, and deli items. It's open Monday through Saturday from 8:00 A.M. to 7:00 P.M. and Sunday from 10:00 A.M. to 5:00 P.M.; 400 Pine Street, Burlington 05401; (802) 863–3968 or (800) 447–1205; www.cheeseoutlet.com.

The **Flynn Theatre** in Burlington is a cultural institution that brings arts of all kinds to Vermonters. All forms of performance art—ballet, musicals, top vocal performers—come to the Flynn, which averages at least three major performances a month. Flynn performances have included jazz and Latin bands and productions by national touring companies of *Gypsy* and *Joseph and the Amazing Technicolor Dreamcoat.*

Call the box office at (802) 86–Flynn for a schedule of upcoming acts. The Flynn is at 153 Main Street, Burlington 05401; (802) 863–5966; www.flynntheatre.com.

To see an expert glass craftsman at work, visit the downstairs workshop at ***Church & Maple Glass Studio.*** The entrance to the studio is off Maple Street, down the driveway and through an unmarked door on the right. There you walk directly into the workshop, where you can sit on a comfortable sofa and watch Mike, the principal glassblower, create beautiful—and useful—bowls, plates, glasses, vases, pitchers, Christmas ornaments, and other tableware and art glass. Our two favorite lines are Emerald Sea, a marbley mix of deep blues and greens, and Ferris Wheel, a beautiful spiral pattern in contrasting monochrome shades. Confetti designs include a cheerful variety created by fusing recycled pieces, sometimes capturing them in clear glass, forming drinking glasses and elegant pitchers.

At the far corner of the workshop is a stunning display of seconds, along with thirds and firsts. Seconds begin with sturdy tumblers in the Confetti design, or you may find a large pedestal cake plate for upwards of $100. Mike is always experimenting with new designs, so you never know what exciting projects he will be in the middle of when you arrive. On the drawing boards are jewelry items created in a combination of glass and metal. Although there will be glass pieces in progress on most days, occasionally the studio will be busy with other things, so it is a good idea to call ahead if you have your heart set on watching works in progress.

Upstairs is the spacious ***Church & Maple Gallery,*** where first quality art glass from the studio downstairs is shown with other art. Graphics, paintings, and sculpture are by Vermont artists, with an occasional show bringing in New York artists. Plans are afoot to add dance and performance events, making this an arts center. Be sure to look in the rest room at the unusual fused glass vanity top. The address for both the gallery and studio is 225 Church Street, Burlington 05401; (802) 863–3880, www.churchandmaple.com. The studio is open Monday through Saturday 9:00 A.M. to 5:00 P.M. and the gallery is open the same days from noon to 6:00 P.M.

While you are at the studio, continue to the end of the driveway to see the work of Bill Heise at **Heise Sculpture.** Even if Bill is not there, you can see some of his work, rain or shine, displayed outdoors in front of his shop. It's the ultimate in recycling metal parts, and you are likely to be greeted by a knight in armor wielding a scythe blade and defending himself with the lid of a cast-iron Dutch oven. You may recognize his epaulets as the legs from a Glenwood range and his delicately drooping mustache as a former pitchfork. Bill's sly sense of humor can transform a tractor seat into the tail of a duck or a keg into a moose body. Heise Sculpture is at 162½ Maple Street, Burlington 05401; (802) 862–8454.

It's hard NOT to hear about the **Five Spice Cafe,** which has become a local institution since Jerry and Ginger opened it nearly two decades ago. Jerry tells us that about one-third of the sales are of the vegetarian dishes he is well-known for, but the menu has plenty of other options. The focus is pan-Asian, and the Five Spice was serving Thai dishes long before Thai restaurants became part of the Vermont landscape. Indonesian hot sauce spices up chicken wings, trout is smoked in a wok, and a stir-fried chicken dish is from northern Burma. Hunan, Szechuan, and Indian influences flavor other dishes. Only the dessert menu of over-rich European-style cakes jars with the rest of the dining experience.

Open for lunch and dinner seven days a week, Five Spice Cafe is at 175 Church Street, Burlington 05401; (802) 864–4045. On Sundays from 11:00 A.M. until 2:00 P.M., they serve traditional dim sum, with a selection of about twenty varieties. You can sample some of these on weekdays by ordering the dim sum sampler at either lunch or dinner. The selection in the sampler changes and might include a delicious dumpling filled with "mock duck," one of the cafe's signatures. Most entrees on the "lunch specials" menu run $9.00 to $10.00, with dinner special entrees at $14.00 (the vegan selection) to $19.00. The last time we were there, a shared entree, a shared dessert, and two cups of tea brought the lunch bill, with tip, to an even $25, so this is not a budget restaurant. But the food is very well prepared, creative, and uses the freshest local ingredients. Reservations are a good idea, especially for the dim sum on Sunday.

Many restaurants and stores have converged on the area to cater to the increasing numbers of college students and savvy transplants who arrived here during the 1980s demanding a variety of ethnic cuisines and culture. Five Spice Cafe is one; the *India House* restaurant is another.

India House is an attractive restaurant on a busy corner near the University of Vermont Medical Center, about a fifteen-minute walk up Main Street from downtown. Tapestries adorn the walls, and painted scenes lie under the glass on each table. Appetizers include the vegetable dumplings called samosas with two sauces; coconut and mulligatawny soup; and a vegetarian platter—all accompanied by puffed bread and rice with four different sauces: yogurt and cucumber, chickpea, lentil, and pea.

Many people believe that a curry is a curry is a curry. Not so at India House, where eight different lamb curry dishes, twelve chicken curries, fourteen vegetable curries, and eight seafood curries are served. India House mixes the spices for its curries fresh every day, combines them in different ways for each dish, and also varies them to different degrees of mild, medium, hot, and extra hot. In fact, this personal attention toward the exact amount of spice for each dish wakes up the taste buds without overpowering them.

The India House is at 207 Colchester Avenue, Burlington 05401; (802) 862–7800. Open Tuesday through Sunday from 11:30 A.M. to 2:30 P.M. for lunch and from 5:30 to 9:30 P.M. for dinner, and until 10:00 P.M. on Friday and Saturday. The Sunday brunch at India House, from noon to 3:00 P.M., is famous in Burlington.

Lest you think that the only choices for dinner are Asian, we should mention *Trattoria Delia,* an almost subterranean enclave of Mediterranean dining. Skip lunch if you plan to order both a *primi* and a *secondi,* since the pasta course is far from scanty. You'll find choices you don't see elsewhere: *oricchiette* with *fricone*—an Apulian fried tomato sauce with plenty of garlic—or *tagliatelle* tossed with roasted duck and rosemary. *Secondi,* priced from $13 to $22, may include wild boar in Barolo wine with polenta, slow-roasted marinated rabbit, or osso buco (braised veal shanks) over saffron risotto. Breads and pastas are made in-house, and the menu changes seasonally. Two days in advance is not too early to call for reservations here on weekends, but if you can't get a table, they also offer a take-out menu. Trattoria Delia, open every day from 5:00 to 10:00 P.M., is at 152 St. Paul Street (just off City Hall Park), Burlington 05401; (802) 864-5253.

Upstairs at the corner of Cherry and Winooski Streets, **Penny Cluse Cafe** serves breakfast and lunch daily, with dinners on weekends. Pancakes are always on the menu, along with other favorites to start the day, often with a southwestern touch to the side dishes. The cafe is at 169 Cherry Street, Burlington 05401; (802) 651-8834.

To see more of Lake Champlain, take a cruise on the *Ethan Allen II,* perhaps combining it with lunch or dinner. Every day in the summer, cruises leave at 10:00 A.M., noon, and 2:00 and 4:00 P.M., lasting about an hour and a half. In addition to the regular dinner cruises, there's the Monday Feast Afloat Dinner Cruises; the $25.95 buffet features a "Luau on the Lake" with Chicken Hawaian, roast beef and pineapple cake. Cruises run from 6:30 to 9:30 P.M., so you get to enjoy the sunset over water. Tuesdays are Lobstah-on-the-Lake clambake days, which include lobster, chowder, steamers, and corn on the cob for about $37. The *Ethan Allen II* leaves from the Burlington Boathouse on College Street. Reservations are essential; (802) 862-8300.

On the lakefront at the end of College Street, look for Vermont's only **All-America Display Garden,** where you'll find the brightest and the best of the new flowering ornamental plant varieties, blooming in profusion all summer.

Shelburne, the next town south of South Burlington, was chartered and settled early. The town charter was granted in 1763, and Shelburne was settled five years later by two German men who had been loggers in Canada. Reportedly, they were killed by soldiers sent from Montreal, supposedly to protect them from Indian attacks, but this story has never been substantiated. Five years after this initial settlement, two of Shelburne's earliest residents were killed by Indians and Tories, acting together to cut down the fledgling village. The entire settlement would have been destroyed, except that some of the settlers put out the fires in the burning dwellings with a stash of home-brewed beer.

At *Vermont Teddy Bear Company,* you can pick out your own teddy bear, stuff it just the way you want it, and someone will sew it up for you. There are bears with just about every personality and theme. The showrooms, open Monday to Saturday from 10:00 A.M. to 6:00 P.M., Sunday from 10:00 A.M. to 5:00 P.M., are on Route 7 in Shelburne 05482; (802) 985– 3001; www.VermontTeddyBear.com.

Shed Sales is like a huge household sale running through a half dozen rooms. The owners buy the contents of entire houses and bring them here for sale, the ultimate recycling. This home of miscellany is 3 miles south of Burlington on Route 7 at 3614 Shelburne Road, Shelburne 05482. It's usually open Monday to Friday from 10:00 A.M. to 4:00 P.M. in the summer and 10:00 A.M. to 4:00 P.M. in the winter. Saturdays are "catch us if you can," so before you make a special trip, call (802) 985–8511 to be sure it's open.

The next town south on Route 7 is Charlotte, pronounced with the accent on the second syllable. Charlotte is a quiet town that belies its close proximity to the bustling urban center of Burlington, a fifteen-minute drive away.

It's worth your while to find your way to *Authentica African Imports* in Charlotte. Follow the signs to the New York State ferry and turn right at the country store in Charlotte. Lydia Clemmons's unusual shop is three-quarters of a mile up on the left. As you drive to her shop, keep looking west; the view of New York State is breathtaking.

Lydia has been operating Authentica African Imports for many years, and every week she receives new pieces of art, clothing, and jewelry from all over Africa. Check out the five-pound ankle bracelets from Zanzibar. Drums, tapestries, pottery, and handwoven scarves from Ghana are crammed into two rooms of Lydia's old Vermont farmhouse, while a woodstove heats the room. The mixture of African items and old-style New England decor works well. Some of the more exotic items include Masai spears and a Yoruba ceremonial drum. Lydia also offers for sale unusual figurines that tell about daily life in Owo and are carved from 2- to 4-inch thorns that grow on egun and ata trees.

For information and a catalog, write to Lydia Clemmons, Authentica African Imports, Greenbush Road, Charlotte 05445; (802) 425–3137. Clemmons is in the shop most days in the afternoon, but several times a year she goes on buying trips to Africa, so be sure to call ahead.

Ferrisburg, on Route 7, is home to **Dakin Farm,** a farmstead that was settled in 1792. Sam Cutting, president of Dakin Farm, marvels that his own family has assumed the heritage of the farm for nearly forty years, with the third generation of Cuttings learning what it's like to grow up on a farm.

Not everyone is so lucky, of course, so if you make a stop at Dakin Farm, you can at least get a taste of what farm life is like. You can watch the family and employees smoking meats, sugaring in March, and waxing cheese to mail it to people all over the country.

Even though Dakin Farm has a large mail-order operation, as well as a retail store in the Champlain Mill farther north in Winooski, it still remains truly a family business.

Dakin Farm, R.R. 1, Box 1775, Ferrisburg 05456; (802) 425–3971.

You might not notice it if you're heading south on Route 7, but you can't miss **The Cottage Garden** as you drive north in the spring, summer, or fall. The entire roadside is suddenly a bright paint-splash of color, with a profusion of muskmallows, delphinium, and poppies in every shade from pale pink to bright orange. The gardens—and more hidden behind the house—are cutting gardens, and you can buy bouquets of fresh flowers or dried flower arrangements displayed in the tiny shop. If you love to arrange flowers or if you just want an armful to brighten your day, you'll find them here. Gardener Annie Agan welcomes you to wander through her gardens Tuesday to Sunday between 9:00 A.M. and 5:00 P.M.; (802) 425–3192.

While you're in Ferrisburg, look for the **Rokeby Homestead** on your left. Rokeby holds twin distinctions: It served as the home of Vermont's most illustrious writer from the nineteenth century, Rowland Robinson, and it was a major stop on the Underground Railroad. Robinson was an accomplished writer and artist who conveyed the Vermont of the 1800s through his writing and pictures.

Many nineteenth-century houses in Vermont are frequently described as having been Underground Railroad stations—most often by zealous real estate agents who want to see a root cellar or hidden cubby space in the basement as having a special historical significance. Usually, however, these claims cannot be proved, since very little written evidence was kept by the owners of such homes, for fear of prosecution.

Rokeby, though, is one house where ample evidence was kept; after all, a writer lived there. The house, which dates from before 1784, contains eight rooms of clothing, furniture, and other artifacts from Robinson's family.

The homestead is open to the public Thursday to Sunday from May through October; tours are conducted at 11:00 A.M. and 2:00 P.M.; admission is $4.00 for adults, $3.00 for seniors and students, and $1.00 for children under twelve. The Rokeby Homestead, Route 7, Ferrisburg 05456; (802) 877-3406.

The town of Vergennes is the third oldest city in the country and, at 1,152 acres, the smallest; its boundaries form a perfect square. Vergennes is also a nautical town, as the Otter Creek cuts through the town, working its way northwest into Lake Champlain.

Lake Champlain Maritime Museum in Vergennes has, in addition to

Make Way for the Champ

*S*amuel de Champlain, discoverer of the lake named for him, was a down-to-earth man who reported things in his diary in a straightforward way. In July 1609, he reported a serpentine creature about 20 feet long, with a horselike head and about as big around as a barrel. As settlers began to establish farms around the lake, occasional other sightings were reported—one in 1819 in the Plattsburg Republican noted that several settlers were frightened by the appearance of a large creature close to Port Henry, New York—and other newspaper accounts have echoed similar descriptions. The largest group ever to report seeing "Champ," as followers of the phenomenon have named it, were on a sight-seeing excursion boat when the creature surfaced.

The similarities to Nessie, the legendary monster of Scotland's Loch Ness, are remarkable, which has led interested scientists to note the similarities in the bodies of water: each large, deep, and cut off from a former connection to the sea. The chances of your seeing this shy beast, if indeed it exists, are pretty slim (unless you've brought along a lot of Long Trail Ale on your lakeside picnic), but you can bone up on the history, scientific investigation, and sightings at the nature center at Button Bay State Park, or in the Lake Champlain Maritime Museum.

Lake Champlain Maritime Museum, Vergennes

traditional museum displays that relate Benedict Arnold's history with the lake and the role Champlain played in a historic battle during the American Revolution, an exact working replica of the 54-foot, square-rigged gunboat *Philadelphia,* which is so real it seems as if it's straight out of the Revolutionary War.

Exhibits are housed in six buildings in a roomy setting on the shore of Lake Champlain; many of the boats you'll see were recovered from its waters. There's a 16-foot rowboat from the mid-1800s, a 1929 speedboat, and the logging boat used in filming the movie *Where the Rivers Flow North.* Blacksmiths and shipbuilders demonstrate their skills, and exhibits show in detail shipwrecks that ended the careers of many vessels in the lake's early days.

Those days are re-created in special events as the museum hosts re-enactors representing the French, English, and Native Americans who lived and traded around the lake. A Kids' Maritime Festival in mid-June includes model boat building and a chance to paddle a kayak. You can rent small boats—sailboats, rowboats, canoes, and kayaks—by the hour or by the day. Admission is $10.00 for adults and $5.00 for ages five through seventeen. AAA members get a $1.00 discount. The museum is open from early May through mid-October, daily from 10:00 A.M. to 5:00 P.M. Follow Basin Harbor Road from the center of town, just south of the bridge. Lake Champlain Maritime Museum, Basin Harbor Road, Vergennes 05491; (802) 475–2022.

After exploring the museum, you'll be ready for lunch or dinner, and you're in the right place. South of town on Route 7 is **Roland's Place** (802–453–6309), which you can learn more about in the Middle West Vermont chapter. It's a little nearer to Middlebury but is such a good restaurant and so close to Vergennes, you need at least to know its name here.

Shortly past the turnoff to Basin Harbor on Route 22A, you'll see the elegant **Strong House Inn** on the right. The completely restored Federal mansion is the home of Mary Bargiel and her husband, Hugh, who live there and who greet each guest. It's their personal approach and involvement that puts the capital *H* in *Hospitality* here, as well as their knack for creating beautiful yet not formidable rooms filled with the little details that make your stay memorable—thick terry robes in each of the private baths match the towels. Each room is different—in size, shape, and style—ranging from frilly Victorian to the Vermont Room, a bright, spacious room overlooking the Adirondacks, furnished in pale pine wood and shades of blue. In the winter Mary serves "proper" teas one Sunday afternoon each month between noon and 4:00 P.M., for $18 and by

Other Cycling Options

*V*BT offers a trip along the Connecticut River Valley from Woodstock to Windsor, Chester, Grafton, and Saxtons River, then back up through Springfield, with a side trip across the river into New Hampshire to the home of sculptor Augustus Saint-Gaudens (from $975 to $1,075). Yet another biking option is the Mad River tour, which starts in Waitsfield and wanders south along the Mad River, then south to Ludlow, before heading north through Woodstock, Bethel, Strafford, Tunbridge, Randolph, and Roxbury. The Woodstock-Windsor trip is rated easy to moderate (daily rides from 25 to 40 miles, with options), and the Mad River trip is rated moderate (daily mileage from 25). Contact VBT at P.O. Box 711, Bristol 05443–0711, (800) 245–3868, www.vbt.com.

reservation (and you'd better reserve early). For all the upscale class of Strong House, it never loses its warmth.

The property is planted in gardens that you can enjoy from the gazebo or tables on the terrace. Cross-country, snowshoe, and walking trails leave from the backyard, and for winter fun a sledding hill (with sleds) is on the property, along with a skating rink. If you don't feel like going out to dinner after a day's skiing, Mary can order an elegant basket dinner for you from Roland's Place, and you can enjoy it in your room on fine china and linens. Rooms and suites range from $75 to $275, with an additional $20 in foliage season. Strong House Inn, 82 West Main Street, Vergennes 05491; (802) 877–3337; www.stronghouseinn.com

Vermont Bicycle Tours (VBT) pedals clients all over the globe, so it's not surprising to find a trip right at home in Vermont. Their trips are typically six-day, five-night tours, and a recent example is one of the Champlain Valley, touching Lake Champlain at Basin Harbor, Vergennes, and the Fort Ticonderoga end. Along the way, clients pass through beautiful rolling farmland on the western side of the Appalachians, stopping at a Morgan horse farm. In addition to biking, there is an opportunity to kayak on Lake Champlain in an area where Revolutionary War–era gunboats fought it out. The rates (which are about $1,200 depending on the season) include lodging, five breakfasts and dinners, and three lunches, as well as use of a VBT bike, helmets, maps, trip leaders, and a support vehicle for those who wither along the way. The terrain is rated moderate to easy, with expected mileage from 20 to 30 miles per day; optional routes available for longer mileage. For more information: P. O. Box 711, Bristol, VT 05443-0711; (800) 245– 3868; www.vbt.com.

The Eastern "Suburbs"

You'll want to travel on Williston Road, which runs parallel to I–89 between the University of Vermont campus, where it's called Main Street, to Taft's Corner, 3 miles south of Essex Junction. It passes through South Burlington, which is a geographical misnomer, since the town lies due east of Burlington. Here you will find three excuses to stop, all within sight of one another.

Fine cheese is expensive, but you can find the good stuff and skip the high prices at *Cheese Traders.* You never know what specials you'll find here, from Kenya AA coffee at half the regular price to creamy chocolate truffles, but you can depend on fine cheeses at prices you won't see elsewhere. Last time we were there, we found French Camembert for $2.00

a pound. We had to buy a three-pound wheel, but at that price, we could afford to share it with friends and still come out way ahead. Look in the big walk-in cheese cooler at the back of the shop for bags of cheese crumbles, which are bite-sized pieces from the major Vermont cheese makers—Grafton, Cabot, and others, similarly priced. More cheeses in smaller cuts are downstairs in the well-stocked wine outlet.

Shelves are stocked with a number of Vermont-made products, along with imports, many at serious discounts. Hot-sauce aficionados should look for the bright red shelf in the middle of the store, where dozens of brands, including the locally made "Vermont Hots," stand row on row. Steve, the owner, tells us that there are over 30,000 producers of hot sauce in the United States—a figure that makes even his impressive collection seem small. Cheese Traders is open Monday through Saturday from 10:00 A.M. to 7:00 P.M.. It's at 1186 Williston Road, South Burlington 05403; (802) 863–0143.

Almost next door to Cheese Traders is a salesroom for **Snowflake Chocolates,** whose "factory" is in nearby Jericho (see page 25). While you can't watch chocolates being made here, the selection is good and they are just as delicious as they are in Jericho. The shop is at 1174 Williston Road, South Burlington 05403; (802) 863–8306.

Food snobs can skip this, but those who long for really good fries, and maybe a corn dog or hamburger, should head a few yards east to the shiny diner facade of **Al's French Fries.** Lines are long at lunchtime, especially on weekends, and you may have trouble finding a spot in the parking lot, so Al's is clearly not undiscovered. A pint of fries will set you back less than $2.00, and you can take them out or munch them at one of the red upholstered booths. Al's is at 1251 Williston Road, South Burlington 05403; (802) 865–3663. Hours are 10:30 A.M. on Monday, until 11:00 P.M. Tuesday through Thursday, and until midnight on Friday and Saturday. On Sunday Al's is open 11:00 A.M. to 10:00 P.M.

The **Inn at Essex** has all the warmth of a vintage country inn, without the squeaky floorboards and thin walls. Rooms are spacious and elegantly decorated, with quality furniture and nice touches, such as a woven lap robe on the rocking chair. Suites have fully equipped kitchens (complete with an apron), dining areas, and comfortable sitting rooms. Whirlpool tubs are roomy enough to share. The bakery provides excellent scones, croissants, and occasionally *pain au chocolat* for breakfast. The inn practices recycling and other earth-friendly and environmentally aware programs. A well-stocked library off the lobby provides travelers with books to curl up with, and the lobby bake shop is ready with cookies, tarts, or chocolate truffles. The inn is at 70 Essex Way, Essex Junction 05452, off Route 15 east of Burlington; (802) 878–1100, www.innatessex.com.

It is rare that you can stay at an inn where there are more chefs than guests, but that's the case at the Inn at Essex, which is also the Burlington campus of the New England Culinary Institute (NECI). Along with the bakery goods sold in the shop, the students and their instructor chefs create all the dishes for both the *Tavern Restaurant,* a casual upscale pub, and the inn's more formal *Butler's.*

The Tavern menu features lighter foods to accompany the wide choice of local brews, as well as sturdier dinner entrees. We have never tasted a better seafood soup—really a stew—than the bouillabaisselike bowlful set before us there. Each type of fish and shellfish—silken scallops, tender juicy shrimp, plump mussels, and delicate whitefish and salmon filets among them—was added to the savory saffron and leek broth at exactly the right moment to cook each to its point of perfection.

Guests enter Butler's by walking past the evening's dessert selections, a mouthwatering start to a meal. Locally grown and produced ingredients are the hallmark of Butler's, and we especially liked finding less common vegetables on the menu, such as fennel. Whatever you choose for an entree, begin with the pâté and rillettes sampler plate. Forget, for a moment, both your waistline and your cholesterol level to savor these delicately flavored morsels. Hope that someone at your table orders the quail stuffed with wild mushrooms, served with an onion tarte Tatin, so you can sample that, too.

Each course gets full attention, even the salads, which often include one pairing green and red apples with curly endive and Vermont blue cheese. Entrees, like the appetizers, change every day, but you are likely to find a duck specialty, perhaps pan-seared with pistachios, coconut, and currants. Butler's is open daily for three meals, with dinner beginning at 6:00 P.M. Both restaurants are in the central building of the inn; reserve for Butler's at (802) 764–1413, the Tavern at (802) 764–1489. For a preview of current menus at either, visit www.necidining.com.

Towns that lie not too far away from the main center of Burlington, such as Winooski and Essex Junction, are like other "suburban" outposts anywhere in the country. Artists and other creative types, as well as families with children who want a quiet life yet crave easy access to the city, live in places like *Richmond.* Providing evidence are a bustling downtown area, a few convenience stores and historical monuments, and an "alternative" restaurant that caters to locals in Volvos and on motorcycles alike.

If the architecture in the downtown district seems newer than that in the rest of Vermont, it's for good reason: In 1908 a fire raged out of control and burned down the entire business section of the town.

Our Daily Bread is a bakery/cafe whose aromas you can smell throughout the town all day long. The main dining room has only six tables, but it's a local gathering place, and the bulletin board in the hall as you first walk in serves as the town crier of Richmond. Posted notices offer trucks for sale, holistic counseling, housemate situations, painting services, and fairs, among other things.

The food inside is hearty and tasty; you can carry out or eat in. Either way, place your order at one of the two windows for black bean chili, tuna melts, tofu sandwiches, calzones, salads, or cookies. What at first looks like kids' drawings hung throughout the dining room turns out to be highly politicized artwork by adults.

The chocolate Vienna walnut bars are fudgy and rich—no carob here—and the calzones don't skimp on the fillings of mozzarella, ricotta, tomatoes, and mushrooms inside a flaky whole wheat crust. If you need to feel virtuous on the way out, there are always the thirty-pound bags of granola that line the hall, ready to be hauled away.

The bakery and cafe are open from 6:00 A.M. to 6:00 P.M. daily, year-round and for dinner until 9:00 P.M. on weekends. Our Daily Bread, Bridge Street, Richmond 05477; (802) 434–3148.

Richmond is also home to the **Old Round Church,** one of the most unusual buildings in the state. It's not exactly round—it has sixteen sides—but it holds the distinction of being the first community church in the country, since its construction in 1813 was the joint effort of five separate denominations: Methodist, Congregationalist, Universalist, Baptist, and Christian. In fact, it's rumored that sixteen men each built one side of the church, and the seventeenth built the belfry.

The congregations initially held joint services at the church, but they eventually broke away, and the church became the town hall. Henry Ford once tried to buy the Old Round Church so that he could bring it back to Dearborn with him, but the town turned thumbs down.

Today the church is a historical site, and regular tours are offered in summer and during foliage season. For more information, write to the Old Round Church, Bridge Street, Richmond 05477, or call (802) 434–2556.

Old Round Church, Richmond

South of Richmond is the village of Huntington. Huntington abuts a parcel of land called **Buels Gore,** most of which is taken up by Camel's Hump State Forest. Buels Gore is one of those pieces of land that were left over when surveyors tried to reconcile the old original land grants—laid out on flat maps—with the irregular contours of the land itself. It was named for Major Elias Buel, who back in 1780 wanted to start his own town of Montzoar in the gore, which totals 3,520 acres. He purchased all the existing land titles to the gore but neglected to have them recorded or to pay the taxes on them. To pay the taxes, the lands were subsequently sold for a grand total of $11.02.

Continue down the main road that runs through Huntington and turn west onto Sherman Hollow Road to reach the **Green Mountain Audubon Nature Center.** The center has an extensive trail system that is equally accessible to walkers and cross-country skiers. The small, slanting shack alongside the barn has trail maps inside.

Inside the main house is a nature museum occupying several rooms of the house. The Nature Discovery Room has a board with dates of recent sightings of common and not-so-common Vermont-based birds. Live turtles and garter snakes, a cubbyhole filled with fifteen different birds' nests—the center calls them avian architecture—and matching games are in this room.

One of the upstairs rooms serves as a teacher's resource center and library. Steel yourself before you pull out the drawers of actual preserved bird species, from blue jays to pine grosbeaks and owls and swans. If you're at all squeamish, head out to the barn, which is filled with more exhibits and examples of taxidermy that are a bit easier to take.

The center is open year-round from 8:00 A.M. to 4:00 P.M. Green Mountain Audubon Nature Center, Huntington 05462, (802) 434–3068; www.audubon.org (click on Vermont).

While every traveler bound for Burlington on I–89 passes the Waterbury exit, and those bound for Stowe or Ben and Jerry's Ice Cream Factory join Route 100 there, not very many people go into the charming old town itself. They're missing a lot, since *Waterbury* has some very fine Victorian buildings (one house has a large horseshoe window overlooking Route 2), a charming little museum, and one of our favorite inns.

What is there about a checkered past that makes an inn irresistible—especially when it's been carefully restored and nicely furnished with unusual antiques and handmade furniture, *and* its innkeepers have a sense of humor. The *Old Stagecoach Inn* began as a coaching stop and town meetinghouse in 1826, and its Victorian facade with porches was added late in the century. Local opinion is divided from that point on, but most agree that the meetings that began to take place here were not of a civic (and certainly not public) nature, and a photograph the innkeepers have does seem to show a lot of women posed alluringly on the porches. Other local residents remember that the house was haunted, and the inn staff admits to some unusual encounters in Room 2, the one with the magnificent carved four-poster bed.

Another Presidential Scandal?

*A*lthough President Chester A. Arthur is known to have been born in 1829, no one is quite sure where. Fairfield, Vermont, claims the honor, and a replica of his boyhood home was erected there in 1953. The town of Waterville, however, based on a memoir of a friend of his mother, has staked a claim that he was actually born in that town and taken to Fairfield when he was five days old. But wait, there's more. His mother came from across the border in Dunham Flats, Quebec, and they claim that she went there for the delivery. If that's true, then he was not born in the United States and shouldn't have acceded to the job of president in September 1881, after the assassination of President James Garfield. But no one in either Vermont town has much truck with that claim, and it's a little late to quibble about the validity of Arthur's presidency.

Today the guest rooms vary in size and shape, reflecting the architectural history of the house itself, a Colonial-style building with significant Queen Anne overlays. Rates are $80 to $120 for rooms with private baths, $50 to $70 with shared baths. As with most inns, rates increase during foliage season. The innkeepers love to cook, and guests are the beneficiaries, enjoying fresh, home-baked croissants for breakfast as well as their choice of hot entree as part of the full country breakfast included in the rates. If the weather's nice, the porch overlooking the garden is the place to eat. The Old Stagecoach Inn is at 18 Main Street (Route 2), Waterbury 05676; (802) 244–5056 or (800) 262–2206.

A walking trail leaves from the inn's backyard, winding through a cemetery with stones from the 1700s and along the river. Just up the street is the town library, and upstairs is the *Historical Society Museum*, a classic melange of local history, curiosities, and treasures brought back by intrepid travelers. It has some excellent examples of miniature Berlin work, beading, and handmade lace; an interesting rocking butter churn, and an armadillo shell. Be sure to look at the album of photos of the 1927 freshet, a flood that washed out much of Vermont's road and bridge system. The library and museum are located at 28 North Main Street, Waterbury, VT 05657; (802) 244–7036, and are open Monday through Wednesday 1:00 to 8:00 P.M., Friday 10:00 A.M. to 5:00 P.M., Saturday 10:00 A.M. to 3:00 P.M.

Free musical programs are presented at 6:30 P.M. on Thursday evenings in summer in *Rusty Parker Memorial Park* near the train depot. (Waterbury is one of the rare towns that has regular train service.) Programs may include the Vermont Jazz Ensemble, a banjo concert, bluegrass, or big band sounds. Bring your own blanket or chairs to sit on; (802) 244–7352.

Green Mountain Coffee Roasters, whose brews you'll see mentioned by name on the menus of Vermont restaurants and cafes, has a factory outlet store in Waterbury, the only place where all the full-bean coffee collection is assembled in one place. You'll also find overstock items, mostly coffee-related, such as espresso cups and grinders. The outlet store, just off Main Street, is open from 7:30 A.M. to 6:00 P.M. Monday through Friday and from 8:30 A.M. to noon Saturday; (800) 223–6768; www.greenmountaincoffee.com.

South of Waterbury, on Route 100, watch for signs to *Grunberg Haus,* a three-story hand-built chalet, where each of the ten guest rooms on the second floor has its own balcony. Although Grunberg Haus is off the beaten path, it is very close to many of northern Vermont's more mainstream attractions, such as Ben and Jerry's Ice Cream Factory in Waterbury, Cold Hollow Cider Mill, and Stowe. Be warned: Grunberg Haus is so pleasant a hideaway that you may have to consciously drag yourself out into the world, away from the queen-size beds with downy comforters. One of the guest rooms even has a tiny built-in alcove that houses a bed big enough for an eight-year-old, or maybe a couple of cats, or you, if you really want to get away from it all. Breakfast is accompanied by piano music.

Call Chris Sellers at (802) 244–7726 or (800) 800–7760 to reserve a room at Grunberg Haus (R.R. 2, Box 1595, Waterbury 05676–9621).

Stowe's reputation as a top ski area undoubtedly owes much to Mount Mansfield's location in Vermont's snowbelt. The first recorded descent of the mountain on skis was made in 1900 on barrel staves, but things moved slowly until the Great Depression years, when Stowe got its start as a major ski area. In 1932 the first skiers from New York City arrived in Waterbury to get to the top of Mount Mansfield—where Stowe's ski area is located— via an electric railway from Waterbury. Although it took the rest of the decade to cut trails and hook up rope tows, by 1940 Stowe could boast of the first chairlift in the country. The town hasn't been the same since.

A quiet place to escape the crowds is the **Helen Day Art Center** in Stowe, which exhibits the work of Vermont-based artists. The building itself was previously the town high school.

A variety of special events and discussions are also held every few weeks at the center, in conjunction with the current displays. In its special exhibits you may find hooked rugs, food labels, paintings, drawings, and other works of art, all by Vermont artists, covering the walls of the gallery.

For a list of current exhibits, contact the Helen Day Art Center, School Street, Stowe 05672. The gallery is usually open Monday, Thursday, and Friday from 2:00 to 5:00 P.M., Wednesday from 10:00 A.M. to 8:00 P.M., and Saturday from 10:00 A.M. to 12:30 P.M.; closed Tuesday and Sunday.

Although Stowe is not exactly off the beaten path, we'd be cheating you if we didn't mention a few of its attractions. Despite the numbers of tourists that come there year-round, it still manages to remain a real town, and one of its most appealing inns overlooks its main street. Rooms in the **Green Mountain Inn** are all different, at least those in the original building, often with quirky charming shapes and approached along corridors with an occasional up or down step. But there are no rough edges—look for carpeted corridors, original artwork throughout, canopy beds, whirlpool baths, fluffy towels, terry-cloth robes, premium bath amenities, electric fireplaces, and a host of other details of fine innkeeping. In the afternoon, everyone gathers for cider and fresh-baked cookies, which you can take to a porch rocker to watch the comings and goings on Main Street. A pleasant dining room overlooks the street, and breakfasts are interesting and varied, including crepes filled with whole pistachios and ricotta.

Rates begin at $99 and include all the facilities of the health club and pool; special off-season rates start as low as $52 per night for two, with continental breakfast. Main Street, Stowe, 05672; (802) 253–7301 or (800) 253–7302; www.genghis.com.

On Main Street, behind *Stowe Hardware Store* (802–253–7205), which conveniently rents bicycles, is the beginning of the 5.3-mile *Stowe Recreation Path,* a paved multi-use corridor that follows the river through meadows and woodlands, roughly parallel with Mountain Road. Walkers, cyclists, in-line skaters, and cross-country skiers share the path—in appropriate seasons—which leads past lodgings, dining establishments, gardens, a farmers' market, and endless views.

Mountain Road is itself about as beaten as a path can get, lined with restaurants and lodgings of every stripe announced by a succession of signs lined up like street touts. In the midst of all this, your senses will be refreshed by the exuberant gardens of *Whiskers Restaurant,* facing Mountain Road. It has a bike rack at its back gate for those who are enticed in from the recreation path. The gardens bloom until October, and in nice weather you can eat on the terrace overlooking a riot of lupine, poppies, iris, daisies, or whatever else is in season. Order, then wander the garden paths until you see your server waving to you from your table. For lunch, try a chilled salmon steak on a bed of crisp greens with a tropical fruit chutney. Dinner entrees range from $12 to more than $20. You can walk here from downtown Stowe in about an hour if you stop to admire the wildflowers along the way; (802) 253–8996.

Across the street, also set in gardens, is *The Gables,* a warm and welcoming family-owned inn without the pretensions of many of its neighbors, and loaded with just as many pampering comforts, including fireplaces, whirlpool tubs, and candlelight dining. Breakfast here is legendary and lasts most people through a full day's skiing. The Gables is a particularly good place for people traveling or skiing alone, since the hosts make everyone feel like they're visiting relatives and will make sure skiers have a ride to the slopes and arrive safely home. Rates are $68 to $148 (for suites) or up to $198 for suites in high season; dinner is also available, and the restaurant is open to the public; 1457 Mountain Road, Stowe 05672; (802) 253–7730 or (800) GABLES–1; www.gostowe.com.

Leaving Mountain Road on nearly any side road, you'll find quiet lanes and mountain views. To the east of Mountain Road (Route 108), on West Hill Road (don't laugh, this seemingly skewed geography does make sense on a map), you'll find *Sage Sheep Farm*, a combination herb and sheep farm with lovely gardens and a shop filled with attractive wool and herb crafts. Owner Elizabeth Squire serves afternoon tea on the wide porch (she designed the house after those in her native Outback) overlooking the gardens, and you can choose a sweet plate, a savory plate, or a veggie plate to go with your big china potful of tea. The savory plate can include a Moroccan lamb puff, summer sausage rounds, and calendula-petal cornbread, along with poppyseed crisps and an herb-cheese dip. It's just enough for an afternoon pick-me-up without ruining dinner. The sweet plate has English scones with jam and cream, scented geranium tea cake, lemon balm cheesecake tartlets, and almond cookies that dissolve on your tongue. The farm is open from noon to 4:00 P.M. every afternoon except Monday, from mid-June through foliage season; (802) 253–8532.

If you continue past Sage Sheep Farm and go left on Sterling Valley Road, you'll come to *Sterling Falls Gorge.* This series of three waterfalls, six cascades, and eight pools is within a short distance of the road. A walking path parallels them; from its dizzying height you can see how the stream carved its way through the schist, forming irregular potholes and swirly rock surfaces. Do be careful here, especially if the trail is wet, and don't lean over to take pictures (photographing the falls is nearly impossible, unless you're a bird). Don't look for this falls on any map—even some Stowe residents looked at us blankly when we asked about it.

Off the west side of Mountain Road is the *Trapp Family Lodge,* which overlooks rolling meadows, a valley, and the Green Mountains. The air is distinctly Austrian, and very von Trapp, but it's never overwhelmingly *Sound of Music.* Music is often in the air, however, with Sunday morning jazz and coffee, evening sing-alongs, and a harpist in the dining room each evening. Rooms are beautifully decorated, and all overlook the valley views. A full schedule of activities keeps guests busy year-round. In the winter you can enjoy cross-country skiing (the trails are open to the public and known as some of the finest in New England), snowshoeing, sleigh rides, and maple sugaring. Summer programs for families and for children of various ages include fishing, birding, hiking, nature walks, swimming, and llama treks.

Rooms are $425 and up in high season, when they include breakfast and dinner. The dining room, serving European specialties such as

Wiener schnitzel along with game, is open to the public, but reservations are essential. Trapp Hill Road, Stowe, 05672; (802) 253–8511 or (800) 826–7000; www.trappfamily.com.

Not far off Route 100 south of Stowe is **Gregg Hill Gardens,** where a natural rock outcrop is the setting for herb, perennial, and annual gardens and a unique PYO cut flower farm. Giant peonies, poppies, dianthus, phlox, iris, daisies—name a color and they can find you a bouquet to match. The gardens are open Tuesday through Saturday May through October. In the late summer and fall you'll find dried flowers, and the owner does gardening workshops as well. For a schedule, contact Gregg Hill Gardens, Box 250, Stowe 05672; (802) 253–4867.

Politics Is Politics and Business Is Business

From the time of the Jefferson embargo of 1808 through the War of 1812, Vermonters defied federal agents and continued to do business with Canada, their natural trading partner. The route through the notch was an important one for farmers seeking to sell their beef to the British in Canada, even while other Vermonters fought to keep British troops at bay— which is how it came to be named Smugglers Notch.

You could easily miss the intersection where you turn to Gregg Hill Gardens because your attention will be drawn to the other side of Route 100 and **The Spinning Wheel.** The entire yard of this shop is a sculpture gallery filled with life-sized (and larger) woodcarvings of moose, fiddlehead ferns, bear cubs, and a larger-than-life Mountie in his red coat.

Between Stowe and Jeffersonville, to the north, lies **Smugglers Notch,** crossed by Route 108. The road through the notch is so narrow at the top that it is impossible to get plows through to keep it cleared of snow, so it closes until spring melts it clear. When it's open, however, the steep, winding road is one of the most interesting in the state, especially at the top, where it weaves among giant boulders. Stop there (there are pull-outs for a few cars) and climb a short distance to see views to Canada and the Adirondacks in New York. You are not allowed to take a trailer over it nor a large RV. (For more information on how this unusual notch was formed, see the book *Natural Wonders of Vermont,* by Barbara and Stillman Rogers.)

There's an old upcountry Yankee story about the flatlander who stopped to ask directions of a farmer, who replied, "You can't get there from here." He might well have been talking about **Smugglers Notch Ski Resort** in the winter. Getting there from Stowe in summer is a simple matter of driving straight uphill on Route 108 through the narrow rock-bordered passage, then dropping down the other side. When this unplowable road is closed in winter, you have to continue north on Route 100 to Morrisville, take Route 15 west through Johnson and Jeffersonville, and drive back along Route 108. Or you can take Mount Mansfield's gondola and ski over the top and down Smugglers' trails. If you are a skier, it's well worth the trip, however you manage it.

The skiing is superb, with state-of-the-art grooming. We've arrived at midnight in a blizzard that dropped more than a foot of snow and awakened to perfectly groomed trails the next morning. The ski school is also tops—instructors actually look at how you ski and tailor the lesson to your skills and weaknesses, even in a group lesson. It's a family resort with all manner of accommodations for kids, including a day care center they won't want to leave. The entire complex is self-contained, with a shuttle bus between two base lodges offering both hotel and condo lodgings. Slope-side condo units are huge, with full kitchens, fireplaces, stereos, VCRs, and whirlpool tubs. Package plans include lifts, lessons, lodging, and such extras as access to the pool, teen center, theater, and other activities. These package inclusions bring the cost of Christmas and New Year's stays down to non-holiday rates. There's plenty to do here in the summer, too, with hiking, climbing, kayaking, nature programs, tennis, kids' camp, and more. Its secluded location and relaxed air make it seem like another world. Smugglers Notch Resort is on Route 108, Smugglers Notch 05464; (802) 644–8851 or (800) 451–8752; www.smuggs.com.

We were serious about *skiing over the top from Stowe*. The two areas are connected by trails that run from the top of one side's lifts to the other's. You can go it alone or on guided trips with a Smugglers ski instructor, and ski both areas on a single ticket if you are a multi-day guest at Smugglers. The trip requires some cross-country skiing on your downhill skis, at a bit of an incline, but the route goes around a mountaintop lake filled with spectacular scenery. While this over-the-top connection is common in alpine communities in Switzerland, Italy, and Austria, it is rare here—in fact, this is the only one in the East.

Smugglers Notch Resort, long an environmental leader, has gone one step further. If you're in the neighborhood, stop in to see the *Living Machine Wastewater Treatment Plant.* The plant is a three-stage process that includes use of a large greenhouse full of tropical and subtropical plants to purify wastewater from the resort. Odor free, the greenhouse has a deck around it with signs that explain the treatment process. It is included on the several different property tours of the resort.

Farther along Route 108 you'll come to Cambridge and the *Boyden Valley Winery,* not exactly what you expect to find this far north, set on a fourth-generation dairy farm in the Lamoille River valley. The owners of the winery use their own grapes, local berries, and apples along with maple syrup to make wines, cordials, and hard ciders. You can tour the 1878 carriage barn to see the process and taste the results from June through December, Tuesday through Sunday from 10:00 A.M. to 5:00 P.M. and January through May Friday through Sunday. The winery is at the junction of Routes 15 and 104, Cambridge 05444; (802) 644–8151.

While on Route 15, just a tad farther east you'll come to Johnson, and in its center, *Johnson Woolen Mills*. The company goes way back, to a century and a half ago, when local farmers brought their wool to the mill to have it spun and woven into cloth. In the late 1800s Johnson began making warm woolen trousers from the cloth. Meeting with the rousing approval of people who had to do farm chores in the dead of winter, a decade or so later the company added jackets, shirts, and vests. That's what it still makes, along with blankets, mittens, and hats, all of which are sold in a shop located in the original mill building. You'll find first quality at factory-store prices and seconds at unbelievable bargains. You also can buy wool yard goods for sewing or rug braiding. The store is open June to January from 9:00 A.M. to 5:00 P.M. Monday through Saturday, and on Sunday from 10:00 A.M. to 4:00 P.M. P.O. Box 612, Main Street, Johnson 05656-0612; (877) 635–WOOL; www.johnsonwoolenmills.com.

If you return to Burlington on scenic Route 15 or the unnumbered, almost parallel route through Pleasant Valley, you'll travel through *Underhill,* which snuggles up against the western slopes of Mount Mansfield. If you happen along on Saturday evening in the last weekend

He Certainly Picked the Right Place to Be From

*W*ilson Bentley of Jericho, known locally as Snowflake Bentley, had by the age of twenty-one developed a photographic microscope that was able to record the intricate patterns of individual snow crystals. The process was not a simple one, requiring a cold working area, great patience, and the ability to hold his breath for a full minute.

He discovered, after photographing thousands of snowflakes, that no two were alike, that they were all six-sided, and that each flake developed from a tiny nucleus into a hexagonal pattern. Today, more than a century later, much of what we know about snow is based on his research, and Bentley's photographs are among the prized collections of several museums, including the Fairbanks in St. Johnsbury and the Peabody at Harvard. Although he never attended high school, Bentley was elected a fellow of the American Academy for the Advancement of Science.

in June, you'll find one of the last of the old-fashioned **Strawberry Socials** that used to fill the all-too-brief season when fields of strawberries ripen. Jericho-Underhill Lions Club members start picking just after sunrise on Saturday morning. By 10:00 A.M. they're back at the United Church of Underhill, washing, hulling, and slicing and baking the biscuits. *Real* shortcake isn't made with sponge cake baked in little molds, or with pound cake; it uses "short" biscuits, and that's exactly what these are. From 5:00 to 8:00 P.M. the Lions hide these biscuits under juicy fresh berries and freshly whipped real cream and serve about 350 people, who stay until they've eaten their fill. No one asks how many bowls you've eaten, only if you'd like another—or a refill on the coffee, tea, or milk that goes with it. Adults pay $4.50, seniors and kids $3.50; if you have a lot of kids, pay $20.00 for the whole family. It's easy to see why the only advertising is the sign out on the village green.

Just down the street from the green is **Sinclair House Inn,** a striking Victorian with one of the loveliest gardens in the valley. When you follow the path from the front porch, you see only a part of the succession of flower beds that flow down the slope to the flat circle of lawn that just begs to have a bride and groom exchanging vows against a backdrop of Vermont farms and hillsides. The owners have lavished the same attention on the house itself, restoring its paneled interior and decorating its rooms in Victorian antiques and country furniture. We like the bright front rooms—one with a lattice window, the other with stained glass. Rates are $95 to $130 in winter and $105 to $140 in summer, and guests get half-price lifts, rentals, and lessons at Smugglers Notch, 18 miles away. One

Fun in the Snow: No Skis Required

*W*hile most people think of coming to Vermont in the winter only for skiing, an increasing number are discovering the joys of this active winter vacation land for its many other diversions. Non-skiing companions of skiers have long known this secret: While everyone is on the slopes, all the après-ski recreation facilities are nearly empty. To learn about other indoor and outdoor diversions, check out the book New England Snow Country: 701 Ways to Enjoy Winter Whether You Ski or Not. In its Vermont section you will find opportunities for snowshoeing, sleigh rides, skating parties, igloo building, dog sledding, ice fishing, winter carnivals, and activities for those who prefer the warmer pursuits of shopping, museums, art galleries, and fine dining. The book is available in bookstores or from Herbitage Farm Bookshelf, Box 232, Swanzey, NH 03446; (800) 639–1099. The price is $14.95 (plus $3.50 shipping).

room is wheelchair accessible, even to the wheel-in shower and low closet hooks. The Sinclair Inn Bed & Breakfast, R.D. 2, Box 35, Underhill 05489; (802) 899–2234 or (800) 433–4658.

North of Burlington

The stretches of the Champlain Valley north of Burlington offer a flatter, more fertile landscape than many other parts of the state. This rich farmland played an important role in the early development of this part of the state.

As you head north on Route 7 out of Burlington and into Winooski, just north of the Champlain Mill, the VFW hall on the left has a **World War II–vintage army tank** perched on its lawn. Route 7 is a pretty stretch of highway as you wind your way into Milton, named after the poet John Milton. Just north of the town is a gorgeous body of water, the dammed-up **Arrowhead Mountain Lake.** In summer there's a lot of traffic on the lake.

In **St. Albans** the **Vermont Maple Festival** is an annual bash in mid-April that signifies the official end of winter. Sugar-on-snow, arts-and-crafts displays, relay races, and other town activities serve to wake up the townspeople in an area of the state where winter hangs on for a good five months of the year. For the dates of the festival, call the St. Albans Chamber of Commerce at (802) 524–2444 or write to the Vermont Maple Festival, 132 North Main Street, St. Albans 05478.

It Was War, You-all

St. Albans was the site of the northernmost battle— more accurately "event"— of the Civil War, when, on October 19, 1864, a group of Confederate soldiers took over the town, robbed all the banks, blew up the Sheldon Bridge, and escaped to Canada. They were apprehended but acquitted of any crimes because the jury felt they were acting on the basis of "legitimate warfare."

Fine Crop of Rocks This Year

The small stones in the fields actually grow there. Ask any farmer, who will tell you that even though a field is clear of stones in the fall, a new crop has grown there when plowed in the spring. It's the truth: As the ground freezes and thaws in the winter and spring, it heaves up rocks from below in a never-ending process. The original settlers, after they'd cleared the land of trees, moved the larger rocks to the edges and used them to build stone walls, which were more to contain livestock than to mark boundaries (although they served both purposes). As each winter turned up more rocks, the settlers would add them to the walls. In some of these fields, rocks are about the only thing that will grow.

On the main drag of St. Albans, which is actually quite a bustling town for these parts, is *Jeff's Maine Seafood,* a gourmet food and seafood shop and restaurant. The takeout section offers fish both uncooked and prepared, along with a large selection of ready-to-eat dishes like pesto lasagna, smoked bluefish, salads, sandwiches, and specials like chicken burritos and spanakopita, a savory Greek pastry made with paper-thin phyllo sheets. Gourmet desserts are available both to eat in and to take out and include Toll House pie and chocolate hazelnut torte. Jeff's also carries a large selection of French, California, and Italian wines.

There's also a sight rarely seen in any part of landlocked Vermont: a live lobster tank. A fish tank sits atop the deli showcase containing two well-fed goldfish. They must feel nervous about overlooking their relatives below, who enter the store from Maine on Tuesday, Wednesday, and Friday.

If you'd rather eat here, try the lobster dinner. It comes with a cup of seafood chowder, coleslaw, French bread, and a tossed salad, all at a reasonable market price. The Chinese sesame noodles are wonderfully nutty and well spiced, with just enough bite to them. Entrees are $13 to $18.

Jeff's retail store is open from 8:30 A.M. to 6:00 P.M. Monday through Friday and Saturday from 8:30 A.M. to 7:00 P.M. The restaurant is open Monday through Saturday 11:30 A.M. until 3:00 P.M. and Tuesday through Saturday for dinner from 5:00 to 9:00 P.M. Jeff's Maine Seafood, 65 North Main Street, St. Albans 05478; (802) 524–6135.

Swanton on Route 7 is the home of a sizable community of Abenaki. The town was settled as early as 1700, when the French sailed through what is today Missisquoi Bay into the headwaters of Lake Champlain and created a settlement in Swanton. An enjoyable stop in this area is *West Swanton Orchards, Cider Mill and Farm Market,* open from June through October. Apple varieties are MacIntosh, Cortland, and Red Delicious, which you can buy at the stand or pick yourself. As the name implies, the stand carries the trilogy of other Vermont products: honey, maple goodies, and cider, in addition to pies and baked goods and Vermont gift items. The farm is on Route 78 West, about 4 miles from Swanton at 32 Church Road, West Swanton 05488; (802) 868–7851. East of Swanton is *Highgate Center.* This part of the state looks noticeably different from the rest. Route 78 parallels the Missisquoi River, a very wide, 86-mile-long rocky river that begins in the town of Lowell, heads north into Canada, and then migrates back to Vermont into Lake Champlain.

This area is almost desolate. It's not much more than a big expanse of fields and pastures of scrub brush and is more representative of the sparsely populated Vermont of the early twentieth century. Lots of farms are situated along the roadside, and the innumerable silos look like giant milk cans. Route 105, which you meet in Sheldon, follows every curve and contour of the Missisquoi River, making for a drive that never gets boring.

Here, and elsewhere in Vermont, you'll see boulders and rocks in the fields, and you may wonder where they came from. The big ones came from nearby mountains, often quite some distance away. As the great glaciers of the last ice age moved over the mountains, they pulled off pieces of mountaintop and carried them along, dropping the rocks as they melted. These boulders are called glacial erratics, and local settlers sometimes cut them up to use as building stones; more often they just plowed around them.

Once you reach Enosburg Falls, take Route 108 north a couple of miles until you reach **Berkson Farms Inn** on the left. This working dairy farm on 600 acres is open year-round and offers guests the opportunity to stay for a night or two or for an entire week, participating in standard farm chores, from milking cows to bringing in sap buckets in the spring to helping to drive a fence post into the ground.

Dick and Joanne Keesler, native Vermonters, run the farm and the inn and, unlike many innkeepers, do accept families with children. The 140-year-old farmhouse has four rooms for guests, and these rooms are furnished with handsome Victorian furniture, quilts, and large, comfortable beds. One room has a private bath, and all rooms come with a country breakfast. Joanne says that the most popular breakfast is French toast with sausage and home fries. The kitchen and dining room are huge and welcoming and feature lots of antique furniture. One of the living rooms has an old pump organ and a Victrola.

If a couple of nights aren't enough for you, the Kesslers will accommodate you for a full week with a room, three meals a day, and a barbecue, hayride, and other activities; the rates are upwards of $300 per adult and $150 per child. The rates for a room by the night—including breakfast—are $75 for the room with a private bath for two adults and $65 for the other three rooms. The Kesslers keep a herd of milking cattle. With an assortment of sheep, swans, geese, chickens, and rams, in addition to a friendly dog named Shaker, the Berkson gives you a good idea of what it's like to live on a farm. Berkson Farms Inn, Enosburg Falls 05450; (802) 933–2522.

Back in the village of Enosburg Falls, drive east on Route 105. You'll pass a Christmas tree farm, then the road will go up and down like a roller coaster. In Enosburg Town you'll see old stone remnants of a bridge and retaining walls in the Missisquoi River. East Berkshire on Route 118 East is frontier land. It's hard to pick up anything but a Canadian radio station in this outpost border town.

The town of **Montgomery** has two villages, 2 miles apart, and is known as the **Covered Bridge Capital** of Vermont. There are seven bridges here, most still in daily use. Most are also within sight of a main road, or very close to one, making them easy to tour. Three span gorges with waterfalls, although these are usually difficult to get a good view of, especially in safety, since the banks are steep and wooded.

As you drive east on Route 118, just before the sign that says WELCOME TO MONTGOMERY is the Longley Covered Bridge, built in 1863 by the Jewett brothers, as were the next two.

The second covered bridge is the Comstock, built in 1883 as a lattice-type bridge. The third covered bridge, which was built in 1890, is the Fuller Bridge, located just off the green past the post office.

Two more stand just to the west of Route 118 as it heads south from Montgomery Center. The first, on Hutchins Mill Road, sits astride a falls and gorge that you can actually get a pretty good look at. The other is on the old Gibou Road. A new bridge now bypasses the old one, situated almost over the falls, but you can see the unused bridge right beside the new road.

Breakfasts at the **Phineas Swann Bed & Breakfast** are not just a meal, they're an event, with home-baked breads and jams made from the berries grown in the backyard. The whole place is welcoming, with well-decorated rooms and big band music in the background at afternoon tea. But it's not a bit fussy, and you'll be perfectly at home here in your hiking boots or ski clothes. The owners are long on sense of humor and short on pretensions, although their inn ranks right up there with the best. Rates are $85 to $145, the higher range for the new suites in the carriage house overlooking the river, with whirlpool baths and fireplaces. Cooking is what owners Glen and Michael love most, so ask ahead if they will serve dinner while you're there. The inn is right on Main Street, Montgomery Center 05471; (802) 326–4306.

Down the street is **Kilgore's General Store.** From the outside it looks like a stodgy old general store. Inside, however, everything from miso soup to granola to salad dressing to wine is found on its shelves. Sewing sundries, books, and baskets are located upstairs; children's toys can be found downstairs, and you'll find a selection of antiques and Vermontiana, too. Besides the unusual collection of items for sale, one of the attractions at Kilgore's is the soda fountain built in 1929. The fountain is topped by a solid slab of Vermont green marble countertop. The back of the store overlooks Trout River, which can be pretty exciting in the spring. A couple of years ago, you could savor your homemade chile at a table on the back porch, but during spring melt-off, the river carried the porch away. The mid-afternoon sun warms the room and the spirit even in winter, as you enjoy soups, sandwiches, milk shakes, and sundaes from the fountain and the store dog, Maxine, dozes by the fire.

The original store was built in 1876 and served as a post office, general store, and town clerk's office at various points in history. During the 1970s the building held the notorious Trout Saloon—the local watering hole—and reopened as Kilgore's in 1989.

Write to Kilgore's General Store, Main Street, Montgomery Center 05471, or call (802) 326–3058. The store is open from 9:00 A.M. to 5:00 P.M. Wednesday through Monday and the same hours Friday though Monday in the winter.

North of Montgomery on Route 242 is *Jay Peak,* the state's northernmost ski area, where the state's highest snowfall means that snow lasts well into spring. It is the home of Vermont's only aerial tramway, too, and a favorite with Quebec skiers, so you'll hear a lot of French spoken there.

In summer the aerial tramway brings hikers and walkers to the top of the mountain. The resort has a self-guided tour called the *Mountain Ecology Nature Trail;* pick up the small guide to the nature trail at the resort welcome center. The trail winds down the mountain and takes about an hour and a half for the average hiker. At the upper end it passes through conifers and by an alpine pond, where the sensitive ecosystem is explained. At lower levels the Forest Loop Trail travels past typical north woods trees and plants. Look for the trees hollowed by woodpeckers, the tracks and droppings of moose and deer, and the headwaters of the Jay Branch. The upper end of the famed Vermont Long Trail passes through the area. Jay Peak Resort is close to the Jay-Westfield town line, west of Lake Memphremagog, on Route 242; (802) 988–2611 or (800) 451–4449; www.jaypeakresort.com.

The record snowfall also brings Nordic skiers to *Hazen's Notch Cross Country Ski Area* on Route 58, where 18 miles of groomed trails and 72 miles of backcountry trails wander along the slopes of the notch; Montgomery Center 05472; (802) 326–4799.

As you leave Montgomery Center, take a left onto Route 58 East, which climbs and twists and turns into a dirt road about a mile up from town. Great views soon abound. The road follows some parts of the Bayley-Hazen Military Road, for which some of the local landmarks are named, including Hazen's Notch State Park. About 5 miles out of the town of Montgomery Center, you'll come across a huge rock outcropping—it looks like you're going to drive right into the mountain. This is **Hazen's Notch,** and Sugarloaf Mountain, with an altitude of 2,520 feet, lies directly behind it.

Past the notch, the second left, where the sign says HAZEN'S NOTCH CAMP-GROUND, leads to **McAllister Pond,** a beautiful body of water for fishing and swimming.

The Champlain Islands

A totally different landscape—at times you'll forget and think it's a seascape, especially if haze fades the Adirondacks across the lake—awaits if you travel northwest from Burlington instead of northeast. North of Colchester, take Route 2 toward South Hero, which you will reach via a long bridge. Just before you leave the mainland, you'll pass Sandbar State Park. Even though you're not on the ocean, these island towns have a vague seaside resort feeling, but without the crowds.

Vacationing families have been coming here for generations, primarily because not much changes in the islands from one year—or decade—to the next. Moreover, the islands are compact enough that you can spend the day exploring from South Hero to East Alburg, see about everything there is to see, and still have time to return to the mainland—or, after collapsing in one of the inns or B&Bs on the islands, still have enough energy to go for a long bike ride the next day.

This sparseness of attractions is one reason it never seems to get crowded up here. Because the islands touch the Canadian border, you'll see a fair number of Quebecois and other north-of-the-border license plates and French summerhouse nameplates here.

If you decide to just stick to Route 2 and its immediate environs, you'll have plenty to explore, from the numerous **antiques shops** that dot the islands to the various historic sites, from **Ste. Anne's Shrine** on Isle la Motte to the **Hyde Log Cabin** on Grand Isle. You don't even need a map to find these places either, as they're well marked and well known.

If you're up in the islands from mid-July to the end of August—which is likely, given that this is the time of year when the population of the islands expands from 4,000 to as many as five times that number—you shouldn't miss the *Royal Lipizzan Stallions,* a performing horse troupe of a special breed, of which only a few hundred survive. Although these noble white horses perform throughout northern New England in the summertime, the *Atkin Herrmann Farm* on Route 2 in North Hero is their semipermanent warm-weather home. The rest of the time, they live in Florida. Call (802) 372–5683 for more information, or get your tickets for the Thursday-through-Saturday performances at the North Hero chamber of commerce. You can visit the farm anytime.

Also in North Hero is an establishment known for its rooms and its restaurant. The *North Hero House* has several different choices for lodging, ranging from the restored inn house to the Cove House, which has rooms with screened porches that directly overlook the lake. These lakeside lodgings are popular with families, since the inn has its own sandy beach below. In the main building, furnishings are often antiques or quality reproductions, and some rooms on the front have delightful screened porches overlooking the lake, as well. Doubles are $75 to $195 in winter, $95 to $255 in summer.

If you plan to eat dinner at the North Hero House, either as an inn guest or as a visitor, be prepared for a wait, since the place is popular with locals and with some of the aforementioned families who have been coming here in the summers for decades. What's ideal is to dine on the screened-in porch that faces the Cove House on a late-summer night just as the sky turns to dusk. The menu offers meat, fish, and pasta dishes prepared simply but very nicely, and there's a well-stocked wine cellar. The chef has a way with seafood, especially salmon, and wows everyone with his maple salad dressing (if you see someone at the next table licking their salad plate, don't be surprised). It's a good idea to reserve a table for dinner on the porch. Entrees are $12 to $25. Breakfast and dinner packages are available with rooms.

Write to the North Hero House, P.O. Box 106, North Hero 05474, or call (802) 372–4732.

To explore the islands or delta on a day trip by sea kayak, reserve a space with *True North Kayak Tours*. All equipment is provided, as is basic instruction in sea kayaking. (802) 860–1910.

MORE PLACES TO STAY IN NORTHWEST VERMONT AND THE CHAMPLAIN VALLEY

(ALL AREA CODES 802)

BURLINGTON (05401)
Lang House on Main Street, 360 Main Street, is handily located between Church Street and the university, in a grand Eastlake Victorian home. Afternoon tea is served, and breakfast is created by a chef; (877) 919-9799.

WATERBURY (05676)
1836 Cabins are modern, comfortable, and in a beautiful pine-woods setting just off Route 100; 244-8533.

STOWE (05672)
Edson Hill Manor,
1500 Edson Hill Road, is a summer base for hiking and in winter for tobogganing, sledding, or cross-country skiing. B&B and modified American plans available, as well as special packages. B&B plan rooms begin at $99 in low season, $179 during foliage; 253-7371 or (800) 621-0284.

VERGENNES (05491)
Emersons' Bed and Breakfast,
82 Main Street, is a comfortable Victorian home in downtown Vergennes; 877-3293.

MONTGOMERY CENTER (05471)
The Inn on Trout River, Main Street, is in the restored mansion of the owner of the town's first automobile; 326-4391 or (800) 338-7049.

Black Lantern Inn, Route 118, is listed on the National Historic Register and has candlelight dining; 326-4507 or (800) 255-8661.

MORE PLACES TO EAT IN NORTHWEST VERMONT AND THE CHAMPLAIN VALLEY

(ALL AREA CODES 802)

COLCHESTER (05446)
Junior's Restaurant,
6 Roosevelt Highway, Southern Italian, with excellent *suppa de pesce* and moderate prices; (802) 655-0000; for the pizzeria downstairs, call (802) 655-5555.

WATERBURY (05676)
Tanglewoods,
Guptil Road, off Route 100 north of Waterbury, has an outstanding New American menu with a penchant for the Southwest; 244-7855.

To Learn More in Northwest Vermont and the Champlain Valley

For Stowe and environs, contact the Stowe Area Association, *Box 1320, Stowe 05672; (800) 24-STOWE; www.stoweinfo.com.*

For information on the far north, contact the Jay Peak Area Association, *R.R.2, Box 137, Jay 15859; (800) 882-7460.*

STOWE (05672)
Blue Moon Cafe,
35 School Street,
has a New American menu
with dishes like
polenta-leek pie, rabbit
braised with mushrooms,
and salmon with
maple-whiskey sauce;
253–7006.

Gracie's,
on Main Street,
is a good stop for
mega-burgers, lunch
sandwiches, and a general
menu of moderately
innovative dishes. Portions
are generous, and they're
open until midnight;
253–8741.

FAIRFAX (05454)
The Country Pantry,
at the junction of
Routes 104 and 128, is open
for three meals daily, with
enormous breakfasts (the
Belgian waffles are wonderful) at $3.00 to $4.00; dinner entrees are all under
$10.00; 849–6364.

ENOSBURG FALLS (05450)
Abbey Restaurant,
Route 105,
is known for hearty
portions and
Sunday brunch;
933–4747 or
(800) 696–4748.

MONTGOMERY CENTER
(05471)
JR's, Main Street, serves
three meals daily from
6:30 A.M. to 10:00 P.M. It's
inexpensive and reliable;
326–4682.

Northeast Kingdom

All of the Northeast Kingdom could be considered off the beaten path, as it's so far removed from everything. Some of the most sparsely populated areas in the east fall within the boundaries of the counties that make up the Kingdom: Caledonia, Essex, and Orleans.

The Northeast Kingdom is rumored to have received its name when Senator George Aiken, who until Jim Jeffords made history in 2001 was Vermont's best known senator of all time, was visiting the northeastern town of Lyndonville in 1949. "You know," he reportedly said, addressing the townspeople, "this is such beautiful country up here that it should be called the Northeast Kingdom." Another version holds that the area was named in anger during a meeting of the state legislature in Montpelier. It seems the people of one northeastern hamlet refused to yield on a certain budgetary matter that representatives from the rest of the state were in agreement on. A member of the opposing side is said to have shouted, "You people think you live in your own kingdom up there!"

No matter what the true genesis of the Northeast Kingdom's name, the area is considered one of the state's most beautiful regions. The Kingdom's sky seems bluer, the trees greener, and the snow whiter.

The Kingdom contains three of the four grants and gores in Vermont, land parcels that were left over when town boundaries were set. The three—Warners Grant, Warren Gore, and Averys Gore—nestle side by side in the extreme northeast, one town south of the Canadian border. Both Warners Grant and Averys Gore contain no roads, although Route 114 does cut through Warren Gore. All three, along with the adjacent town of Lewis, add up to a population of zero. In fact, most of the towns in the Kingdom have populations in the three figures, and sometimes less than that.

Towns in this northeastern frontier were settled later than towns in other parts of Vermont. While parts of southern Vermont attracted pioneers from "overcrowded" Connecticut and Massachusetts as early as 1764,

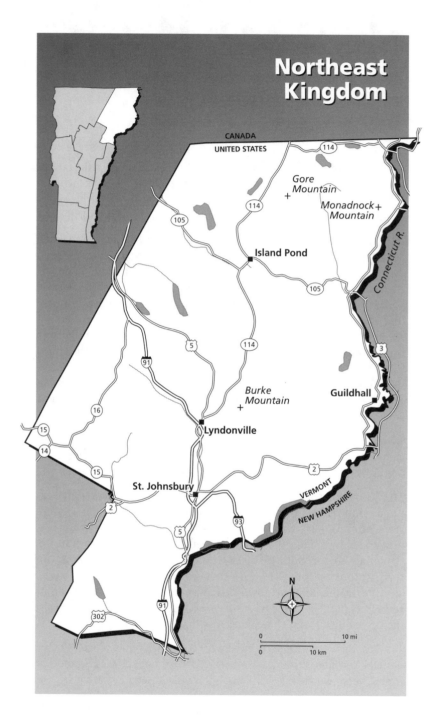

Northeast Kingdom

CANADA
UNITED STATES

114

Gore
Mountain
+

Monadnock +
Mountain

Connecticut R.

105

Island Pond

105

3

114

Burke
Mountain
+

Guildhall

91

5

16

Lyndonville

15

14

15

2

St. Johnsbury

VERMONT

NEW HAMPSHIRE

2

5

93

N

91

302

0   10 mi
0   10 km

much of northeastern Vermont was settled after 1785 and even well into the nineteenth century.

It's interesting to note that some of the farms in Kingdom towns that front the Connecticut River—farms in towns like Lemington, Guildhall, and Brunswick—still follow the boundaries of the settlement grants and charters of their first settlers. Farmland was laid out in long, narrow strips to allow every settler to have enough of the rich, fertile land that bordered the river, which also served as a water and transportation source.

The Kingdom holds a way of life that disappeared from other parts of the country long ago. Cherish this as you drive over its back roads.

Route 14 North

Route 14 gently climbs out of Montpelier and twists past farms and pastures, while the Kingsbury Branch River plays tag with the road, appearing first on the east side of the highway, then on the west, and finally feeding into Sabin Pond at the northern end of Calais (pronounced *callus*) and the southern border of Woodbury.

After a gradual climb (this, by the way, is what Vermonters call flat), **Woodbury Lake** appears, its shoreline a bustling community in summer and all but dead in winter. Here and there you'll see old abandoned houses, sagging barns, and granite block walls, remnants of earlier, more prosperous times. Woodbury holds at least two distinctive claims in the Vermont Hall of Fame: (1) The town affirms it sent more soldiers per capita to the Civil War than any other Vermont town, and (2) of the twenty-eight lakes and ponds found in Woodbury, all of their streams and brooks flow out of the town, not into it. (As you go farther north in Vermont, many of the rivers flow north, too, into Canada, although the Lamoille recrosses the border farther west.)

By contrast, Hardwick is a relatively busy center of commerce in the Kingdom. Hardwick served as the final destination for the Hardwick and Woodbury Railroad, which was built in 1896 to transport the mammoth blocks of granite from the quarries in Woodbury north to the mills in Hardwick. The railroad had the distinction of having the steepest grades and most hairpin turns in the East. The tracks were taken up in 1940 when the quarries were abandoned.

The *Brick House Shop/Perennial Pleasures* off Route 16 in East Hardwick is an extensive English herb garden with everything from catnip and lemon thyme to shrubs, roses, and lilies, all clearly marked.

According to local legend, in 1796 pioneer Samuel Stevens was exploring what a year later would become the town of Hardwick, named after Hardwick, Massachusetts. He stabbed a spot in the ground with his walking stick near where the house currently stands, and the stick grew into a willow tree.

There's a tea garden with a gazebo and afternoon tea ($8.00) is served Tuesday to Sunday, Memorial Day through Labor Day from 12:30 until 4:30 P.M. Reservations are appreciated. Cucumber sandwiches on thin whole wheat bread with a cream cheese dressing made with mayonnaise, horseradish, dill, and pepper are served, along with scones, homemade jams, cakes, and a variety of teas. The gift shop has many garden-related items and such kitchenware as teapots, honey dippers, twig baskets, oils, ceramics, and both marble and wooden mortar and pestle sets.

The nursery is open from May through late September, Tuesday to Sunday from 9:00 A.M. to 5:00 P.M. (it's closed Monday). Brick House, Brick House Road, East Hardwick 05836; (802) 472–5104.

To drive along a piece of Revolutionary War history, take Route 16 north for 3 miles until you see a road on the left with a sign reading GREENSBORO. Follow this road for 2 miles and continue straight past Tolmans Corner until you see Caspian Lake on your right. This stretch of road is part of the *Bayley-Hazen Military Road,* a 55-mile-long road originally authorized by George Washington in 1776 so that Revolutionary War troops could have an easy access route into Canada to launch surprise attacks against the British. A monument can be found on the east side of the road, overlooking Caspian Lake and just past the first road on the left past Tolmans Corner. Colonel Jacob Bayley of Newbury directed 110 workers in building the road from his hometown on the Connecticut River to the town of Cabot, 20 miles away, in forty-five days. He paid the laborers $10 a month and half a pint of rum per day.

After one month construction was halted when Washington realized that if the road would make it easier for the colonists to reach Canada, then the British would also be able to reach the colonists that much quicker.

In April 1779 construction on the road began anew. This time Colonel Moses Hazen led his road builders to continue the road 35 miles farther into Westfield. But work again ceased six months later when Hazen thought the Brits were gathering steam, and the construction, which was planned to go through Swanton and then up to St. John, Quebec, ended for the final time. Two years later the war was over, and the road was used as a major artery for development by settlers.

Willey's Store on Main Street in Greensboro Village has frequently been called the quintessential Vermont general store, as have many others around the state. Once you step inside, you'll see that it's the clear winner.

Willey's has camping gear, nails, hinges, fishing lures, greeting cards, toiletries, trashy summer paperbacks, a deli department, a selection of wines, phyllo pastry, and, of course, maple syrup and Ben & Jerry's. Open daily, Willey's Store is on Main Street, Greensboro 05841; (802) 533–2621.

Greensboro has long been a haven for famous members of the intelligentsia who want to keep a low profile when they retreat here in the summer. Its winter population can easily quadruple in summer. Supreme Court Chief Justice William Rehnquist is possibly the most famous summer resident; others are top book editors, educators, and writers. The village and summerhouses are scattered around the perimeter of Caspian Lake, which is shaped like an hourglass.

Right across the street from Willey's is *The Miller's Thumb,* a typical Vermont vacation area crafts shop, but with a distinct difference. Besides offering clothes, stuffed animals, cow-adorned T-shirts, potpourri, assorted gifts, and imported Italian and Portuguese ceramics, it's located in a former gristmill, John Barrington's Greensboro Grist Mill to be exact. At one side of the first floor, you can look down into the old grain chute and see the waters of the Greensboro Brook rush by below. Other vestiges of the old mill remain. Outside, the original grindstone has been embedded in the patio surrounded by slate tile, and the cogs and wheels are displayed at the side of the shop. The Miller's Thumb is open from 10:00 A.M. to 5:00 P.M. year-round; call (802) 533–2960 or (800) 680–7886, or write to The Miller's Thumb, 4 Main Street, Greensboro 05841.

People consider *Craftsbury* to be the gold medalist in the picture-postcard division of Vermont attractions. But back in 1781, when the town was first chartered, not many of the original grantees could envision the town's promise. In fact, the grantees of most Vermont towns were residents of Massachusetts and Connecticut; a relatively tiny number of them actually acted on their land grants, which were typically one hundred acres. Most sold the land to people who had little to lose by heading north and settling the wilderness. The original grantees were moderately wealthy men who did not want to forgo their luxuries of "civilization" for the unknown territories.

The founder of Craftsbury, however, was one of the few exceptions. Ebenezer Crafts, one of the original grantees of Craftsbury, was from Sturbridge, Massachusetts, and served as an officer in the Revolutionary War after graduating from Yale University. He founded the village in 1788 (seven years after the town was chartered) and sent his son, Samuel, to Harvard. After Samuel graduated from Harvard, he returned to Craftsbury to serve as town clerk and later was governor of the state for two terms.

People still follow Samuel Craft's example by returning to Craftsbury, but unlike Sam, they stay only for the summer. North of the village center is Craftsbury Common, where the *Inn on the Common* offers lodging, along with breakfast and family-style dinners.

The inn is an amalgam of new and old: antique beds and clawfoot tubs together with VCRs and tennis courts, giving guests the best of new and old Vermont. The inn's eighteen rooms are scattered throughout several buildings on the grounds, on both sides of the main thoroughfare through town. There's an old, immaculately kept cemetery right next to one of the buildings. The gravestones of both Ebenezer and Samuel Crafts are in the graveyard, right up near the front. On summer evenings after dinner, stroll through the cemetery and read the inscriptions, some of which date from 1790.

The Inn on the Common offers a modified American plan, which includes breakfast and dinner. All rooms have private baths, and rates range from $250 to $310 for a double room. If you choose not to have dinner at the inn, the rate is $20 per person less. Nearby activities include swimming in either a pool or a lake, tennis, croquet, and hiking. Special packages at the inn include a skiing and a honeymoon package. For more information, write to the Inn on the Common, Box 75, Craftsbury Common 05827, or call (802) 586–9619 or (800) 521–2233, or visit www.innon thecommon.com.

WORTH SEEING

Cabot Creamery,
Main Street, Cabot. You can tour their cheese-making operation and sample Vermont cheddars,
(802) 563–2231.

Groton State Forest,
Groton, where you'll find camping, recreation areas, hiking, geological and natural points of interest, and plenty of the great outdoors.

Regular guests at the inn will be pleased to learn of the newly opened **Coachworks Farm,** a day spa and fitness facility about ten minutes away, in Albany, reached from Route 114. Along with a variety of spa services, you can enjoy the lap pool; (802) 755–6342.

The **Craftsbury Sports Center** was begun in 1976 in a defunct private boys' school. A variety of sports weeks are held here year-round, from

Inn on the Common, Craftsbury

running and sculling camps to walking weeks. You can stay here without enrolling in one of the special programs and participate in all sports. There are 140 acres, with 600 more acres serving as a nature preserve. Currently, 65 miles of trails exist for skiers and hikers to explore, with a few more miles to be added during the next several years. The rooms are what you would expect of a former boys' school, but it hardly matters, since most of the guests spend their time outside being active. The daily rate includes a room, some sports fees, and three meals a day. The food is delicious and served buffet-style, with the emphasis on complex carbohydrates to fuel all the exercise you'll get at the center. Vegetarians are amply accommodated, and during summer the vegetables are from the center's own gardens.

The center is open year-round, and the room rate of $136 to $144 (shared bath) or $198 to $208 for two includes three meals and the use of ski or snowshoe trails in winter, the beach and canoes in summer. Cottages run about $210 to $230 a night with meals. Special multi-day programs are priced according to their length and the recreation activities included. For more information write to the Craftsbury Sports Center, Lost Nation Road, Craftsbury Common 05827, or call (802) 586–7767; www.craftsbury.com.

Newport, just south of the Canadian border on Lake Memphremagog, is a utilitarian kind of town, blending touches of the twenty-first century and bilingual traffic signs with the ambience of an old Vermont town. Downtown it looks like exactly what it once was, a lumber mill town. Even though Newport has always depended somewhat on border trade, it's not especially geared to tourists; it's more for Canadians and Vermonters who need to get their business done as quickly and cheaply as possible.

The town—it's actually a city, the only incorporated city in the Kingdom—rises from the shore of Lake Memphremagog, which means "beautiful waters" in the Algonquin language.

As you're driving through Newport and the vicinity, turn your radio to *WMOO–FM,* or 92MOO–FM, as it's popularly called. The station plays a combination of country, light rock, oldies, and folk.

St. Mary Catholic Church has a fine view of Lake Memphremagog from its commanding position high on Prospect Street, on the west side of town. This church with twin granite towers is a mariners' church, uncommon so far inland. The dedication stone reads MAY 1904, and an inscription reads AVE MARIS STELLA, a statement that combines Mary and the nautical reference point of the North Star. An anchor is carved into

WMOO—FM, Newport

the stone, and a lighted figure of Mary stands between the two towers. This landmark is visible from most of the town at night. The church is open to the public only for Saturday and Sunday services. Call (802) 334–7371 for hours; 5 Clermont Terrace, Newport 05855.

If even Newport's relative hustle and bustle is too much, take Route 105 west to *Rose Apple Acres Farm,* a quiet B&B on a working farm that is just under 1 mile from the Canadian border as the crow flies, but is 3 miles by car. Cam Mead has owned the fifty-two-acre farm with her husband, Jay, since 1986, and she says that even though the farm initially appears peaceful and quiet, you'll have to get used to a different kind of "noise" here: the sounds of the birds, the sheep, the occasional bee, and the wind chimes on the porch.

The farm has sheep, goats, and Belgian horses and looks out onto the Canadian Sutton Range on one side and Jay Peak on the other. The faraway blinking lights to the northeast are in the Quebec town of Mansonville. The house was built in the early 1900s and at one time drew a crowd from both sides of the border on warm Sunday afternoons, when the Augers, a family of local circus high-wire walkers, performed at the farm.

"People used to line up on the road and watch the Augers walk on a wire 100 feet off the ground without a net," says Cam. "Today I feel that the house gets real excited when an Auger comes to visit."

That accounts for the name of the house cat, Auger, who is a bit finicky that you pronounce its name using the proper French accent, making it sound a lot like "O.J." Cam makes porcelain dolls and teaches three-day courses, which you can combine with your lodging for a nice getaway package. At the end, you have a handmade doll to take home. Prices vary with the complexity of the doll. Dexterity seems to run in the family, since the Meads' son runs Henderson Forge, a blacksmith shop on the same property, where you can find hand-forged home accessories or have custom pieces made to order.

The Meads are among the few innkeepers we know who do not raise prices during foliage season; you pay $50 for a room with a shared bath no matter what time of year you visit. If you're hiking the Long Trail, they can arrange for transportation to and from the trail or the hiker bus.

To meet the Meads, write to Rose Apple Acres Farm, R.R. 2, Box 300, East Hill Road, North Troy 05859, or call (802) 988–4300.

The Northeast Corner

Snuggled into the far corner of the state, this region north of St. Johnsbury and bordered by Canada, New Hampshire, and I–91 is to many people the heart and soul of the Northeast Kingdom. While its border with New Hampshire is pretty easy to identify—in all but one tiny spot, you must cross a river to change states—crossing into Canada is less obvious.

What about border guards? When you cross on a road that actually goes somewhere in Canada, there will be the usual border formalities. But at other places, back roads may stray across the line and back again without your even being aware of it. The rule is that if you can't get anywhere from the road, no one cares much. Or so it seems. In reality, however, the entire boundary between the two countries, which is the longest undefended international boundary in the world, is closely watched. Surveillance cameras alert authorities on both sides to any unusual crossings, even on foot. These illegal crossings are investigated, so the casual appearance of the border on remote roads is misleading.

The border is even more fun in ***Derby Line.*** As you might guess from its name, the town sits right on the boundary line, with residential streets wandering back and forth randomly. The colors of street signs change at the line, but it is otherwise invisible. The town's opera house and library is an impressive building that ties Derby Line firmly to its neighboring town in Quebec. The international border is marked by an inlaid wooden strip across the center of the reading room floor. You can read a book there while sitting in two countries.

Upstairs, the theater has the stage in Canada, while the audience applauds from the United States. Anyone who plays there instantly becomes an international star. Some homes sit astride the line, too, so you can imagine what fun this was for revenue men during Prohibition. Guests could enter through a "dry" front door and drink quite legally in the kitchen.

Westmore and Lake Willoughby are a popular summer camp area. Westmore was chartered in 1781, but its grantees decided not to organize until twenty-three years later. Since then, the population has grown at a snail's pace, still totaling only a few hundred. Lake Willoughby has a lot to do with it; virtually all of the tiny town's industry is geared toward summer visitors, from the campground and two restaurants to the six inns and clusters of cottages that overlook the lake.

For all its proximity to tiny Vermont towns—East Haven and Victory— **East Burke** is a relatively sophisticated area, with a high-quality restaurant and shopping. Nearby Burke Mountain Ski Area doesn't hurt, but those who come to ski the big mountains and do the Vermont nightlife in places like Killington, Stowe, and Stratton usually ask, "Where's Burke?" when the topic of Green Mountain ski areas comes up.

Between West Burke and Burke Mountain Ski Area, you'll drive for 5 miles through the West Burke Municipal Forest as well as on some pretty back roads. Before you make the left to head to Burke Mountain, drive into the downtown area of East Burke, making a sharp right-hand turn where you see the sign for the Friendly Art Gallery, a.k.a. *The Art Cache.*

The retailers and storekeepers who have chosen to do business here in East Burke haven't come for the nightlife. By her own admission, Mary

Visit an Artist

*T*he Vermont Crafts Council sponsors an annual Memorial Day **Open Studio Weekend,** which gives visitors an opportunity to go into the studios of more than 120 artists and fine craftspeople all over the state. In addition to artists in many media, studios include those of makers of fine reproduction and contemporary furniture, potters, and photographers. You can get a map of the arts tour from the Vermont Arts Council, 1344 State Street, Montpelier 05602, and from any state welcome center, or call the council at (802) 223–3380 or check out Vtcrafts@aol.com.

Martin, who runs The Art Cache, says that things in town just about die after the lifts close. But Martin doesn't care. She came to East Burke more than twenty years ago specifically to have an art gallery, and she hasn't looked back.

Martin exhibits established artists from all over, not just from Vermont, on a knoll looking up to Burke Mountain just across the valley. Her art is reasonably priced and follows a broad range of styles: oil, watercolor, acrylic, pen and ink, and prints. Her clientele is equally diverse, ranging from locals to people who come from California. Every June The Art Cache has an Annual Sports Art Show, with art themed around golf, tennis, water sports, equestrian activities, and, of course, skiing. Martin keeps a scrapbook of press clippings, brochures, and photographs of all the artists whose works are currently displayed at the gallery.

Housed in two rooms of a house built in 1856, the Art Cache is open daily from 10:00 A.M. to 5:00 P.M. The Art Cache, One Darling Hill Road, East Burke 05832; (802) 626–5711.

Down the main road of East Burke is **Bailey's & Burke Country Store,** an institution for decades for skiers and snowmobilers. If you've ever had any desire to furnish your entire house in Vermontiana, you can do your one-stop shopping here. Household goods, clothing, toiletries, toys, stuffed animals, knickknacks, wicker furniture, live bait, groceries—these are just a few of the items available. In fact, you can't drive through East Burke or go skiing at Burke Mountain without stopping at Bailey's—it's physically impossible. And Bailey's is the reason there's no mall within a good two-hour drive of here, for it goes one step beyond a mall by filling a number of rooms, balconies, and alcoves with souvenirs and necessities alike.

Along with the groceries, fresh bagels, trendy condiments, and decorator items for those who want to make their home look "Vermonty," you'll find tucked into a back corner, next to the nail-and-screws bin, a community bulletin board with menus from area restaurants and other useful information. Bailey's has achieved the perfect blend of serving both the local residents and the great variety of travelers and skiers who pass through. The store's hours testify to the owners' dedication to being there when townspeople need them: Monday through Saturday 6:30 A.M. to 9:00 P.M. and Sunday 7:30 A.M. to 8:00 P.M. Bailey's & Burke Country Store, Route 114, East Burke 05832, or call (802) 626–9250.

Burke Mountain is a family-friendly ski area where Olympians train but intermediate and beginning skiers can find plenty of comfortable runs, including a novice trail from the top. Facilities are low-key and good, not flashy or "Ye Olde Swisse," as has become the trend farther south. Burke Mountain's cross-country area has 50-odd miles of trails through mixed forests and across meadows with mountain views. It begins right at the base of the ski slopes, handy for families who have both kinds of skiers. Rentals and lessons are available at either. For the downhill area, call (802) 626–3322; for cross-country, (802) 626–8338; Burke Mountain Ski Area, P.O. Box 247, East Burke 05832, www.skiburke.com.

In the summer and fall, you can drive to the top of Burke Mountain on the Toll Road, which is the other use for that long novice ski trail from the top. At any time of year, the view is lovely and includes the ridges of Mounts Pisqah and Hoar, with Lake Willoughby between them. From this distance, they look like a single ridge with a giant bite chewed out of the center.

When the O'Reillys, who had several children, tired of being consigned to look-alike motels when they traveled with their family, they resolved to create a fine inn where children were not only welcome but could also pursue their own pleasures without interfering with adult guests' enjoyment of theirs. They have succeeded admirably with the warm and hospitable **Wildflower Inn,** on a hilltop with views over the mountains. Stunning gardens frame every view in the spring, summer, and fall, while autumn brings a panorama of brilliant foliage. The swimming pool is set in the gardens, with a view of its own.

Kids of all ages get a lot of attention—teddy-bear-shaped pancakes at breakfast (parents get a full hot breakfast, too, starting with homemade granola chock full of giant pecan pieces), a barn full of baby animals to pat and watch, bunk beds in many of the rooms, a sledding hill (with sleds) and lighted skating rink, playground equipment, a batting cage, a pitching machine, a basketball court, a playhouse, and a playroom with games and a trunkful of costumes. Mealtimes are planned so parents can have an early prelude while kids eat dinner (from a separate menu filled with their favorites, complete with drink and dessert at $5.95), then enjoy their own dinner later while the kids are entertained elsewhere—or sound asleep.

Guests without children are just as much at home in these well-decorated rooms and suites, the latter with kitchenettes. We liked the Old Schoolhouse, a separate building that's perfect for a honeymoon suite. A dozen miles of cross-country ski trails (free to guests) wind through the property, and weekend winter carnivals in March bring skating parties, contests, and dogsledding. Sleigh rides and hayrides are available regularly.

Room rates range from under $100 to about $140, summer or winter, with only a modest increase during foliage season. Suites are $160 to $250 in winter, $165 to $280 in the summer.

The dining room, which overlooks impeccably kept gardens and mountain views from a glass-enclosed porch, has an eclectic and creative menu. Grilled chicken breast is served with a tomato salsa or marinated in lemon and dill and served with Vermont chèvre over a coulis of blackberries. Shrimp and scallops are blended in a Thai curry, yellowfin tuna is topped with tequila-lime butter, and salmon is glazed in orange and basil. The wine list is reasonably priced, and the dining staff can describe preparation details. Have you guessed yet that we've had some great meals here? Dinner is served to guests and the public, with entree prices ranging from $14 to $22.

The Wildflower Inn is on Darling Hill Road, Lyndonville 05851; (802) 626–8310 or (800) 627–8310; www.wildflowerinn.com.

On the same property is *Vermont Children's Theater,* which for the past twenty years has produced two musicals each summer, one a Broadway show and the other written especially for eight-to-thirteen-year-old actors. Performances are held in mid-July and August; tickets are inexpensive, or you can watch rehearsals in the afternoons in the 200-seat barn theater on Darling Hill Road.

The entire property was once part of the 8,000-acre farm of Elmer A. Darling, an enormously successful hotelier in New York and a major benefactor of the town. You can see his mansion and huge main barn farther up the road, both privately owned. Beyond the mansion, and also part of the original farm, you'll find the *Inn at Mountain View Farm.* Although it no longer produces cream, butter, or crops on what was once the largest farm in Vermont with 953 acres, its 440 intact, quiet, acres of farmland hold farm buildings that will entice you to explore them.

The stately brick main house, which once served as the creamery for the farm, is now a seven-room B&B, with each room named after a local town: Sutton, Sheffield, and Wheelock are three of them. There's an understated, casual elegance to the inn that owner Marilyn Pastore has worked hard to attain. There are several sitting rooms downstairs, an ice chest in the lobby, and braided rugs on all the floors, which are painted cement. The breakfast room still contains the old steam engine that provided the power to run the creamery machines; today antique furnishings are found in the common areas and in each bedroom.

A number of restored farm buildings are scattered across the land, and the weathervane atop each tells its purpose: The dairy barn has a cow weathervane that measures 5 feet in length, and on top of the creamery is a butter churn. The clock on top of the 1912 post-and-beam barn chimes on the half hour, and the structure was a model for nineteenth-century agricultural efficiency. Upstairs, hay was stored. Farmhands would spread hay evenly throughout the barn, almost up to the rafters. When it was time to feed the horses, they'd rake the hay over to what looks like half-moon hot tub structures at the sides of the barn, lift up the covers, and let the hay drop. The horses kept here were about sixteen hands high, and you can see where they chewed on the bottom of the barn's windows.

Rates at The Inn at Mountainview Farm start at about $115 mid-week and $145 on weekends. A suite is $175 to $245, and a condo with whirlpool tub, fireplace, and washer/dryer is priced from $370 a night. You'll find the inn on Darling Hill Road, East Burke 05832; (802) 626–9924 or (800) 572–4509.

South of the Burkes, you'll find another cluster of villages, all some variation on Lyndon, around the town of *Lyndonville.* You can't just buzz through this town because Route 5 makes two abrupt right-angle turns in the center of it. That's OK, since you'll want to look at some of the interesting architecture in the downtown business blocks, not to mention stopping for ice cream at Carmen's.

The *Miss Lyndonville Diner* on Route 5 is related to the Miss Vermonter diner down in St. Johnsbury, but it's not as big as its sister, and there are fewer out-of-state plates in the parking lot.

The original dining car has been enclosed but is still very much in evidence. The just-greasy-enough burgers are served plain and simple or as the Vermonter, a hamburger-and-thick-steak-fries combo with gravy spooned over both, with a side of slaw. Old-timers and locals on lunch break hang out at the counter, read the paper, and catch up on local news and the weather.

A slice of cream pie arrives at the table looking like Mount Everest. It's relatively lighter, though, and the coconut cream pie has a layer of toasted coconut sprinkled on top of both the pie crust and the whipped cream layer. You can't eat this thing without a cup of coffee.

The Miss Lyndonville is open from 6:00 A.M. until after supper, whenever the last person leaves. Call (802) 626–9890 for information, or write the diner at Route 5, Lyndonville 05851.

We're not sure how **Trout River Brewery** got its name, since there is no Trout River that we know of in East Burke, where the brewery used to be, nor in Lyndonville, where it is now. But the name inspires some clever titles for the excellent brews: Hoppin' Mad Trout, Rainbow Red, and Rising River. Hoppin' Mad is an IPA, and Rising River is a seasonal ale made from rye but tasting very much like a wheat. Scottish Ale is always on their list, as is the Chocolate Oatmeal Stout, which is hearty enough to substitute for dinner. Speaking of which, the brewery serves good pizza after 6:00 P.M. on Friday evenings. They serve pints and sampler trays daily from 11:00 A.M. until 6:00 P.M. at their brewery at 58 Broad Street, Lyndonville 05851; (802) 626–9396.

If you need to walk off the cream pie or the ale, go to White Market on the green (open daily from 8:00 A.M. to 10:00 P.M.) and ask for the directions for the 6-mile **Lyndon Covered Bridge Walk.** If you are a member of the American Volkssport Association or IVV, its international counterpart, you will quickly recognize this as a sanctioned Volkswalk (and you can get credit if you pay a $2.00 fee), but anyone can take the walk free, any time between May and October. Simply sign in at the beginning and follow the directions through four covered bridges, past the Lyndon Institute, the college, a small museum, and some fine mountain and valley views. Other Volkswalks are sponsored by the Kingdom Kickers, the area's very active Volkssporting group, which also sponsors cross-country ski events and an Oktoberfest (see events listing). To learn more about Volkssporting, contact Merrily Wieland, P.O. Box 17, East Burke 05832.

Three miles north of West Burke on Route 5 in Sutton is **Laplant's Sugar House,** where you'll find an old-fashioned 1,000-bucket sugar bush. During sugaring season you can visit the sugar bush and sample some syrup. Laplant's Sugar House, Sutton 05867; (802) 467–3900.

The Vermont towns that have evolved as busy summer communities have done so because of their proximity to large bodies of water. **Barton,** on Route 5, is no exception. Like Lake Willoughby in Westmore, Crystal Lake is the main draw in town during the summertime, and traffic jams can form even in this northern outpost. The wintertime population of Barton, however, is ten times that of Westmore.

Orleans is a village within the borders of Barton, and the two villages have shared an intense rivalry, ranging from good-natured athletic contests to outright fistfights. Orleans was originally settled as Barton Landing in 1821, and the rivalry started soon after. The final straw came in 1909, when the people of Barton Landing decided to change the name to

Orleans, so as not to appear as an underling of Barton. In the past few decades, however, the rivalry has been changed to almost a friendship, since the two villages decided to build a union school together.

The town of Glover, to the south, was settled in 1797 by General John Glover, who was granted the town in gratitude for his service in the

The Pond That Isn't There

*T*he well-named Mud Pond was the source of the Barton River, which flowed north providing power for the grist- and sawmills of Barton and Glover. But in dry summers, such as that of 1810, even the mud dried up, and the mills lay idle. About a mile south, but almost 100 feet higher, was the larger Long Pond, with plenty of water year-round. With his mill idle, owner Aaron Wilson did a little investigating in the mile of marshy brush between these ponds and discovered that their ends were really only 700 feet apart.

A little information can be a dangerous thing, so Wilson persuaded the men of Glover to dig a trench between the two, allowing some of the ample water in Long Pond to spill out and fill Mud Pond, providing water to run the mills downstream. Enough were convinced (possibly by his promise of a keg of rum when the work was done) that a group assembled on June 10 with picks and shovels. By noon, a trench was finished through the soft sand, and most of the men were sampling the rum as a few dug through the last few feet at the north end of Long Pond.

What no one knew was that inside the mound of fine sand holding the lake's end was a lining of packed clay, like the rim of a pottery bowl. When the

first pickax broke that rim, the water quickly washed away the supporting sand, and the rim shattered. By the time the slightly more than one billion gallons of water had reached Lake Memphremagog seven hours later, only one house was left in Glover, few more in Barton, and the fields and pastures were 6 feet deep in sand and mud. Wilson's mill and all the other mills were gone. Trees and boulders were swept away by the wall of water, along with houses, barns, mill machinery, dams, and livestock. Water rose as high as 75 feet above river level in narrow places.

When the pond broke loose, several men ran ahead to warn people to run for high ground, so not a single life was lost. Everyone lost crops and livestock, but they had more than five tons of fish to salt for winter, which they found stranded along the shore, pulled from the mud, or caught in tributary streams into which the fish had fled as the turbulence entered the lake.

Foundations of the church and other buildings you see in Glover are built of stones cut from a 100-ton boulder swept into the village by the flood. And up on Route 16, look for a small sign on the west side of the road marking the low muddy area that was once the 300-acre surface of Long Pond.

military during the Revolutionary War. But today Glover's most popular residents are a 180-degree turn from the town's military founder.
Near the Glover General Store, turn onto Route 122 to find social com-
mentary at the **Bread and Puppet Museum,** less than a mile up the
road on your left.

Bread and Puppet is a theater troupe that travels all over the world pre-
senting its political ideas to eager audiences. It was begun in 1963 on
New York's Lower East Side by an artist-actor named Peter Schumann.
He began Bread and Puppet by traveling around New England with a
stick-puppet show telling stories from the Bible. Then the organization
became more radical, using life-size puppets and performing in
parades in New York. Schumann moved his troupe to Plainfield, Vermont, in 1970, then to its present location in Glover in 1974.

You'll never mistake them for conservatives, but all types of people
used to show up at Bread and Puppet's annual Domestic Resurrection
Circus, a two-day event that thousands of people participated in on the
theater's pastures. But the big annual show, so famous that several
alternative restaurants as far away as Brattleboro used to close for
"Bread and Puppet Day," is no more. Instead, smaller shows are performed at 3:00 P.M. on Sunday afternoons in July and August. Call for a
schedule of other performances and events. The museum is open all
summer through October, and if you've never seen the theater's actors
in performance, the museum can be a little overwhelming. The sign
reads ENTER AT YOUR OWN RISK. Don't say you haven't been warned.

Bread and Puppet makes its point using 12-foot-high, larger-than-life-
size puppets with huge heads and tiny bodies. But the exhibits do what
a museum should do: make you think. Downstairs in the former horse
stable—this was the former Dopp Farm—are montages of previous
performances.

If downstairs is striking, then upstairs is an absolute assault on the
senses, for everything hangs from the ceiling—a visual cacophony of
papier-mâché globes, 12-foot-tall Ben Franklin look-alikes, and more.
There's also a box of puppets for adults and kids to play with if inspira-
tion hits. Across the road is the **Cheap Art Bus,** an old school bus filled
with art and prints ranging from 10 cents to $15.00, though most go for
around $5.00. The museum and shop are open every day from 10:00
A.M. to 6:00 P.M. June through October, and the museum is open the rest
of the year by appointment. Bread and Puppet Museum, Route 122,
Glover 05839; (802) 525-3031.

St. Johnsbury

S t. Johnsbury developed as a busy northeastern Vermont outpost due to its location at the confluence of three major waterways: the Passumpsic River, the Moose River, and Sleeper's River. The Fairbanks family from Massachusetts also influenced the growth of the town—despite its appearance, St. Jay, as it's commonly called, is a town, not a city. By building a factory, Thaddeus Fairbanks, inventor of the lever scale, made good on the initial patent he was awarded in 1830.

Today, the town seems to have two separate parallel main streets running through it, each with a totally different atmosphere. The lower one, Railroad Street, is the commercial area with facing rows of brick business blocks. Up the hill is **Main Street,** an avenue of fine Victorian residences, churches, and public edifices, several of which were designed by the architect Lambert Packard. Some of these are based on the Richardson Romanesque style (which Bostonians know well from the imposing Trinity Church on Copley Square). The centerpiece is the red sandstone Fairbanks Museum, a classic of Richardson style, which contrasts with the also Victorian (and also Lambert Packard) but much more perpendicular Gothic style of the North Congregational Church opposite it. These and other outstanding Victorian buildings on Main Street—including Grace Methodist Church, which has a large Tiffany window—are described in a flyer mapping a thirty-minute walking tour of the street.

You can get this map and other fascinating brightly colored information sheets from the **Fairbanks Museum and Planetarium,** where you will certainly want to stop. This wonderful Victorian "cabinet of curiosities," which began as the private collections of the town's favorite son and benefactor, has an oak barrel-vaulted ceiling with an arcade of cherry and oak display cases forming an upper gallery. The building is as fascinating as its exhibits, which range from an interactive examination of Vermont's wetlands and the creatures that inhabit them to a bizarre collection of Victorian "bug art" portraits of Washington, Lincoln, and others. Be sure to stop at the wildflower identification table, where you will see fresh examples of wild plants in bloom locally during the current week. The requisite stuffed birds are from all over the world, as are the other natural history collections, although the wildlife displays concentrate on Vermont habitats.

Upstairs are old toys, dollhouses, books, and stone tools from an Abenaki grave in Swanton. The *Vermont in the Civil War* exhibit shows everything from medical and dental implements to a saddle used in battle. Downstairs is for the kids—a hands-on nature center complete with wasp hives, frogs, iguanas, and turtles, as well as machines that show some of the basic properties of physics. The museum also serves as an official U.S. weather observation station, and its planetarium offers in its fifty-seat theater informational programs on the weather and sky above St. Johnsbury.

The museum is on Main Street and is open year-round. Its hours are from 9:00 A.M. to 5:00 P.M. Monday through Saturday and from 1:00 to 5:00 P.M. Sunday. In July and August the museum is open 10:00 A.M. to 6:00 P.M. Planetarium shows are scheduled during open hours, but you should call ahead for the times. Admission is $5.00 for adults, $4.00 for seniors, and $3.00 for ages five through eighteen. A family rate is available. For more information, write to the Fairbanks Museum and Planetarium, Main and Prospect Streets, St. Johnsbury 05819, or call (802) 748–2372.

Although Lambert Packard did not design the **St. Johnsbury Athenaeum and Art Gallery**, he did supervise the building of the art gallery, which was constructed to house Albert Bierstadt's *The Domes of Yosemite,* still displayed there.

The building, which is a National Historic Landmark, serves as the town's public library, but visitors are welcome into the athenaeum, an immense dark room with a lone skylight overhead and quietly whirring ceiling fans. The sign at the door says WELCOME TO THE NINE-

Really Do Be Wary of Moose

*A*s you drive in this part of the state, especially along Route 114, which parallels the international border, you'll see an increasing number of signs warning MOOSE CROSSING or MOOSE NEXT 12 MILES or MOOSE NEXT 5,000 FEET. These are not tourist advertisements to tell you the best sites for wildlife watching. They are serious warnings to sharpen your peripheral road-scanning skills in order to avoid a collision with the most dangerous animal in the northern woods. Slow down when you see these signs, and be especially watchful on overcast days, in the early morning and evening, after dark, and early in the spring. Moose don't dent cars—they total them, and often the driver and passengers as well. Nearly everyone up here knows a family that has lost someone to a moose collision, a more frequent occurrence as the moose population increases. Take a good look at the stuffed moose in the Fairbanks Museum in St. Johnsbury, and picture it flying over the hood of your car. You'll understand why you should slow down in moose country.

TEENTH CENTURY, which is true if you ignore the current best-sellers out in the main part of the library.

The paintings include several religious subjects from the Italian school, as well as classic ships-at-sea and others. The art is a mix of American and European styles, and the collection, as well as the building, was financed by Governor Horace Fairbanks. The showcase at the entrance has books and ephemera from the early days of St. Johnsbury.

The athenaeum is open Monday and Wednesday from 10:00 A.M. to 8:00 P.M.; Tuesday, Thursday, and Friday from 10:30 A.M. to 5:30 P.M.; and Saturday from 9:30 A.M. to 4:00 P.M. St. Johnsbury Athenaeum/Art Gallery, 1171 Main Street, St. Johnsbury 05819. (802) 748–8291; www. stjathenaeum.org.

An entire block of downtown St. Johnsbury burned in the winter of 2000, taking, among other businesses, the **Northern Lights Book Shop and Cafe.** The good news is that the rebuilding is complete, and the same cheery staff will serve up delicious hot scones in the morning and homemade soup of the day at lunch, along with their famous low-fat vegetarian chili, portobello burgers, and the "kitchen sink omelet" that begins so many of our days in Saint Jay. The cafe is open from 9:00 A.M. (maybe earlier in summer) and remains open for dinner until 8:30 on Thursday and Friday evenings—the only days dinner is served. The bookstore keeps standard downtown business hours, staying open until

They Carried It to the End of the Earth

*W*hen Albert Bierstadt's monumental painting The Domes of Yosemite *was brought from New York to St. Johnsbury in 1873 to be displayed in its specially built gallery, New York critics lamented it as a "profound loss to civilization." The 10-by-15-foot painting is one of the largest landscapes in the United States and is appropriately (well, maybe not, according to nineteenth-century New Yorkers) housed in the country's oldest Victorian art gallery still in its unadulterated original form. Most other galleries have been modernized, but like the neighboring Fairbanks Museum, this building remains a pristine monument to the age of great public museums.*

This appropriation of things from the Big Apple didn't end with the painting, however. The street clock at the corner of Main Street and Eastern Avenue in front of the Athenaeum was formerly in the old Grand Central Station and was placed here in 1910, where it has told time (but not always the correct time) ever since.

The Artist Will Not See You Now

In the nineteenth century, a self-educated artist named Russell Risley lived in the town of Kirby, which lies north of Route 2 as you head east out of St. Johnsbury. Russell and his sister devised a series of levers, pulleys, and trapezes to transfer full and empty milk pails between their house and the barn. They lived as virtual hermits; instead of visiting with real people, Russell painted pictures of neighbors and prominent figures on the side of his barn. Although people came from all over to see his creations, Russell was, after all, a loner at heart; thus, he painted a sign that said SMALLPOX and thereby solved his problem.

9:00 P.M. on Thursday and Friday. It is on Railroad Street, in downtown St. Johnsbury 05819; (802) 748–4463.

If you happen to be in St. Johnsbury on a Monday night, June through the end of August, then you're lucky enough to be able to hear the **Courthouse Park Band Concerts** held in the town center. If you thought these outdoor band concerts had gone the way of the Edsel, guess again, because you'll be able to hear everything from oompah bands to Glenn Miller tunes. For more information and a calendar of upcoming performers, call (802) 633–3757.

Molly Newell's **Broadview Farm Bed & Breakfast** is on a quiet side road that was once part of the Boston Post Road. In fact, the house itself, which is on the National Register of Historic Places, once served as a stagecoach inn on the route.

The road doesn't see much traffic, but Molly Newell doesn't mind; her bed-and-breakfast brings her plenty of company from Memorial Day weekend through October, when it's open.

The four guest rooms up a steep flight of stairs are filled with the artifacts of the lives of Molly's relatives. In what she calls the Children's Room, there's a picture of her father and his twin sister as children in front of the farmhouse. A pair of Molly's aunt's shoes hang above the bureau, and in the Whittier Room, named for her opera singer–aunt, Harriet Whittier, a pair of old pointe shoes and old silver brushes and combs rest on the table. Outdoors, guest can swim or fish in the new pond Molly's children have built for her. Write to Broadview Farm Bed & Breakfast, 2627 McDowell Road, Danville 05828; (802) 748–9902.

Concord, on Route 2, claims the distinction of being home to the first school in America specifically founded to train teachers. The **First Normal School,** as it was called, was founded in 1823 by the Reverend Samuel Read Hall. The house is 2.5 miles south of Route 2; follow the signs to Concord Corners. The house is not open to the public.

From Route 2, follow signs to Granby and Victory, a left turn as you're headed east. The first few miles of the route are paved, and lots of young hardwoods line the road, which follows the curve of the Moose

River. At the Victory town line, the road turns to dirt as you enter the *Victory Bog Wildlife Management Area,* a protected area of almost 5,000 acres where deer, bear, grouse, and woodcock roam freely. There are 5 miles of old logging roads and unmarked trails to explore, as well as several parking areas.

A couple of miles into the bog, if you're sharp-eyed you'll see to your left a boulder with a plaque that reads IN MEMORY OF FRED MOLD, WHO WORKED TO PRESERVE VICTORY BOG. IN HIS ROUND OF DAILY LIFE, HE GAVE OF HIMSELF. HE CARED ABOUT THE 'LEAST OF HIS BREATHREN' AND TOOK THE TIME TO EVEN FEED THE BIRDS. WHERE HE MET A STRANGER, THERE HE LEFT A FRIEND. 1921–1975.

It's a nice place for a picnic, surrounded by a quiet pine forest and giant spruce trees. You'll have no doubt that you're in a bog, with the wetlands and stands of ghostly trees that line both sides of the road.

On the other side of the bog, a right turn in the village of Gallup Mills (which is still part of the town of Victory) brings you through little *Granby,* the last town in Vermont to get electricity. That was in 1962. As you head on toward Guildhall, watch the right-hand side of the road for an old *garage covered with license plates,* literally *covered.* There are plates from Vermont and other states and from many years—1962, 1959, Maine, California, New York, New Hampshire, Nevada, Connecticut, Washington. Old vanity plates read SALTY, TOPCAT, TEACH, CHESSS. An old rusting car in back is slowly becoming part of the land. The sign reads NO TRESPASSING.

Guildhall is the only town in the world with this name. The Essex County Courthouse is here, along with more houses than you've seen for many miles if you arrived here via Victory Bog. Route 102 wends its way north, playing tag with the Connecticut River to the town of Maidstone. This is prime hunting country, and landowners are pretty liberal about allowing hunters on their land. Instead of the posted NO TRESPASSING/NO HUNTING signs that are common in the southern part of the state, HUNTING BY PERMISSION signs abound. Often the landowners offer themselves out as hunting guides to people who don't know the territory.

The entrance to *Maidstone State Park* is in the town of Brunswick. The 5-mile dirt access road proceeds to Maidstone Lake and the park, which even in summer is uncrowded throughout its 469 acres. There are eighty-three campsites, rental boats, fishing, swimming, and plenty of picnic tables. Listen for the loon cries from the lake. The park is open daily Memorial Day through Labor Day from dawn to dusk. For more information, call (802) 676–3930, or write to Maidstone State Park, Box 185, Guildhall 05905.

In Lemington, the **Columbia Covered Bridge** crosses over into Cole-brook, New Hampshire. This is sparsely populated land, which appears to revel in its isolation. It's thrived for years, hidden away from the rest of the world and from most human influence, with scarcely more than 100 residents in the 20,532-acre town.

This makes **Canaan,** the next town north, seem like a metropolis by comparison, with a number of Christmas tree farms, dairy farms, and a couple of restaurants in town. Many Canaanites say they feel more of an affinity with New Hampshire than with Vermont up in this corner of the state, where bridges lead over the Connecticut River into the Granite State. The radio and TV stations and newspapers they receive are from New Hampshire and Canada; delivery of Vermont newspapers takes a day longer.

At **Beecher Falls,** just north of Canaan, is the one tiny place where New Hampshire and Vermont share a land border. At Beecher Falls, the Con-necticut River turns due east, while the border continues to run generally north. Canada is directly north, and although the line of the U.S.-Canadian international boundary was set in the 1800s by the Webster-Ashburton Treaty, the two states continued to dispute the exact location of the line for many years. The issue finally went to the supreme court of the U.S. Boundary Commission in 1934, and the definitive line was drawn.

You can cross it on a road that leaves Beecher Falls and follows the river to the right, while the main road continues left to the international line and the customs control point. The river is a lazy stream here, and as you follow it, you can see cars on Route 3 in New Hampshire on the other side. After the pavement ends, and just as you're sure you must have sneaked over into Canada by mistake, you'll see a **granite bound-ary marker** set at an odd angle on the left side of the road. Its position is skewed because it sits directly astride the border, and on one half is carved TOWN/CANAAN VERMONT and on the other LINE/PITTSBURGH NEW HAMPSHIRE. Cross that line and you'll need a copy of *New Hampshire: Off the Beaten Path* to guide you.

About 3 miles north of the center of Canaan on Route 114, **Wallace Pond** is on the right. The Canadian border is somewhere in the mid-dle of the pond. If you can find the exact point with a boat, you can fish in two countries at once. The boat access ramp is located just off the road. There are a couple of camping areas nearby with good views of the pond.

Averill is large, with an area of 24,320 acres, and was one of the first towns in the Kingdom—not to mention the state—to be chartered, in 1762. But the town was never organized and today has only a dozen or so year-round residents.

Quimby Country is a sixty-two-acre, rustic resort tucked into the woods on the shore of Forest Lake. The best way to describe it is as a summer camp for families. Guests are also close to Great Averill Pond and Little Averill Pond, remote bodies of water that are superb for fishing, swimming, and boating. Meals are family-style; lodging is either in the big lodge or in one of twenty cabins.

Quimby's motto is "Where nothing ever changes," and apart from the addition of a more dependable electrical system, that's quite true. During the summer, rates (which include meals) are about $120 to $140 per adult, with lower rates for children based on their age. In spring and fall (Quimby's is open from mid-May to mid-October) cottages with kitchens begin at $50 per person, but without meals. In the spring, these cottages are popular with fishermen and birders, who enjoy seeing the migrating flocks that stop around the lake. Wildflowers are at their best in June, with lady's slippers carpeting the ground in places. In September the lake shores are painted in bright leaves. All the boats, tennis courts, and other facilities are there off-season, but you have fewer people to share them with.

In the summer, Quimby's rates also include a full program for children, with counselors. For more information, write to Quimby Country, Forest Lake, Averill 05901; (802) 822–5533.

Norton's claim to immortality is that, while it was the first town to be granted a charter in the state, it was among the last to be settled, in 1860. To reach Norton from any other part of Vermont, travelers first had to go into Canada and then come down south into the town center, which straddles the international boundary line. This rate caused the delay in settlement.

Brighton incorporates the village of *Island Pond*—a place with quite an illustrious past. A religious group lives in town, and after some initial tensions between the group and the townspeople, both groups now live

You Might as Well Hear It from Us

It's a classic border tale, one of many told along the Connecticut River, and you're bound to hear it if you hang around long enough. When the exact location of the border was finally established, the local selectmen went to visit an elderly Vermonter whose home, according to the new line, was now in New Hampshire. They feared that the shock would be too much for him and took the local doctor along just in case. But they needn't have worried. A happy smile broke out on the old gentleman's face at the news, and he replied with fervor: "Good, b' God, I don't think I could've survived another one of those Vermont winters!"

side by side, some say peacefully, others say by merely tolerating each other. Mystery writer Archer Mayor, who lives down near Brattleboro, based his 1990 novel *Borderlines* on the religious group.

Right in the center of Island Pond, you'll find ***Jennifer's Restaurant,*** where you can get hot sandwiches with gravy and fries for $4.95, a BLT packed with bacon for $2.50, or full dinners for $8.00 to $12.00. A fisherman's platter is $13.95. It's casual and friendly, and you'll overhear a lot of local news while you eat. Jennifer's also serves breakfast, and only a truck driver from Quebec could finish off a platter of their pancakes. Jennifers, Cross Street, Island Pond 05846; (802) 723–6135.

Lakeside Park is right on the village's namesake, Island Pond. In the middle of the pond is a twenty-two-acre island, which measures 1 mile wide by 2 miles long.

Stand on the shore of Island Pond, close your eyes, and listen for the long-ago bustle of a town where the most valuable resource in the midst of the Industrial Revolution was this body of water. The pond once served as the outlet for the tributary off the Pherrins River that was used as a transport for floating logs from Norton and Canada. Island Pond—the village—was also known as the halfway point between Montreal and Portland, Maine, on the Grand Trunk Railway, where the lumber from the Great North was transferred to the railway.

South of St. Jay

The valley south of St. Johnsbury is a pretty, rural area where many artists have been inspired to call such towns as Peacham and Barnet home. Farms are interspersed with crisp white Capes and rolling vistas of the mountain ranges and lakes that characterize Vermont.

At the ***P&H Truck Stop*** in Wells River, in the north end of the town of Newbury, *thick* is the watchword, whether you order omelets, meat loaf, pork chops, fish chowder, or onion rings. This is an old-fashioned kind of truck stop where locals, truckers, and travelers all converge to chow down on delicious and hearty real food. The truckers have their own section upstairs to eat in and relax, while families sit downstairs.

The menu is written in both French and English. Don't pass up some of the homemade bread at P&H: white, oatmeal, whole wheat, or cinnamon raisin. P&H is open twenty-four hours a day, seven days a week, and more than a few southern Vermonters have been known to drive up to Wells River at 3:00 A.M. for a piece of Reese's Pie—made with chocolate cream, chocolate pudding, and peanut butter, an exact replica of the candy—or maple cream pie. If only they delivered . . . via Federal Express. Write to P&H, Route 302, Wells River 05081, or call (802) 429–2141.

The *William Scott Sleeping Sentinel Monument* is just down the road west of the village. During the Civil War, Groton native William Scott enlisted in the Union army. He drew night duty one evening, then stood in again the next night for a fellow soldier who was ill. Scott fell asleep and was court-martialed; however, President Lincoln stepped in and pardoned him, rescuing him from the firing squad. Scott went back into battle, and not too long after his pardon he was killed in Virginia.

Route 232 North cuts through *Groton State Forest* just west of the village. Old railroad lines within the forest are now hiking trails.

On Route 2 in Danville, *Deerfield Village Furniture* is on the north side of the street across from the high school. This is the showroom for antique furniture reproductions made in a workshop in St. Johnsbury. The setting is an historic Danville home, the Smith House, which dates to 1797.

The showroom is open Monday through Saturday from 10:00 A.M. to 4:30 P.M. Deerfield Village Furnture, 198 Route 2, Danville 05828; (802) 684–2156.

Also in Danville is the *American Society of Dowsers,* which is open to the public. Dowsing is the ancient art of locating underground water sources, and you can take free lessons here Monday through Friday between 9:00 A.M. and 5:00 P.M. There are also weekend workshops; call for a free information packet. The society's annual convention is held in late July or early August at Lyndon State College, where you can sit in on basic, expanded, and specialized classes and a wide variety of lectures on dowsing and related topics, including earth energies, feng shui, and labyrinths. Behind the headquarters building is a labyrinth that you are welcome to visit whether the society headquarters is open or not. The society's store, at 99 Railroad Street in St. Johnsbury 05819, carries tools and books on dowsing and other New Age subjects. The store is open from 10:00 A.M. to 5:00 P.M. Tuesday through Saturday; (802) 748–8565. For a free book catalog, classes, or convention information, call (802) 684–3417 or (800) 711–9497.

If you leave Danville on Brainerd Street, where the Society of Dowsers is located, you will see some of the state's finest views of its neighbors, the White Mountains of New Hampshire. To the left is the Killkenny Range; to the right is Cannon Mountain and Franconia Notch, with Mounts

Lincoln and Lafayette, with Loon Mountain showing in between their peaks. If you continue straight at the fork, along the top of the ridge, you will enjoy more mountain views before dropping to the *Greenbanks Hollow Covered Bridge*. Built in 1886, it spans a rushing river that drops a significant distance as it cascades past the stone foundations of old mills. The sides of this small, one-lane bridge are open, not enclosed, as most others are.

If, however, you bear left onto Joe's Brook Road, you will come to the *Danville Morgan Horse Farm,* stretching along a hillside with more White Mountain views. You can visit the farm any day between 9:00 A.M. and 3:00 P.M. Small signs point the way from Danville or from Route 5, where you will end up if you continue along Joe's Brook Road. The address is 1906 Joe's Brook Road, Danville 05828; (802) 684–2251; www.dmhf@kingcon.com.

MORE PLACES TO STAY IN THE NORTHEAST KINGDOM

(ALL AREA CODES 802)

GREENSBORO (05841)
Highland Lodge has comfortable, homey rooms, good food (have lunch on the veranda overlooking Caspian Lake), and an accommodating staff. The lodge is open from mid-December until mid-March (when they have cross-country skiing) and from Memorial Day to Columbus Day; 533–2647.

WESTMORE (05822)
The WilloughVale Inn has views from each of its seven unique rooms and four lakefront cottages, all furnished in handcrafted Vermont furniture. The inn is closed in November and

April. Overlooking Lake Willoughby on Route 5A; 525–4123; www.willowvale.com.

EAST BURKE (05832)
Bed & Breakfast at Moose Crossing, on Route 114 about 2 miles from Burke Mountain, has two guest rooms with private baths in a recently renovated farmhouse. Rates are very reasonable, especially so close to a ski area; (802) 626–0989; www.moosecrossingbb. com.

ISLAND POND (05846)
Overlooking Island Pond, in the center of town, the *Lakefront Motel* is a nicely kept property where snowmobilers congregate in the winter, and people who enjoy water sports can moor their boats or beach their canoes; Cross Street; 723–6507.

LOWER WATERFORD (05848)
Rabbit Hill Inn, afroth with lace, canopied beds, fireplaces, whirlpool baths, and an air of detachment from the mundanities of

To Learn More in Northeast Kingdom

For information on the lower Northeast Kingdom, contact the Lyndon Area Chamber of Commerce, *P.O. Box 886, Lyndonville 05851; (802) 626–9696,* You can learn more about the entire area on the Internet at www.travelthekingdom.com or by calling *(888) 884–8001.*

life, is set on extensive grounds; 748–5168 or (800) 76–BUNNY.

Information on local B&Bs is available at www.travelthekingdom.com.

MORE PLACES TO EAT IN THE NORTHEAST KINGDOM

(ALL AREA CODES 802)

WESTMORE
The WilloughVale Inn has a casual tap room and a more formal main dining room overlooking Lake Willoughby; 525–4123.

DANVILLE (05828)
Danville Restaurant and Inn is a family-run dining room that has long been a local favorite. Breakfast is served Monday through Saturday, lunch Monday through Friday, and dinner on Friday and Saturday; Main Street; 684–3484.

The Creamery is an upscale restaurant open lunch and dinner Tuesday through Saturday; Hill Street; 684–3616.

EAST BURKE (05832)
Old Cutter Inn, on Mountain Road, East Burke, is highly recommended by local people for its continental menu. It's closed in November and April and on Wednesday; 626–5152.

River Garden Cafe, in the center of East Burke, serves lunch and dinner year-round (except Monday) in an upbeat setting. Jamaican jerked chicken with black beans, fajitas, pesto salmon, or rack of lamb may be on the menu; 626–3514.

COVENTRY (05825)
Heermansmith Farm Inn is intimate and gracious, serving healthy dishes with style. Look for the roast duck, and enjoy the fresh berries grown on the farm. Open for dinner, mid-June to mid-September, Wednesday through Sunday; Heermanville Road (off Route 5); 754–8866

NORTH TROY (05859)
North Troy Village Pub and Restaurant combines good food with a lot of history, which owner Irene will be glad to share if asked. It's open from 5:00 P.M.; closed Tuesday; School Street; 988–4063.

Buon Amici is a cheery Italian-American restaurant; closed Monday and Tuesday, open 5:00 to 9:00 P.M. other days. Railroad Street; 988–2299.

NEWPORT (05855)
East Side Restaurant and Pub, 47 Landing Street, with solid menu featuring prime rib and pot roast, is also known for its chowder. It overlooks Lake Memphremagog; 334–2340.

ST. JOHNSBURY (05819)
Cindy's Pasta Shop makes pasta and serves a good variety of pasta dishes at reasonable prices; Route 5 North; 748–4848

Central Vermont

Central Vermont has long been defined by its massive granite quarries, whether you look at the many Scottish, Irish, and Italian granite workers who flocked to the area during the last half of the nineteenth century or at the rough topography that determined where residential areas cropped up, where the best access routes to the quarries were, and where the railroad tracks were laid. And given the region's "landlocked" status—it didn't share any borders with other states or with Canada—Vermonters in this central area had to learn to rely on themselves to a greater extent and in different ways than people in other parts of the state.

But this region of Vermont also has its own particular rugged beauty that is unlike the Green Mountain range to the west or the almost-nautical air of the towns that skirt Lake Champlain. Central Vermont's beauty stems from the rocky riverbeds of the first, second, and third branches of the White River, branches that eventually wind their way down and through the mountains to empty into the Connecticut River. The region's beauty also comes from the stands of second- and third-growth forest that line the sides of the state highways through towns such as Chelsea and Corinth. And it's hard to miss the beauty in the wide valleys that cut a swath along Route 12 in Braintree and Brookfield. Only occasionally does a house pop up in some of these spots.

So drive down an unmarked dirt road on impulse, or follow the signs to the quarries in Barre, to see a part of Vermont that is unlike any other.

Barre/Montpelier

The Barre/Montpelier area is the thriving, active heart of this central region and of the state. Barre has been home to thousands of immigrants over the years, from the Italian stonecutters who came to Vermont via Ellis Island to work in the granite quarries to the Irishmen who were recruited in droves to work on the railroad, first to lay track and then to operate the trains.

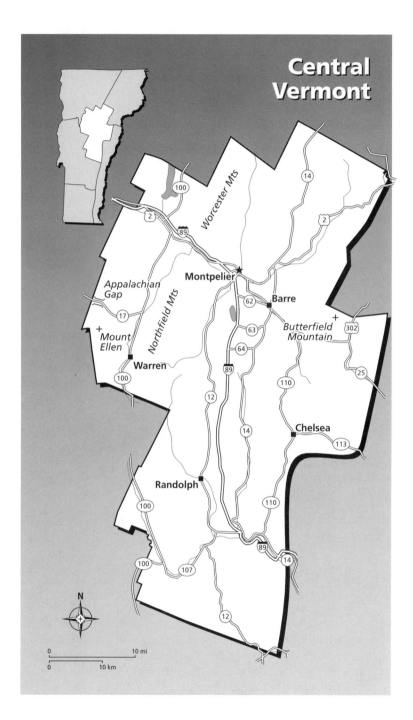

Central Vermont

Worcester Mts

Montpelier

Barre

Appalachian Gap

Northfield Mts

Mount Ellen

Warren

Butterfield Mountain

Chelsea

Randolph

N

0   10 mi
0   10 km

AUTHORS' TOP HIGHLIGHTS:

Hope Cemetery

Covered bridges in Tunbridge and Randolph

Brookfield Floating Bridge

The granite quarries were founded shortly after the end of the War of 1812. Three grades of granite are still taken from the mountains: a coarse stone ideal for millstones and doorsteps; a less sandy stone for house foundations, much like the stone used to build the state capitol in Montpelier; and the beautiful, almost flawless stone that is used for gravestones and monuments all over the world.

Despite the retail development both downtown and on the Barre-Montpelier Road, Barre has managed to retain its working-class, melting-pot flavor for more than a century.

Hope Cemetery, a seventy-five-acre cemetery that dates back to 1895, is on Route 14 just north of Route 302. The cemetery is known for its elaborate carvings of Vermont's early-twentieth-century stonecutters. New stones are interspersed with old ones, and Italian names are plentiful. When you first enter Hope Cemetery, turn right and drive around its perimeter to see some remarkable granite statuary stones.

The lifelike sculptures of some of the grave markers are the attraction at Hope Cemetery. Far left and back look for the Brusa stone: A brooding angel, with legs crossed, trumpet on lap, sits beneath a Greek pillar and balustrade sculpture. Here, so as not to detract from the elegance and detail of monuments, small stones with the name of each family member are placed in front of the sculpture.

Population Burst

*B*arre holds the distinction of having the largest increase in population in Vermont to occur within a decade: With the opening of Ellis Island in New York City and the great influx of skilled granite workers from Scotland, Italy, and Scandinavia, the population of Barre increased from 2,060 in 1880 to 6,812 in 1890. Social unrest soon followed, when the underpaid granite workers got together to demand better working conditions and higher pay.

Though today Barre looks like the solid, conservative, working-class town that it is, back in the late nineteenth century the politics in town were quite radical. Long before Vermont sent Bernie Sanders, the only independent in the U.S. House of Representatives, to serve in Washington, D.C., Barre elected a socialist mayor to serve its people. Early twentieth-century anarchist Emma Goldman was arrested in Barre and charged with aiding and abetting the murder of a mayor.

Also look for Elia Corti's stone, a life-size monument at the crossroads near the back of the cemetery. Corti was a stonecutter who died in 1903. His stone shows his full-size likeness sitting and gazing at the surrounding forest. A few stones away from Corti's is the Cole/Spence stone, complete with contemplative Greek goddess.

Another Brusa monument—located in another patch of stones downhill and secluded from the main yard—depicts a wife comforting her dying husband, who succumbed to silicosis, a lung disease many stonecutters contracted from breathing in stone dust. And directly in front is a sculpture of Gwendolyn and William Halvosa, a husband and wife holding hands, with the inscription SET ME AS A SEAL UPON THINE HEART FOR LOVE IS STRONG AS DEATH.

Heading back out of the cemetery, stop to walk among the stones that don't face the road. Look for a chair that serves as a grave marker, a soccer ball stone, and another with a classic Green Mountain view—complete with fence posts, a rifle, a fishing rod, a dune buggy, and lots of trucks. One shows a Shell Oil truck driving through the mountains; another serves as a belated advertisement for the Benedini Well Company, depicting a truck in the process of digging an artesian well.

You will notice a number of art nouveau and art deco influences in the designs on stones and on the bronze doors of the family vaults along the back row. On the Calcagni monument, an Erte-like angel stands in a colonnade. You will also notice that all the flowers are fresh, not plastic. Bouquets of cut flowers and carefully tended blooming plants decorate many of the burial places, and on weekends you're likely to see families tending these. Since people from the area still bury their loved ones here, Hope Cemetery is not a historical icon from bygone days. It is an active cemetery where Vermonters come to remember their dead, whether they died a century ago or last week. A cemetery is a place to pay one's respects, so remember to show courtesy to people who might not like to be reminded that visitors are taking a casual, interested stroll through the cemetery's grounds.

As you might expect, Barre has a lot of public statuary, from the traditional monuments to a war memorial—granite, of course—in 1930s heroic Realist style. In Dante Park, in honor of

That's Some Rock Band

Rock of Ages quarry in Barre is 550 feet wide, a quarter of a mile long, and 450 feet deep, the largest in the world. The high-quality granite is used for monuments and headstones because its exceptionally fine grain makes it the perfect medium for finely detailed but long-lasting, durable outdoor sculpture. The quarry is the basis of a $200 million-a-year industry that employs more than 1,500 Vermonters.

CENTRAL VERMONT

ANNUAL EVENTS IN CENTRAL VERMONT

the contribution made by Italian Americans to the city, region, and state, is a large statue of a gentleman with a kindly face, so well sculpted that his character seems to shine from within the stone. You will also notice a lot of business signs—real estate offices, the credit union—carved in granite.

The **Snack Shack** is run out of a little camping trailer on a vacant lot just across the street from the *Times-Argus*. In fact, many of the newspaper's employees grab a bite here between deadlines. Hot dogs will run you $1.00, and a handmade burger—not stamped and frozen—will set you back $1.25. Add-ons like chili, cheese, and peppers and onions will cost 25 cents extra. Besides burgers and dogs, you can get hot or mild sausage, onion rings, scallops, homemade fries, clam rolls, and ice cream. Try the chocolate ice cream and peanut butter milk shake if you crave peanut butter cups. The Snack Shack is usually open Monday through Saturday from 11:00 A.M. to 9:00 P.M. and Sunday from noon to 9:00 P.M. Contact the Snack Shack at Route 14, Barre 05641; (802) 479-5508.

In East Barre, you can visit quarries; the hills that surround the town are actually tailing piles from the quarries. In the center of this town, where the quarry workers lived, is a large antiques mall, a craft center, and the factory store of Vermont Flannel, where you can get good bargains on flannel clothing and fabric. They have a half-price sale in April.

East Barre also has one of the largest multi-dealer shops in the state. The **East Barre Antique Mall,** with over 12,000 square feet of display space, features antiques and collectibles from glass to furniture, which is one of their strong points. A basement level area is set aside for bargains. The shop is at the junction of Routes 302 and 110, 133 Mill Street, East Barre 05649; (802) 479-5190.

Though they're joined at the hip, Barre and Montpelier could never be mistaken for twins, fraternal or otherwise; they're hardly even siblings. Their temperaments are too different. From January through April Vermont's state legislature is in session in Montpelier. Elected representatives from all over the state come to the capital to decide how their

July–August: Free Summer Band Concerts, State-house lawn, Montpelier, Wednesdays at 7:00 P.M.

July 4: Annual Fourth of July Parade and Celebration, Warren; (802) 496-3409.

Mid-July: Annual Vermont Quilt Festival, Norwich University, Northfield; (802) 485-7092.

Mid-September: Tunbridge World's Fair, Tunbridge; (802) 889-5555. (Note that about 30,000 people cram into this tiny town, creating the state's longest and worst traffic jams on record.)

December: Live Nativity Pageant, Joseph Smith Birthplace, South Royalton, has live animals; Thanksgiving weekend through New Year's; (802) 763-7742.

Musical Capitals

Montpelier was established as the state capital in 1805, with the first statehouse completed in 1808. Previously the capital had rotated throughout the state, its legislators meeting in towns from Burlington to Randolph. In 1838 another, more regal statehouse was constructed and Vermonters thought the matter was settled. But the debate flared up again in 1859 after the second statehouse burned down, leaving only the shell. Montpelier remained the capital, however, rebuilding the statehouse in the same location.

state will run for the rest of the year. Then, in May, representatives in both the House and the Senate turn back into their regular selves for the rest of the year—farmers, officeworkers, and homemakers among them.

Montpelier is a dynamic state capital and the smallest in the nation, with a population of under 10,000. Several colleges are located here, and students, teenage skateboarders, conservative lawyers, and activists who live on nearby communes all know one another and frequently share a dish of Ben and Jerry's on Main Street. It's not unusual to see men with long hair and batik clothing sitting next to women in suits and high-heeled shoes.

The New England Culinary Institute is one of the foremost in the country, and as part of its training program it operates three dining rooms in Montpelier: ***Main Street Grill and Bar, Chef's Table,*** and ***La Brioche Bakery and Cafe***. Main Street Grill and Bar and Chef's Table are at 118 Main Street, the former on the street level and open for breakfast, lunch, and dinner and the latter on the second floor and open for dinner only. La Brioche is diagonally across the street at 89 Main Street.

Main Street Grill and Bar's dining room is sleek, modern, and attractive, with big sliding windows overlooking the street and al fresco dining on the portico in good weather. As expected from a culinary school, the menu is interesting and the fare well prepared. Soups and salads include a roasted eggplant and tomato soup and Asian roasted chicken salad with peanut sauce and are in the $1.95 to $5.95 range. Entrees might include Copper Ale fish and chips, Pan-seared Cajun catfish, and grilled pork satays in the $6.00 to $7.00 range. Lunch is served 11:30 A.M. to 2:00 P.M. Monday through Saturday, and dinner from 5:30 to 9:00 P.M. Monday through Sunday. Sunday brunch is served from 10:00 A.M. to 2:00 P.M. 118 Main Street, Montpelier 05602; (802) 223–3188.

Chef's Table is the domain of second-year students. A bit more formal, its innovative menu is always changing to incorporate the freshest in-season ingredients with an emphasis on Vermont products, including native lamb, duck, hams, and cheeses. It opens for lunch Monday through Friday 11:30 A.M. to 1:30 P.M. and dinner Monday through Saturday 5:00 P.M. to 9:30 P.M. 118 Main Street, Montpelier 05602; (802) 229–9202.

CENTRAL VERMONT

La Brioche is a European-style bakery, a good place for a light continental breakfast, a croissant, or baked goody in the afternoon. There are tables indoors and outdoors on a plaza raised just above sidewalk level; 89 Main Street, Montpelier 05602; (802) 229–0443.

WORTH SEEING

Morse Farm Sugar House and Museum, Main Street, Montpelier; (802) 223–2740.

Rock of Ages Quarry, tours and visitors center, Barre; (802) 476–3119.

Sugarbush Ski Resort, Mountain Road, Warren 05674; (802) 583–2381. *(The ski area offers 110 trails on three mountains.)*

Although there are a few motels located in Barre and on the outskirts of Montpelier, a better choice for lodging—one that's not too far removed from the bustle but is quiet enough that you will forget you're in a city—is *Betsy's Bed & Breakfast,* just up a hilly side street from the main street in the capital. During the early 1990s it was a decrepit-looking Queen Anne home complete with turrets crying out for rescue. Jon and Betsy Anderson, lawyers who work for the state government, have carefully restored the building to its previous glory. They did such a good job, in fact, that the house won the Montpelier Historical Society's award for best commercial renovation in 1993.

Today the B&B has three rooms in the main house and a private suite in the carriage house out back. All rooms have cable TV, telephones, and private baths. The plentiful and delicious breakfasts feature cereal, compote, blueberry pancakes, and omelets.

For more information, write to Betsy's Bed & Breakfast, 74 East State Street, Montpelier 05602, or call (802) 229–0466.

Betsy's Bed & Breakfast, Montpelier

The **Vermont State House** is interesting with its ornate halls and floors of—what else would you expect?—marble. Flags from the Civil War decorate the walls, along with portraits and other paintings. You can wander on your own or take a more formal tour with a guide, offered weekdays July through mid-October on the half hour from 10:00 A.M. to 3:30 P.M. and Saturday from 11:00 A.M. to 2:30 P.M. The building, on State Street, Montpelier 05602, is open weekdays from 8:00 A.M. to 4:00 P.M. year-round, and admission is free; (802) 828–2228.

State Street presents a remarkable architectural heritage, and a walking tour is the best way to admire all the buildings that line it. As you leave the State House, look to the right, across State Street, at number 128, the Edward Dewey House. It's as Queen Anne as you can get, with all the variety this late-1800s style embodied. Notice the different shingles, roof lines, and windows. Turn left and walk down State Street, past the flamboyant Romanesque Department of Agriculture building. Nothing could be farther from the simple lines of the farms this agency represents; like the Queen Anne house up the street, it seems never to repeat anything, with a tutti-frutti of different windows and roof styles. A tower, bay, and turret further complicate its design, which is even more embellished with a carved wooden frieze above the front door.

The clean, symmetrical lines of the 1870 building next door are a nice contrast with their tall windows and straight columns. Opposite is the elegant reconstruction of the Pavilion Hotel, which once housed legislators during sessions and now houses state offices and the Vermont Historical Society (see below). Its bricks were made from molds dating from the 1800s, and some of the original architectural ornaments, such as keystones and spindles on the porch, are originals from the earlier building.

Three buildings on the same side of the street in the next block represent different stages of the Federal period, with its clean, well-balanced shapes based on the Georgian style then popular in England. Number 107, behind the service station, shows more of the Georgian lines in its steep roof and balanced chimneys. Number 99 is more Federal, with the characteristic recessed doorway topped by a fanlight. Number 89, next to it, is quite similar and may have been one of the first houses on State Street. On the corner is the Greek Revival courthouse, and behind it on Elm Street is the old brick jail, which was transformed in the early 1900s to a flat-roofed business block; you can see where the new brickwork began.

Across the street from the courthouse is the Episcopal church, a Gothic design built of local granite. Inside you can see its vaulted ceiling and a rose window. The bank building across Elm Street from the courthouse

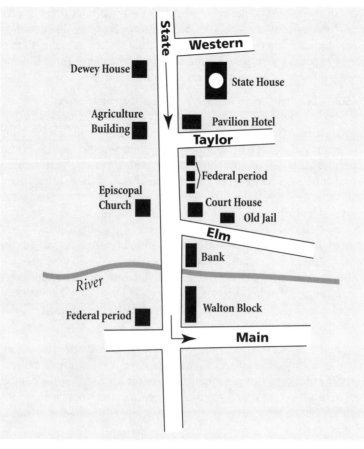

Dewey House

Agriculture Building

Episcopal Church

Federal period

State

Western

State House

Pavilion Hotel

Taylor

Federal period

Court House

Old Jail

Elm

Bank

Walton Block

Main

River

A Walking Tour of Montpelier

was built in 1874, but the mansard roof and round dormers were added about twenty years later.

The Walton Block, next to it, is a beautifully restored 1870s commercial building decorated in cast-iron columns and stamped sheet metal, a style popular in that period. Opposite, on the corner of State and Main Streets, is Montpelier's only remaining example of a Federal-period commercial building. You can recognize its Federal lines in the steeply sloping roof and the gables at the ends.

To see more fine examples, most of them Victorian, wander up Main Street to your left, past the residences that show Greek Revival and Federal origins—often mixed as the earlier Federal homes were modernized.

Some of the "newer" homes are more purely Victorian, built after two fires in 1875 destroyed many older ones. To learn more about the distinguished public and business buildings and the beautiful Victorian residences that line Montpelier's streets, seek out a copy of the brochure *Three Walking Tours,* published by a local historical group.

One of the structures you will see as you walk up Main Street is a lovely brick Federal building, almost encircled by a veranda supported on delicate columns. This is now the elegant ***Inn at Montpelier,*** its interior also beautifully restored, with fireplaces, fine woodwork, and grand staircases. It is warm and comfortable, with individually decorated rooms furnished in antiques and reproductions, each with telephone and television. Plan to be there long enough to enjoy the wraparound front porch overlooking the shady street. It is one of the nicest you'll sit on anywhere, and the relaxing atmosphere of the inn will make you want to do just that. A new addition is a little in-house bar, so you can enjoy a glass of wine on the porch. The inn is only a block from the center of Montpelier, but in a town so small this means you're still in a quiet residential neighborhood. Rooms run from $94 to $177 in high season. The inn is at 147 Main Street, Montpelier 05602; (802) 223–2727; www.innatmontpelier.com. e-mail:mail2inn@aol.com.

Next to the capitol building is the ***Vermont Historical Society,*** with an extensive library and a museum. Fortunately, you don't have to be a member of the society to visit either the library or the museum—people travel here from all over the country to conduct genealogical research, for which the library has a treasure trove of old papers, letters, and reference works.

The museum also has exhibits about the numerous stages of the state's history, and these exhibits change about once a year. One year the featured exhibit showed how Vermonters coped with the rigors of World War II on the home front. Newspapers, canned goods, and piped-in music helped create the atmosphere.

The library and administrative offices of the society have new quarters at 60 Washington St., Barre 05641. The museum is being expanded into the former library space and is closed for renovations until early 2003. The new hours for the library and museum house have not been determined but will be posted on the Web site, as will the new phone number for the library. Visit www.state.vt.us/vhs.

A donation is welcome for admission to the museum and library. Write to the Vermont Historical Society, 109 State Street, Montpelier 05602, or call (802) 828–2291 for more information.

One attraction that many friends begged us not to disclose is **Manghis'
Bakery** (pronounced "Mang-high").

Although Manghis' bread is available fresh in general stores and markets around the Barre-Montpelier area, it's best to buy it direct from
the source. Manghis' is located in a yellow semi-Victorian house that
has real estate offices and a few other small businesses. How could
anybody work in that building without succumbing to a loaf from
Manghis' at least once a day?

Manghis' bakes bread Monday through Friday. Although the bakery is
open from 7:00 A.M. to 5:00 P.M. Monday through Thursday and from
7:00 A.M. until 2:00 P.M. on Friday, the best times to stop in are from noon
to closing on Monday, Wednesday, and Thursday, or you can call ahead to
order a special loaf. Manghis' offers anadama, maple walnut, six grain,
cracked wheat, onion herb, challah, and whole wheat oatmeal breads, as
well as special breads at holiday times, like hot cross buns at Easter and
stollen at Christmas. Manghis' Bakery is located off Main Street, 2 blocks
northeast of its intersection with State Street. Or just follow the aroma of
baking bread to 28 School Street, Montpelier 05602; (802) 223–3676.

The **T. W. Wood Art Gallery** was founded to give Vermonters access to
the art of their time, and it still fills the mission with changing exhibits
of contemporary artists. But you will also see art from earlier times,
including the work of the nineteenth-century artist T. W. Wood, who
endowed the gallery. Permanent collections feature a selection of
Depression-era work. The gallery is open Tuesday through Sunday, noon
to 4:00 P.M., and admission is free. It is part of the Vermont College campus on College Street, 05602; (802) 828–8743.

Montpelier is nothing if not compact; everything is either within a
long 2-block or a short 2-block radius of everything else. Tucked away
a few steps from the main drag is **Angeleno's,** a local favorite for pizza
and pasta. Situated in an old Victorian house, Angeleno's makes the
best pizza in Vermont. The pizza has a thin crust, and the tomato
sauce is just a little bit spicy. You can choose from thirty-one different
toppings, with the more obscure ranging from peanut butter and
pickles to turkey and eggplant.

All the pasta is homemade, and daily pasta specials include baked
mostaccioli and linguine tossed with olive oil and shrimp; one side of the
menu is devoted to heart-healthy dishes and suggestions for diabetics.
Wine and beer are available, and the desserts are variations on traditional
Italian themes. The frozen tortoni is made from a slice of rum-soaked

pound cake with vanilla and chocolate ice cream and rum custard between the layers and a thick, hot, bittersweet fudge sauced ladled on top.

And, of course, Angeleno's has cannoli, a crunchy shell with a light ricotta filling that tells you it was prepared seconds before arriving at your table.

Angeleno's is open at 11:00 A.M. Monday through Saturday, closing at 9:30 P.M. Monday through Thursday and 10:00 P.M. Friday and Saturday. They are open 4:00 to 9:30 P.M. Sundays. The restaurant is at 15 Barre Street, Montpelier 05602; call (802) 229–5721 for reservations or takeout.

Sarducci's overlooks the river, with an enclosed porch for dining on the water side. Low walls separate the large dining room into several smaller areas without obscuring the view of the big wood oven or the flamboyant chef-ly show with the pizza dough in the open kitchen. But pizza, however good and tender of crust, is only part of the menu. Pasta dishes usually have more meat than pasta, a refreshing change from the usual. Nice pairings may include mussels and Italian sausage with roasted onions in a white wine sauce or sea scallops with tomatoes and asparagus in a basil broth. The menu balances well between the *haute* of northern Italian dishes and the red-sauce circuit. Sarducci's doesn't make pretenses and provides a thoroughly satisfying dinner, cheerfully served in a most pleasant atmosphere at a very reasonable price. Who can ask for more? Sarducci's is open daily, with lunch entrees at around $7.00 and most dinner entrees $8.00 to $14.00, on Main Street, Montpelier 05602; (802) 223–0229.

The *ReStore* is a shop that recycles a bit of everything and sells it to local craftspeople, schoolteachers, and others with a little imagination.

Everything at the ReStore is considered to be clean industrial scrap from Vermont businesses. And since the ReStore receives new shipments every week, the inventory is always changing.

The Great Green Mountain Pumpkin Show

*W*hile most of the spring and summer **Ellie's Farm Market** sells plants and fresh produce from their stand on Route 12, south of Montpelier, it is in October that half the population of Vermont (or so it seems) appears at Ellie's. On October 30 and 31 every year, the staff carves over 1,000 jack-o-lanterns, which are then placed about the property, even in the trees. Come after dark has settled in, preferably after 9:00 P.M. to avoid the crowds. Admission is free, but donations are taken to benefit a local charity.

All types of fabrics, wooden beads, polished marble bases, packing materials, and clay flowerpots are accepted from businesses. The ReStore has also begun to accept items from local homeowners—old lamps, bubble wrap, magazines, cookie tins, office supplies, and the like, items that would otherwise end up in Vermont landfills. Most of the items are unpackaged and displayed in large bins so that you can pick as few or as many as you need.

The ReStore is open Monday through Friday from 10:00 A.M. to 5:30 P.M. and Saturday from 9:00 A.M. to 1:00 P.M. ReStore, 186 River Street, Montpelier 05602 or P.O. Box 885, Montpelier 05601, or call (802) 229–1930.

Maple syrup and its relatives—maple sugar, candy, and cream—are perhaps the quintessential Vermont products. A good place to see these made the old-fashioned way and to experience the pleasures of a maple grove is *Bragg Farm Sugarhouse and Gift Shop.* Take the personal guided tour of the operation, or watch it all on the video. The shop sells candy, syrup, and even maple soft ice cream. The farm, open daily November through April from 8:30 A.M. to 6:00 P.M. and May through October 8:30 A.M. to 8:00 P.M., is a mile north of the village on Route 14, East Montpelier 05651; (802) 223–5757.

North of the Capital

The town of *Plainfield,* on Route 2, is home to the progressive Goddard College and many of its graduates. Because of the college, which has retained its bohemian and independent reputation, Plainfield was a mecca in the 1960s for communes and hippies of all stripes, some of whom are still here. Town kids and adults hang out on "the Wall," a few doors up and across the street from the Winooski River Valley Co-op, while dogs run leashless in the street. A visitor might have to check a calendar or newspaper to be sure of the year.

The *Maple Valley Country Store* only enhances this aura. Locals come here, including those who commute from St. Johnsbury, about 25 miles away via Route 2, to Montpelier or Barre—a not-uncommon routine in these parts. They'll stop in for coffee and a pastry on their way to work.

At Maple Valley the Tiger Balm sits on the shelf right next to the Tylenol. Locally made greeting cards, soy milk, books, candles, incense, and Ben and Jerry's factory seconds—ice cream the company's quality control division has judged does not meet Ben and Jerry's high standards, which often means only that there are too many chocolate chunks in a pint— are available here. The cafe has hummus, corn chowder, vegetarian chili, sandwiches, and cappuccino available to go or to eat in. You can even buy a futon here.

The store is open in summer from 6:00 A.M. to 10:00 P.M. seven days a week and in winter 6:00 A.M. to 8:00 P.M., Sunday 7:00 to 8:00 P.M. Maple Valley Country Store is on Route 2, Plainfield 05667; call (802) 454–8626.

Up at the town's main attraction, "Camp Goddard"—as Goddard College is referred to by some—does indeed resemble a camp in certain ways, and students carry on the school's traditions of participating in a certain number of chores each day and in group meetings.

On Route 2 east of Plainfield, near the Maple Valley Country Store, Hollister Hill Road heads up the hill to a long ridge. Some of the oldest families and houses in town are on this road, not to mention a one-room schoolhouse that is furnished and offers the public an opportunity to peek inside the windows for a glimpse of how education in Vermont used to be run.

A mile and a half up from Route 2, the road will fork. Bear left. A half mile later is an intersection with a red barn on the left and a white farmhouse on the right. Go straight and you'll immediately see the white schoolhouse on the right, the former **Hollister Hill School.** Arnold L. Tibbitts, the present owner, occasionally changes the messages on the blackboard. Old gaslights and the original desks and wood stove are still there. The school dates from 1856, and the "lesson" Tibbits records on the blackboard is intended to put history in context. As he explains, the white farmhouse that immediately precedes the schoolhouse was built during the presidency of John Adams, the second president. The addition was put on when James Polk was president, and the schoolhouse was built during Franklin Pierce's term. You can't go in, but you can see the entire school through the large windows.

Impatience Is a Virtue

The servers at Rainbow Sweets usually try to bring the dessert before they bring dessert forks. We couldn't wait, so we started stabbing the tart with our knives. The waitress brought the forks over a minute later and smiled. "It's a test," she said, "to see if you can wait." Obviously, we failed.

Back on Route 2, continue east into Marshfield and **Rainbow Sweets** in the village. Ask owner Bill Tecosky if the empanadas have just come out of the oven. These Mexican turnovers, stuffed with onions, green and red peppers, raisins, and spicy beef, all wrapped up in a slightly sweet, flaky crust, come with a side of chips and hot salsa. Rainbow Sweets also offers stuffed brioche, which is its trademark; smoked Danish trout; and gnocchi.

People of lesser willpower and greater determination come in, sit down, and cut right to the sugar. The chocolate tart is light, sweet, and chocolaty, a three-layer cake liberally strewn with almonds and cocoa-butter cream. The almond meringue tart is mild, with a thin layer of sweet almond filling on top. There's a big display case filled with that day's desserts, and the staff patiently describe each one to you.

For those who visit and can't wait until the next visit, several offerings can now be shipped to your door. Linzertorte, walnut caramel kirsch torte, English fruitcake, almond chocolate butter crunch, and chocolate cherry almond torte are the delectables from Rainbow Sweets that travel well on a UPS truck, and many patrons take advantage of this service.

Rainbow Sweets is open summers from 9:00 A.M. to 6:00 P.M. Monday through Thursday and from 9:00 A.M. to 9:00 P.M. on Friday and Saturday. On Sunday the restaurant is open from 9:00 A.M. to 3:00 P.M.; it's closed March and April. During the winter, they are closed Monday and Tuesday, opening at 10:00 A.M. the rest of the week, closing at 5:00 P.M. on Wednesday and Thursday, 9:00 P.M. Friday and Saturday, and 3:00 P.M. on Sunday. Write to Rainbow Sweets, Box 121, Marshfield Village 05658, or call (802) 426–3531.

From the town center of Marshfield, take the road west that leads to East Calais and Route 14. Follow the signs to Kents Corner. At the Kents Corner crossroads, turn right onto Robinson Cemetery Road. A short way up on the left is **Robinson Sawmill,** a reconstructed sawmill with original parts that were used to build the mill back in 1803. A display gives the history of the mill and shows the development of the area with photos that date from 1875. Set on the Aldrich Nature Preserve at Mill Pond, the sawmill still has its old turbine, saw blades, and machinery intact.

Robinson Sawmill was a busy place. One miller wrote out his invoices on shingles that were milled here, kids floated on sap pans in the pond, and local farmers and merchants traded gossip and news. The mill sits on extremely thin fieldstones as pilings, one atop another. You're almost afraid to sneeze, lest the impact set the mill tumbling down. But the mill can take a lot more than is obvious, as it was in full operation from 1803 to 1958.

Camp Meade in Middlesex is a World War II enthusiast's dream. Camp Meade was founded in 1929 as a Civilian Conservation Corps (CCC) camp after the flood of 1927 destroyed the town. The CCC was sent in to rebuild, and the camp was named after the first family to settle in the town of

Middlesex in Washington County. In fact, its namesake, Thomas Meade, had quite a reputation as a hunter, having shot three bears in one morning shortly after he settled here with his family in 1783.

After the CCC left, the barracks and dining hall were opened to the public as rental cottages and a filling station. A museum focuses on the 1930s and 1940s, with documentary films and newsreels from the period and World War II artifacts. It is open from mid-May through mid-October, Monday through Saturday 9:00 A.M. to 4:00 P.M.

Outside on the campgrounds, walk over to the checkpoint and the mannequin inside the booth. The poster hanging behind the fake MP dates the place. It shows a picture of a woman and reads, GEE! I WISH I WERE A MAN. I'D JOIN THE NAVY. BE A MAN AND DO IT.

Around the grounds are assorted tanks, jeeps, a howitzer, fighter planes, and even a bunker. The cabins around the perimeter of the vehicles are named for famous generals, admirals, and colonels, among them Omar Bradley and George Patton. There are fourteen units available for rent.

The cabins are open mid-May through mid-October, and breakfast is included in the rates, which are around $50. The camp is off exit 9 of I–89 on Route 2, Middlesex 05602; (802) 223–5537, www.campmead.com.

If you're in central Vermont in late October, don't miss the Halloween-night display at the *1782 Settlement Farm* on Route 2 in Middlesex. Driving south on I–89, you'll see the glow from hundreds of pumpkins illuminate the dark autumn night; the pumpkins rest on platforms out in a field, showing off their last rays of glory before being consigned to the compost heap.

The whole area, including local schools, becomes involved in the carving, scooping, and setting up that this massive operation entails. Political messages declaring VEGETATION WILL SAVE THE NATION cover one of the displays; animal faces, tombstones, flowers, and fish are other examples of the separately themed exhibits, each of them expressed through the pumpkins. For sale inside the farmhouse are cider, syrup, fruits and vegetables, cookies, and, yes, pumpkins. Don't park on the interstate, though; state troopers are out in throngs on this night. Instead, head south on I–89 and take the Montpelier exit. Follow Route 2 heading west for a few miles, and the farm will be on your left.

The Mad River Valley

amel's Hump, a 4,083-foot mountain that straddles the borders of Duxbury and Huntington, is the third highest mountain in the state, after Mount Mansfield and Killington, and has variously been known through the years as the Sleeping Lion, the Couching Lion, and Camel's Rump. The *Long Trail* passes by Camel's Hump, and trails to access the mountain's summit run through Huntington and Duxbury.

South of Duxbury on Route 100 are Waitsfield and Warren. This is prime tourist country, very busy in summer and winter. The ski resorts Mad River Glen and Sugarbush are in the area.

To say that **Mad River Glen** is a skier's mountain is a bit of an understatement; it is, in fact, the only ski mountain in the country that is actually owned by the skiers. Founded in 1948 by Fred Palmedo, it was not primarily a business but rather a place for people who loved the sport. That philosophy stuck with the next owners, Truxton and Betsy Pratt. When Betsy decided to retire, she almost closed the place down because she didn't want it to become like the other areas. That's when the skiers who loved it got together and bought it.

The vertical drop of about 2,000 feet is among the greatest in the state. Mad River has such a reputation among avid skiers that many beginners hesitate to try it. That's a mistake, because beginners have their own separate section of the mountain with their own lift. Intermediate trails run from the tops of two of the peaks of the ridge, as do expert trails. One of the really nice things about the trail layout here is that you won't get a nasty surprise if you start down a beginner or intermediate trail. Trails here either keep their own rating or merge into trails of the next lower category, so you won't suddenly find yourself over your head (literally or figuratively). For experts, the terrain here is probably the most challenging anywhere in the East, over natural snow covering wild bumps and down through narrow trails and glades.

Their "ski it if you can" motto ought to tell you something. Remember, this place is for skiers—there's no huge lodge with a big bar and lots of snow bunnies. But if you like it, you can become an owner for $1,750 (800–850–6742). If you're a snowboarder, however, pass this one by, because snowboarding is not allowed, a policy that suits most skiers just fine.

Rates during the week still stay close to $32 (those under sixteen and over sixty-five pay $20) and are higher on weekends and holidays

Not a Corner to Hide In

Designed by the Shakers, round barns are a classic example of the Shakers' inventive and practical improvements on farming. The farmer could drive a team in, load or unload, and circle around and drive out. The raceway, a ramp to the loft, led directly into the top, where hay was stored. The middle level was for dairy cows, which were also easier to herd in and out in a circle and whose straw litter and manure could be removed by trapdoors to the ground floor. There it could be removed easily—or even allowed to fall directly into the wagons.

($42). Half-day tickets are available at slightly reduced prices during the week and after noon on weekends; student passes are a bargain, as is a midweek season pass. Mad River Glen, Waitsfield 05673; (802) 496–3551; for snow reports, (802) 496–2001; www.madriverglen.com.

Palmer Sugar House looks a lot like it did in 1840, when it was new. Open for visits to the working sugar house in late February and early March, Palmer's sells syrup at the farm year-round. Palmer's Sugar House, Palmer Lane, Waitsfield 05673; (802) 496–3696.

The great round Joslyn Barn, overlooking the valley from East Warren Road, is a local landmark, one of very few remaining in the state of the twenty-four known to have been built. After the Simcoes renovated the family farm into the *Inn at the Round Barn Farm,* they tackled the restoration of the 1910 barn. But more on that later. The inn fits so well into the rambling home with its attached carriage sheds that you'd never guess what guest luxuries await inside. The large rooms are beautifully designed and furnished, with windows big enough to make the mountain views part of the decor. Hearty breakfasts are filled with home-baked breads and served in a bright sunporch overlooking the gardens below. In the winter the inn has its own cross-country ski center for guests and the public. Hosts are relaxed about everything but the maintainance of the inn, which is meticulously cared for, and they enjoy conversations with their guests. The Inn at the Round Barn Farm, RR 1, Box 247, East Warren Road, Waitsfield 05673; (802) 496–2276. www.roundbarninn.com; e-mail: roundbarn@madriver.com.

Back to the barn. It took the Simcoes two years to restore it, from the time they began jacking up the entire structure and pouring a new foundation until it was insulated and re-roofed. Then they had to decide what to do with it. When a couple asked to be married at the inn, they had part of their answer. The rest of it came when they held a music festival there, and it was a success, and the *Green Mountain Cultural Center* was born. Now with more than 200 members, the barn is a venue for performing and visual arts and hands-on workshops year-round, with the Vermont Mozart Festival, soloists, ensembles, and an annual art show filling its schedule.

To get off the beaten path around here, head for the **Warren-Sugarbush Airport,** a bucolic area where you can take gliding lessons or have one of the airport's experienced pilots fly you over the valley in a sailplane.

The airport is perfect for a day's outing. You can enjoy the swing set, an outdoor barbecue, a volleyball net, a gazebo for contemplation, and a feeling of being on top of a mountain. There's even a snack bar, the Diner Soar Restaurant, where you can grab a sandwich or bowl of soup, sit outside on the second-floor deck, and watch the gliders soar in and out of the fields. Sugarbush Soaring at the Warren Sugarbush Airport has been in operation for twenty-five years, yet people still don't think of spending the day at the airport. Decades ago people sometimes spent the entire day at an airport, picnicking, visiting with friends and family, playing games, and watching the planes fly in and out. You can spend a similar day at the Warren-Sugarbush Airport.

Rides in a classic 1940 WACO biplane range from a twenty-minute adventure called the Mad River Valley to the half-hour Top Gun at Sugarbush, which includes a few acrobatic twists and turns if you're so inclined. Sugarbush Soaring also offers multiday, learn-to-soar camps. An introductory lesson includes ground school and a soaring session, in which you'll pilot a two-person training sailplane with an FAA-certified instructor. Another offering is a three-day soaring package, which includes eight training flights. The ultimate indulgence, however, is the sixteen-flight package.

For more information, write to Warren-Sugarbush Airport, P.O. Box 123, Warren 05674, or call (802) 496–2290.

The tiny town of Washington is part of Orange County but not of Washington County, its immediate neighbor. Washington—the town— was named for George Washington. Washington—the county—comprises the towns of Barre, Montpelier, Plainfield, and Waitsfield, among many others, and was originally called Jefferson County (in 1810) after Thomas Jefferson. Four years later, however, the locals and many other Vermonters turned against Jefferson for his influence on the Embargo Act and the War of 1812. The name of the county was therefore changed, but the name of the town— which again, is in Orange County—wasn't. Got it?

The White River Valley

The first and second branches of the White River rise in the hills south of Barre, paralleled by Routes 110 and 14, respectively. Either route takes you through rolling farm country, and at the southernmost end of each, past covered bridges. A third north-south road, Route 12, parallels these to the west of Interstate 89. To make the choices even more varied, Routes 64, 65, and 66, as well as several unnumbered back roads, go east-west between these. You could spend a couple of days wandering about in these hills and valleys and see a Vermont that even most Vermonters have never explored.

Route 12, the westernmost of these roads, goes through Northfield Falls, where four covered bridges cluster in a group, then drops into Northfield Gulf, one of several gulfs in Vermont. The easternmost, Route 110, goes through Washington, and from here it is only a short trip east—on unpaved but good road—to East Orange and its unique *Mosaic Church.* With its needlelike spire, pointed windows with stained glass framing the panes, and riot of fancy-cut shingles, the structure is atypical of Vermont village churches. A nice four-bay carriage shed and a small schoolhouse complete the ensemble in the center of this tiny town.

Route 14, the center option, passes through Williamstown, where you should look on the southern end of the village for a sign to *Knight's Spider Web Farm.* One day Will and Terry Knight decided to maximize the beauty of the spiderwebs they saw in their barn. Both artists, the Knights devised a system of spraying a spiderweb with a combination of white paint and glue before mounting it on a wooden plaque and allowing it to set.

The Knights initially scouted out webs in their own and neighbors' barns, then opted for mass production by constructing a series of frames protected by a roof where spiders could spin their webs in peace and where you can watch them at work. Some of the Knights' designs incorporate painted flowers onto the plaque for an additional decorative touch. Webs cost from $10 to $15. The gift shop is open year-round, but to see the process of creation, go from mid-June to mid-October.

Knights' Spider Web Farm is open from 9:00 A.M. to 5:00 P.M. daily or call for an appointment. They ship a 7-by-9-inch web portrait for $15.00, plus $5.00 shipping. Write to Knights' Spider Web Farm, Spider Web Farm Road, Williamstown 05679, or call (802) 433–5568; www.spiderwebfarm.com; e-mail: webfarm@together.net.

Farther south on Route 14, a right turn onto Route 65 will bring you to the town of Brookfield, home of the 320-foot-long *Floating Bridge.* To reach the bridge, you'll first come to a dirt road, then take a right. Floating Bridge is a one-lane bridge that floats on 380 tarred wooden barrels and is connected to the land by hinges that allow for variations in the water's height. Still well traveled by local foot and auto traffic, Floating Bridge spans what is called at various times Sunset Lake, Mirror Lake, and Colts Pond. When you walk on the bridge, there's a certain buoyancy to it, which becomes more obvious when a car crosses over.

The bridge is located in a tranquil spot, with lots of trout. As if to attest to the bridge's popularity as a fishing spot, fishing lines and sinkers hang suspended from the phone and power lines that cross over the lake, parallel to the bridge. There are some boggy areas to the lake. When a car passes over the bridge, the water comes up between the wooden planks. Puddles of water gather in strategic spots on the bridge, which is part of Route 65. The bridge has been under repair and may be closed.

In the late 1800s and early 1900s, Brookfield was known as one of the best sources of high-quality ice, and harvesting ice from Sunset Lake was one of the town's primary businesses. The general store had a large icehouse near the floating bridge and stored enough ice there to supply the town. The rest was sent to nearby Randolph, where it was used to cool the milk train to Boston.

For the past quarter century, the people of Brookfield have revived this industry for one day each winter. On the last Saturday in January, they haul out all the old ice-harvesting tools and equipment, which visitors and townspeople alike can use to cut, saw, and haul ice blocks. As one local told us, "After you see all the work involved, it makes you want to go home and hug your refrigerator." So unusual is this activity, which takes place at the Floating Bridge, that 200 people may show up to watch.

Within a stone's throw of the bridge is *Green Trails Inn,* whose several buildings range from Federal to Greek Revival style. Of the thirteen guest rooms, some have private baths, some shared, some with whirlpool baths. Trails originally cut for the inn's stable of riding horses now serve as hiking trails in summer and cross-country and snowshoe trails in winter. Winter also brings sledding and skating, and on the last weekend of January inn guests join in the annual Ice Harvest Festival at nearby Sunset Pond, reliving a tradition that dates from 1875 or earlier.

Cool Facts

- *It took 5,000 pounds of ice a year to cool food for an average family.*

- *It took 1,500 pounds of ice to cool the milk produced by a single cow during a year.*

- *A cube of ice measuring 1 foot in all dimensions weighs about fifty-seven pounds.*

- *Brookfield ice was so clear that people claimed they could read the* **Boston Herald** *through a piece 16 inches thick.*

- *Ice blocks stored in sawdust would keep through the summer.*

Green Trails Inn, Brookfield 05036; (802) 276–3412 or (800) 243–3412; greentrails@quest-net.com; www.quest-net.com/gti.

Farther south, and on the west side of I–89, is *Randolph,* a busy, thriving town, with farms and manufacturing plants, along with the Vermont State Technical College.

Randolph was chartered in 1781, and the origin of Randolph's name is somewhat confusing. General John French, an early settler in the town, was born in Randolph, Massachusetts, but the town was not named by or after him. The first settler in Randolph was known to be from New Hampshire; the exact town of his origin is not known, however, though there is a Randolph, New Hampshire, as well. Local history has it that Randolph, Vermont, was named by Vermonters, without any outside influence, selecting the name of the town merely because they liked it. Incidentally, early towns in Vermont were named by the governor of New Hampshire, Benning Wentworth, when Vermont was part of the New Hampshire grants.

In the village of Randolph, the *Chandler Art Gallery and Music Hall* serves as the area's cultural oasis for locals who don't want to travel to either Montpelier or Dartmouth College in Hanover, New Hampshire, for their dose of art.

The music hall holds several performances each month, ranging from works by local theater groups and children to swing bands to the acclaimed folksinger Odetta. The gallery next door holds exhibits centering on the history of Vermonters' use of art. Recent offerings include displays of decoys, children's art, antiques, stenciling, and art from the Abenaki; often workshops and demonstrations are conducted on the theme of a given month's exhibit.

The Chandler Art Gallery is open from March through November; hours are noon until 2:00 P.M. Saturday, Sunday, and Wednesday and during performances. Call ahead for exact dates (802–728–9878), or write for a schedule of exhibits and a schedule of music and other events in the music hall. Chandler Art Gallery and Music Hall Main Street, Randolph 05060; (802) 728–6464 (box office), open 3:00 to 6:00 P.M. and until one hour before performances.

East of Randolph on Route 66, west of I–89, you'll see a sculpture just off the south side of the road that seems a bit incongruous for Vermont apart, of course, from the stone it's carved from. *Whales' Tails/Reverence* is a sculpture of polished marble that celebrates Vermont's commitment to environmental harmony. The statue is of two behemoth yet graceful whales' tails mounted into the mountain, atop a slight rise in the land. The work overlooks the Green Mountain range in the distance.

Artist Jim Sardonis created the work, which was sponsored by the Environmental Law Foundation in Montpelier and dedicated in 1990. The inscription reads that *Whales' Tails/Reverence* is A TESTAMENT TO OUR COMMITMENT TO THE ENVIRONMENT. A small parking area and a stone wall are nearby the sculpture.

Route 12 leads from Randolph to Bethel, a funky town that was the first town chartered by the erstwhile Republic of Vermont. One of the most unusual street signs in the state is located in Bethel. If you're headed north on Route 12, the state highway makes a sharp left turn over a bridge. If you miss the turn and instead go straight, you'll soon discover your error, for there is a big red-and-white sign on the right that says THIS IS NOT ROUTE 12. The residents got sick of answering travelers' questions after too many wrong turns and remedied it with the sign. Whoever said Vermonters lack a sense of humor?

On Route 107 West is the **White River National Fish Hatchery.** If you go fishing in Vermont, chances are that the next salmon you catch will have originated in Bethel. The best time to visit the hatchery is in November. It is then that two million Atlantic salmon eggs are hatched in the incubation room that the visitors' room overlooks. The sight is something out of a sci-fi movie: huge, circular tanks that look as if they're ready for takeoff.

The fish are transferred to outdoor tanks before they're let loose to stock the Connecticut River and its tributaries in spring and again in fall. Also at the hatchery are displays of old photos that show how incubation and stocking were done in former times and how the breeding of salmon occurs without human interference. The hatchery is open daily from 8:00 A.M. to 3:00 P.M. For more information, call (802) 234–5241, or write the hatchery at Route 107, Box 140, Bethel 05032. E-mail: Ken_gilette@fwf.gov.

The Brick Store, on Main Street in Bethel, 05032, has a 1930s soda fountain, along with penny candy. They also carry items made by nearby Johnson Woolen Mills, including vests, coats, hats, backpacks, and ladies' bags. The adjoining **Specialty Shop** represents over one hundred exhibitors, with quilts and other crafts; (802) 234–5378.

South on Route 12 is the Barnard General Store and **Silver Lake,** a recreational area that's popular with both locals and visitors. Provision with a picnic lunch from the store, then sit on the shores of the lake in warm weather. If you wander up North Road—you'll see the sign—you can have greater access to the lake through Silver Lake State Park, complete with camping and paddleboat rentals. Barnard is a small town with a real sense of community, and even though it's a couple of towns away from bustling Woodstock, once you hit it, you know you're in a different kind of Vermont.

If you follow Route 107 east from the village of Bethel, you'll reach **Vermont Castings** on your right. You've probably heard of this maker of wood stoves, since the company ships its stoves all over the world. Some of its models—the Defiant, the Vigilant, and the Resolute—have been responsible for Vermont Castings' reputation for powerful, reliable stoves that go all night. The company has kept up with technology by introducing gas-powered stoves as well as the pellet stoves that cut down on pollution and wood use.

If you've never considered owning a wood stove, a visit to the Vermont Castings showroom will make you yearn for a cold winter's night even if it's the middle of summer. For information, write to Vermont Castings, Route 107, Bethel 05032, or call (802) 234–2300.

At the **Vermont Sugar House** in North Royalton, a variety of chainsaw-art sculptures may greet you outside the building. The best times to catch an artist in action are in the fall before hunting season and in the spring after sugar season.

Inside the Vermont Sugar House are a restaurant with picnic table seating and a gift shop in the back. Of course, you have to get pancakes with a pitcher of that season's maple syrup—no bottle of Log Cabin has ever touched the lips of anyone on the premises. The Vermont Sugar House also serves breakfast all day, as well as soups, sandwiches, and burgers at lunchtime, but, again, the maple sugar and syrup are the primary reasons to eat here.

The Vermont Sugar House is open for breakfast and lunch seven days a week, from 7:00 A.M. to 3:00 P.M., except Sunday, when it opens at 6:30 A.M. The gift shop stays open until 3:00 P.M. Write to the Vermont Sugar House, Junction of Routes 14 and 107, Royalton 05063, or call (802) 763–8809.

After you leave the Vermont Sugar House and drive south on Route 14, watch out for a couple of low overhead railroad trestles that transform it into an instant one-lane road. In other places in Vermont, abandoned railroad trestles are kept intact and not torn down, partly because of their history, since the railroads helped to build the state, but also because it costs money to take them down. So they remain, a monument to bygone Green Mountain Railroad days.

While in the South Royalton area, call **Sabra Field** to ask if she's receiving visitors at her studio in East Barnard that day. If she is, get directions and head out there. Sabra Field is a top Vermont artist who opens her studio to visitors while she works. Her work ranges from the official Vermont postage stamp to food labels to her own prints that are sold in top galleries all over the state.

When Sabra Field and her husband, Spencer, first began their studio in East Barnard, they intended it to be a place for serious work. "I chose to live out of the way because it gives me time to work," says Sabra. "But people started coming here and seeking me out even though I was represented at galleries elsewhere. Our work didn't look very nice on the walls of the workroom, so ten years ago we built this little gallery so we could have things looking the way we wanted them to look."

East Barnard is a bit off the beaten track, and Sabra says there's a certain breed that goes to the trouble of venturing there. "People who come out here are usually interested in comparing impressions or seeing work that is out of print," she notes. "They might also be interested in the process, and if they come on a day when we're printing, we're very happy to have them watch."

Write to Sabra Field, 75 East Barnard Road, South Royalton 05068, or call ahead at (802) 763–7092. Her studio is open by appointment or by chance; www.sabrafield.com.

Routes 14 and 110, which, as you'll remember, follow the respective branches of the White River, join in the Royaltons, where their streams also meet the main body of the White River. A trip up either one of these or, better yet, a loop that combines the lower ends of each by a road over the ridge that lies between them will show you one of the heaviest concentrations of *covered bridges* in the state. Heading up Route 110 you will pass five, all but one within sight of the road (and that one's close, but hidden in a little hollow).

You will pass, in turn, the Howe Bridge (on the east side of the road), the Cilley Bridge (on the left), and the Larkin Bridge (on the right). The next is the Flint Bridge, on the right, which you can cross to find the *Morgan Horse Cemetery.*

After you go through the Flint Bridge, turn right and follow the dirt road up the hill until you come to a small grassy triangle at a fork. To your right, beside the right-hand road (which turns into a driveway here), you'll see a granite stone marking the grave of the Morgan Horse Lippitt Mandale. What you may not see, unless you look downhill from the first, is the other stone monument, which reads as follows: ON THIS FARM LIES THE BODY OF JUSTIN MORGAN, FOALED 1789 DIED 1821 PROGENITOR OF THE FIRST ESTABLISHED AMERICAN BREED OF HORSES. On the stone is a portrait of the famous horse.

The next bridge is not visible from Route 110, but you can cross it if you follow the riverside road instead of recrossing the Flint Bridge. You will cross the 1883 Moxie Bridge and return to Route 110, just before the left turn that will take you over the ridge (with nice mountain views) to Route 14 at East Randolph. About a mile south of the intersection is Braley Covered Bridge Road on your right, at the bottom of which you will find a small covered bridge. Farther along Route 110 is the Gifford Bridge on the left and the Hyde Bridge on the right. Not far south of the last bridge, Route 14 joins Route 107 to complete the loop.

MORE PLACES TO STAY IN CENTRAL VERMONT

(ALL AREA CODES 802)

WAITSFIELD (05673)
Lareau Farm Country Inn, Box 563, 35 Lareau Road, Route 100, has thirteen homey rooms with private or shared baths in a rambling farmhouse; 496–4949 or (800) 833–0746; www.lareaufarminn.com.

MORE PLACES TO EAT IN CENTRAL VERMONT

(ALL AREA CODES 802)

MONTPELIER (05602)
McGillicuddy's Irish Pub, Langdon Street, has pub fare, with hot and cold sandwiches at about $5.00 and a selection of ales.

Barre (05641)
A Single Pebble on Route 302 (also known as Montpelier Road) is an out-of-the-ordinary Chinese dining experience. The menu re-creates dining region by region across China. We suggest going with at least four people so you can sample a wider variety of dishes and regions; (802) 476–9700.

Brookfield (05036)
Ariel's Restaurant and the Pond Village Pub, Stone Road and Route 65, Brookfield Village. Fine dining in a nineteenth-century farmhouse or a bit more casually in the pub; (802) 276–3939.

WAITSFIELD (05673)
American Flatbread, Lareau Farm, Route 100, bakes pizzas in a wood-fired oven and serves them in an informal setting on weekends only; 496–8856; www.americanflatbread.com.

WARREN (05674)
The Common Man Restaurant, German Flats Road, offers an uncommon menu of New American and European dishes, expertly prepared; 583–2800.

To Learn More in Central Vermont

Central Vermont Chamber of Commerce; *(802) 229–5711,* *http://www.central-vt.com.*

Connecticut River Valley

The Connecticut River cuts a wide swath between Vermont and New Hampshire—at least in this area—as though underscoring the differences between the two states. Beside it, and in sight of it for much of its route, runs Interstate 91, high along a shoulder of the hills that rise on the river's western bank. The views are among the best from any interstate highway in the country, over rich fertile farmlands, the wide winding river with its oxbows and tributary streams, and across at the hills and mountains of New Hampshire. It's New England scenery at its best at any time of year, and a spectacular panorama in the fall.

Route 5 also parallels the river, often weaving back and forth across the straighter interstate, and passing through some of the most fertile farmland in New England as it strings together the towns from Brattleboro to Newbury—and beyond, an area you've already read about in the Northeast Kingdom chapter.

Early settlers homesteaded along the river so that they could easily receive supplies from their previous homes in Connecticut and Massachusetts. They weren't dissuaded by the countless bends in the river that are especially common between Thetford and Newbury. In fact, Bradford's high school is called Oxbow.

In some towns in what is known as the Upper Valley—the towns that fall between Springfield and Newbury—the line between Vermont and New Hampshire across the river begins to blur. A phone call from Norwich to Hanover, even though it's from Vermont to New Hampshire, is not a toll call; there are ample bridges for residents to travel from one state to the other. Since the area is touted as a region and not two different states, the line gets even fuzzier. In fact, the Norwich/Hanover school district is the only multistate local school district in the country.

White River Junction

White River Junction, in the center of the valley, is an old railroad town that, like many others, had its heyday when the trains made

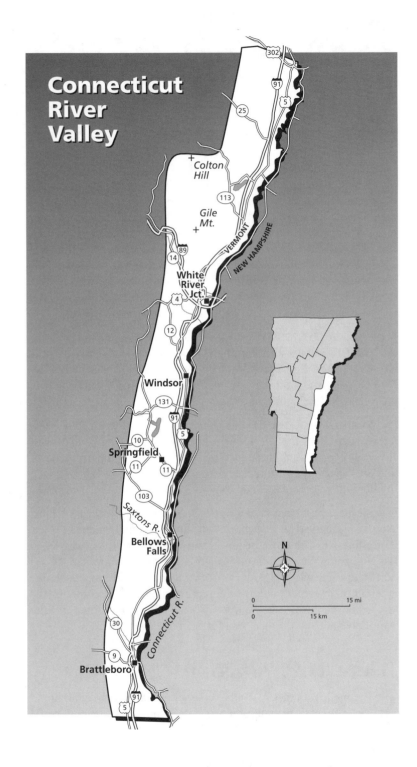

Connecticut River Valley

Colton Hill

Gile Mt.

VERMONT   NEW HAMPSHIRE

White River Jct.

Windsor

Springfield

Saxtons R.

Bellows Falls

Connecticut R.

Brattleboro

N

| 0 | 15 mi |
| 0 | 15 km |

AUTHORS' TOP HIGHLIGHTS

The Montshire Museum

Chester

Justin Smith Morrill Homestead

the air thick with smoke. In the past few decades the owners of many long-established businesses have either pulled up stakes or moved across the river to tax-free West Lebanon, New Hampshire.

Today the town still has many thriving retail stores, a food co-op, and a couple of restaurants. And, yes, White River Junction still serves as a stop for Amtrak.

Funkiness helps in White River. The **Vermont Salvage Exchange** is funky and utilitarian at the same time, a used-house-parts store where you can find everything from stained-glass windows to doors, wainscoting, and heating grilles, all in one place.

Amid the three floors of boxes of doorknobs, light fixtures, and gargoyles are creative decorating hints intended to help you make the most of your purchases. A hand-printed sign atop a cart of old solid oak doors asks, HAVE YOU EVER THOUGHT OF MAKING WAINSCOTING FROM 5-PANEL DOORS? The decorator-in-residence then offers drawn diagrams to help you envision this unusual wainscoting and offers three or more doors at $25 apiece to help you out.

Sometimes the human element of these spare parts becomes evident when you see a sticker announcing a security system or a PetFinder or

It's a Long Way to White River Junction

*B*oston & Maine Railroad's Engine 494 is not just any old steam locomotive; it has a unique history of its own. Built in Manchester, New Hampshire, in 1892, Engine 494 hauled passengers on the company's Eastern Line, then was used on the uphill run from Fabyan Station to Marshfield Station, 2,700 feet up the side of New Hampshire's Mount Washington. It hauled coal to fuel the Cog Railway, which ran from Marshfield to the summit. Over its lifetime, many improvements were made in train construction, and with each, Engine 494 was modernized to

keep up with the times. It was retired in 1938.

But not quite. In 1939 Engine 494 was chosen to represent Boston & Maine at the New York World's Fair, and it was unmodernized, its steel cab replaced with wood, its electric headlamp replaced with an oil light. After the fair it was stored and almost scrapped, but a group called the Railroad Enthusiasts was unwilling to see this unique example of a restored nineteenth-century locomotive die, and a new home was found for it in White River Junction.

TotFinder sticker on a screen door that probably came from the next town over. In fact, many houses could be assembled from materials found here.

The store is open Monday through Friday from 8:00 A.M. to 4:30 P.M. and from 8:00 A.M. to 3:00 P.M. Saturday. Vermont Salvage Exchange, Railroad Row, White River Junction 05001; call (802) 295–7616 for more information about what's come in on a given day.

In the center of town, within sight of both the Briggs Opera House and Vermont Salvage, stands steam locomotive **Engine 494** with its tender and caboose, a reminder of the days when as many as fifty trains a day brought passengers to and from the depot here.

While a locomotive seems quite natural in this trackside setting, the restaurant across the street does not. Instead of the usual opposite-the-station burgers and fries place, you'll find **Tastes of Africa,** which is exactly what its name suggests. Here, in a bright setting of plants and bold-colored Kente cloth hangings, you can order *akara* (fried rice balls) or peanut chicken stew from Mali, jasmine pilaf or curried goat from Kenya, Moroccan couscous or a salad of red onions, red cabbage, corn, and yams from Ghana. The menu is varied, with plenty of choices for both vegetarians and carnivores, with each dish described fully and its ingredients listed. The restaurant is at 2 North Main Street 05001, next to the Opera House; (802) 295–4250. Open Wednesday through Sunday, 5:00 to 9:00 P.M. for dinner.

In the same block you'll find the inviting **River City Cafe,** the kind of place everyone's hometown ought to have. Order your sandwich or bowl of soup (or both for the daily special) at the counter, then choose a booth, table, or comfortable chair, where you can read if you're lunching alone. An astonishing selection of good teas are made into custom teabags as you watch; coffee choices are just as varied. Look for the cafe at 17 South Main Street, 05001; (802) 296–7113.

North of White River, off Route 5, the town of Hartford has established the **Hurricane Forest Wildlife Refuge,** thanks to the gift of Windsor and Bertha Brown. The entrance to the 142-acre tract is off of Old King's Highway. Four trails are from $2/10$ miles (Pond Loop) to $8/10$ miles (Beacon Hill Loop) in length. Benches are placed at strategic points for resting or observing nature. Look for the turn on the left, close to the I–89 underpass on Route 5. For more information, contact the Town of Hartford Parks and Recreation Department at (802) 295–9353, ext 31.

ANNUAL EVENTS IN THE CONNECTICUT RIVER VALLEY

Late February: Winter Carnival,
Brattleboro, one of New England's
oldest, with events for all ages;
(802) 254–4565.

Mid-July: Cow Appreciation Day,
Billings Farm Museum, Woodstock,
where you can try your hand at milking and enjoy freshly churned butter
and hand-cranked ice cream;
(802) 457–2355.

Mid-July to mid-August: Marlboro
College Music Festival, Marlboro,
features professional and student
musicians, who perform for the public
on weekends; (802) 254–2394.

Late June to early August: Yellow Barn
Music Festival, Putney, brings a series
of concerts by well-known musicians;
(802) 387–6637.

Early August: Annual pilgrimage to
Rockingham Meeting House,
Rockingham, where for more than
ninety years this fine example of an
early meetinghouse has been commem-
orated annually with music and historical programs; (802) 463–3941.

Late August: Annual Scottish Festival,
Quechee, with bagpipes, dancing, foods,
rugby, sheepdogs, and massed bands;
(800) 295–5451.

Mid-October: Annual Heritage
Festival, Newfane, featuring crafts,
Vermont products, a flea market, and
entertainment on the common;
(802) 365–7855.

Mid-October: Harvest Celebration,
Billings Farm Museum, Woodstock,
when the fall activities of a nineteenth-
century farm are demonstrated and
celebrated: cider pressing, the pumpkin
harvest, a husking bee, preserving, and
more; (802) 457–2355.

Late October: Apple Days,
Brattleboro, with crafts, foods, art
and musical events, orchard tours,
and cider pressing;
(802) 254–4565.

Early December (usually the first
Saturday): Brattleboro Farmers
Market Annual Craft Show,
Congregational Church, Main Street,
Brattleboro; (802) 254–4565.

Norwich–Strafford

Visitors to Norwich, just north of White River Junction, frequently
marvel on their approach to Hanover, New Hampshire, and Dartmouth College just across the Connecticut River how courteous Vermont drivers are. As you approach the Ledyard Bridge, there's a
left-turn-only lane that—mirabile dictu—drivers use only to make left
turns. Most other places motorists would use that lane to squeeze ahead
of one another. This notoriety regularly wins wide-eyed wonder from
city people who think this brand of courtesy is long extinct.

Norwich is like that. Home to hundreds of Dartmouth College employ-
ees, professors, and students, as well as a number of eighth-generation
Norwichers, the town has a countrified, genteel air about it. From the
Montessori school and *trés cher* restaurant to the green that serves as

playground for the town's elementary school and the three-way stop where, again, drivers actually stop for one another, Norwich is a curious blend of nouveau-haute culture and country.

Located right on the banks of the Connecticut River, the **Montshire Museum of Science** is a place where both adults and children can let loose the kid inside. "Montshire" is an amalgam of Ver*mont* and New Hamp*shire*.

The first Montshire opened in Hanover, New Hampshire, in January 1976 in an abandoned bowling alley as a community museum for the public—which was a novel idea at the time. From the beginning it was operated as a learning center instead of a museum. Montshire moved across the river to a new facility in Norwich in November 1989 and was designed top to bottom to be a hands-on science museum, from the color-coded ventilation systems to the exposed trusses.

Kids may take a few minutes to make the transition from a world of "Don't Touch" to the freedom of the Montshire, where even adults feel as if they're getting away with something. You can play with light switches, shoot baskets, blow bubbles, and splash around in soapy water.

Hail the King!

In the 1920s, when barrels of King Arthur Flour were delivered throughout New England by truck, the company's advertising consisted of a white truck with a life-size wooden statue of King Arthur on his horse. It was a three-dimensional version of the logo used today, complete with standard flying over his head. Just in case no one noticed this king and his horse hitching a ride through town, the white truck was equipped with a calliope to draw attention to the royal visit.

Parents especially like the Montshire because the only snacks offered are apples, yogurt, trail mix, and Gatorade.

Upstairs are a variety of beetles (dead ones) and boa constrictors (live ones). There's also a dinosaur-size ant colony with hundreds of thousands of ants climbing through eleven Plexiglas chambers. Even if you had an ant colony as a kid, the Leafcutter Ant Colony will make your skin crawl. The Montshire also hosts a number of traveling exhibits—one year it was a collection of dinosaur eggs—so you'll never know what you'll find when you visit.

The Montshire is open from 10:00 A.M. to 5:00 P.M. seven days a week. It's closed on New Year's Day, Thanksgiving, and Christmas. Write to the Montshire Museum of Science, Montshire Road, Norwich 05055, call (802) 649–2200 for information on special programs and daily highlights, or visit www.montshire.org.

CONNECTICUT RIVER VALLEY

On Route 5, just south of the I–91 exit, is a mecca for home bread bakers. *The Baker's Store* is the walk-around version of the King Arthur Flour catalog, which supplies bakers all over the country with everything from the right pan to the right type of yeast and plump dried currants for real scones. Here you can see it all and taste the breads that the catalog only gives you the recipes for (we wonder if they've thought of a scratch-n-sniff patch so readers will have the aroma of fresh-baked bread to inspire them). The store would inspire anyone to get elbow-deep in bread dough, and it offers some specialty items not shown in the catalog. You'll never again think of King Arthur as just flour. The store is open from 9:00 A.M. to 5:00 P.M. Monday through Saturday and 11:00 A.M. to 4:00 P.M. Sunday; Route 5, Norwich 05055; (800) 827–6836; www.bakerscatalogue.com.

WORTH SEEING

The Billings Farm and Museum, Route 12 and River Road, Woodstock 05091; (802) 457–2355.

Basketville, Main Street, Route 5, Putney 05346; (802) 387–4351.

Green Mountain Flyer Scenic Train Ride, P.O. Box 498, Bellows Falls 05101; (802) 463–3069.

Quechee Gorge, Route 4, Quechee (east of Woodstock) 05059; (802) 295–7600.

Vermont Institute of Natural Sciences and Raptor Center, Church Hill Road, Woodstock 05091; (802) 457–2779.

Just past the three-way stop in the village, on your left is *Dan & Whit's,* a country store that's unusual even by Vermont standards. Whenever anyone in Norwich gives out directions, he or she inevitably uses Dan & Whit's as a benchmark: "Oh, go a mile past Dan & Whit's, turn left onto Turnpike Road, and keep going."

The immense outdoor bulletin board on the front of the building serves as the contemporary version of a town crier. Notices about everything from rooms for rent to goat's milk for sale to pancake suppers are posted here. Inside, Dan & Whit's is the antithesis of the modern-day supermarket. No scanners here, just shelves with loaves of locally baked bread next to boxes of doodads. Wander around the aisles up front, but the real treasure is through the door next to the meat counter, a door that looks like it should have an EMPLOYEES ONLY sign hanging over it. The hardware department is in here. Stovepipes, birdseed, shovels, sleds, and inner tubes compete for space and more often than not haphazardly spill over onto the cement floor.

Dan & Whit's General Store is on Main Street; the hours are generally from 7:00 A.M. to 6:00 P.M. seven days a week. Call (802) 649–1602 for information, or write the store at Main Street, Norwich 05055.

Look for signs opposite the common at Main and Elm Streets directing you to the almost-hidden *Alice's Bakery & Cafe.* Sandwiches are built on slabs of crusty sourdough bread, or ask for a baguette packed with imported cheeses and exotic cold cuts. A few small tables in the cafe provide a place to perch while you eat. We like to stop at Alice's in the morning to prepare for the day's picnic with a loaf of bread and a rondel of cheese, which might be a local chèvre or a complex vintage cheese from a remote valley in France. It's one of the best selections of hard-to-find and rare cheeses in New England. Alice's Bakery & Cafe is open Tuesday through Saturday from 9:30 A.M. to 5:30 P.M.; Main and Elm Streets, Norwich 05055; (802) 649–2846.

If you continue on Main Street heading west, the road ascends, climbing up into the mountains from the Connecticut River basin, winding past working farms. Some 5.5 miles from Dan & Whit's, the road forks. Bear left onto Route 132 and about 8 miles from the fork take a sharp right. You'll be in the village of South Strafford.

On the right is *Eileen Collins Rainments and Adornments,* a shop that sells Victorian-era, new, and gently used clothing. It's not exactly a thrift shop, but it's not retail either. The owner gets some clothes on consignment from locals but also spends one day each week shopping in Boston and Connecticut at clearance sales, by-the-pound sales, and retail stores. Her main rule of thumb is that the clothing must be of high quality—some sophisticated and some fun—and must fit the character of the store.

Along with high-end designer wear, extraordinary consignment clothing, and jewelry are home accessories. You will also find teapots, dishes, lamps, glassware, pottery, picture frames, and mirrors in this most unusual shop.

Eileen Collins is on Main Street, South Strafford 05070; call (802) 765–4335 for information about special sales. The shop is open from 11:00 A.M. to 5:00 P.M. Thursday through Saturday and from 1:00 to 5:00 P.M. on Sunday.

If instead of continuing west on Route 132, you bear right at the T on the Justin Smith Morrill Highway and drive 2 miles, you'll be in the Strafford town center. Justin Morrill served Vermont in the U.S. House of Representatives from 1855 to 1867 and in the U.S. Senate from 1867 to 1898. He is remembered for the Morrill Act of 1862, which provided land grants to help found state colleges to promote agricultural, mechanical, science, and classical studies. He is often called "the Father of the Agricultural Colleges." It's hard to miss his home, now a museum dedicated to his memory. The *Justin Smith Morrill Homestead* is a large peach-colored Victorian fantasy with steep gables and generous gingerbread trim, sitting on a hillside along the road in the center of town. The seventeen-room mansion was built in the Gothic Revival style and remains as it was designed, complete with original furnishings, gardens, outbuildings, and an exquisite hand-painted window in the ceiling of the library. It's open from 11:00 A.M. to 5:00 P.M. Wednesday through Sunday Memorial Day through Columbus Day. Justin Morrill Highway, in the center of the village of Strafford 05072; (802) 765–4484.

Facing the green is the *Stone Soup* restaurant. There isn't any sign for the restaurant—the laws of Strafford place certain restrictions on the types of signs retail establishments can hang outside—so the owners decided to buck the trend and not have any sign at all. Look for the picket fence surrounding a house on the left side of the green. Gardens out back provide many of the vegetables served in the restaurant; there are baskets filled with handwoven rugs up front; and requests for special music—from Patsy Cline to Beethoven—are cheerfully filled.

Stone Soup is housed in an old stable, with dried flowers hanging from the rafters and the old wallboards left intact. The place doesn't smell like alfalfa, but the essence is there and goes nicely with dinner.

The menu changes nightly and includes a fish entree, poultry, and meat. Turbot with three-peppercorn shallot butter, roasted hens with a sauternes glaze, and lamb tenderloin with a cabernet sauce are some of the possibilities. All entrees are served with fresh vegetables in season, and if you're lucky enough to get there in the spring, more likely than not your plate will include a few precious fiddlehead ferns—a Vermont delicacy that gets Vermonters' attention because its presence in markets and restaurants signals the end of winter.

Stone Soup is open Wednesday through Monday from 6:00 to 9:00 P.M. July through October; from November through June the restaurant is open Thursday through Sunday only. Reservations are a must, as is saving room for dessert. Stone Soup is on Main Street, Strafford 05072; call ahead at (802) 765–4301 for the nightly specials.

Norwich to Fairlee

Route 5 North out of Norwich parallels the Connecticut River and the old Boston & Maine tracks. This is a route that's popular with bicyclists, and in the river you may see the Dartmouth sculling team.

About 10 miles north is Route 113 West. Just north of the turnoff on the right is *Pompanoosuc Mills* in East Thetford. Pompanoosuc Mills produces and sells finely designed furniture at its seven stores located throughout New England. But all the furniture is made here.

Dwight Sargent is a native of the area. He attended Dartmouth both as an undergraduate and as an MBA candidate at Dartmouth's Tuck Business School. While he was at Tuck, he decided that starting up Pompanoosuc Mills was the best way he could apply what he had learned about furniture making from his grandfather.

Dwight proved to be a good student. The East Thetford showroom is spacious and airy and shows off Pompanoosuc's beds, tables, cabinets, and other furniture to their best advantage via decor suggestions and floor layouts. Each piece of furniture is available in cherry, oak, maple, birch, walnut, and occasionally bird's-eye.

Head upstairs for another showroom and a picture window that looks out onto the mill floor, where you can see workers sanding, shaping, and creating the furniture. Several times a year Pompanoosuc Mills conducts tours of the mill for the public. Call for the dates of its next tour.

Write to Pompanoosuc Mills, Route 5, East Thetford 05043, or call (802) 785–4851 or (800) 841–6671. Pompanoosuc Mills is open Monday through Friday from 9:00 A.M. to 6:00 P.M., Saturday 9:00 A.M. to 5:00 P.M., and Sunday from 11:00 A.M. to 5:00 P.M.

Route 113 heads west, through several of the villages of Thetford. At Thetford Center you'll see a cluster of nice brick homes, and if you turn left there you'll drop into a little hollow with a covered bridge, waterfall, and old mill foundations. Farther along Route 113 is Post Mills Airport, where Post Mills Aviation offers scenic balloon and glider rides over the Connecticut Valley. You might see their brightly colored balloons drifting above the treetops as you drive along the interstate.

Got Milk?

*T*he old joke about Vermont having more cows than people, although once true, has gone the way of the family farm. Over the past decades, Vermont has been losing dairy farms at a rate of about 4 percent a year. But the trend seems to have slowed, then reversed.

Not that you can expect to find an overflow of cows grazing on the State House lawn in Montpelier—the increase amounts to fewer than a dozen new farms a year. But it's progress in keeping the dairy farmer from joining the piping plover on the endangered species list.

From Post Mills, Route 113 wanders on to West Fairlee. Less than a mile past the village center take a left where the sign reads SOUTH VERSHIRE AND STRAFFORD. This road is known in various parts as Beanville Road, Copper Mine Road, and, farther west, Algerin Road. The road parallels Copper Creek on the left and follows several of the river's twists and turns. Stay on this road, and three-tenths of a mile from Route 113 you'll see copper-colored rocks on the left in the creek. Just one-tenth of a mile later is a reddish parking area on the right that is the entrance to what used to be the **Vermont Copper Mining Company,** an old copper mine. Pull in here and walk in at the gate to see the rusting and crumbling remains.

Vershire was first known as Ely, and this area was called Copperfield. This road used to see a lot of traffic. At its height in 1880, there were 600 miners and 225 horses working here at the mine, which produced more than 60 percent of the copper in the United States.

Vegetation grows to the left of the road, but other sections remain spookily barren. The fumes and smoke from the copper smelter and the roasting beds up ahead killed off most of the area's vegetation by 1875, after only twenty years of operation. No vegetation meant that the thin layer of topsoil was easily washed away, and the land is still recovering.

Scraps of iron and slag are scattered throughout the old roasting beds. Straight ahead 100 yards or so is the path the old tramway took to bring the copper ore down from the mines. There's an old cellar hole, quite elaborate, that, judging from old maps, photographs, and descriptions,

Wouldn't That Steam You?

*O*riginally from Orford, across the river in New Hampshire, **Samuel Morey** invented a steam engine and used it in a tiny skiff that he operated on the Connecticut River on a quiet Sunday morning in the early spring of 1793. Morey later moved to Fairlee, Vermont, and worked on his invention while plying the waters of the nearby lake that bears his name. There is a strong tradition that says that somewhere on the bottom of Lake Morey are the remains of the very first steamboat, and it wasn't invented by Robert Fulton. Robert Fulton reportedly visited with Morey in New York and at Orford, and with another Rhode Island steamboat inventor, years before he built his own steamboat and claimed the patent on steam navigation, denying Morey recognition as the inventor of steam propulsion for boats and ships.

was the smelter. Parts of the wall still stand, and where the bricks lie used to be the furnace. If you go back a little farther, about 50 feet or so, you'll see what looks like a heap of copper-colored dirt with large spidery cables sticking out of it. A couple of huge rusted bolts and nuts also stick up out of the concrete walls.

There are plenty of trails to explore at the mine, summer or winter. In fact, local snowmobile clubs and cross-country skiers use the trails in the winter.

Fairlee on Route 5 is blessed with two sizable lakes that have attracted summer visitors for almost as long as Vermont's been a state. Fairlee can become quite congested during July and August, but at any time of year it's a pretty detour from Route 5 to drive around the wooded shore of Lake Morey.

If Fairlee is known by a few for the first steamboat, Bradford, the next town north of Fairlee, is known for James Wilson, who created the first geographic globes sold in the United States in the early part of the nineteenth century.

Bradford is also an important early mill town. Lots of the old mill buildings have been converted for new businesses and residential use. But there's no mistaking them.

At *Colatina Exit* you can enjoy Italian veal, chicken, and seafood entrees and your choice of spaghetti, linguine, or fettuccine heaped with a thick tomato sauce that's made fresh every day. Antipasto and good, hearty soups such as an Italian white bean and sausage soup with a touch of tarragon are among Colatina's appetizers.

But most people come here for the pizza, available in four sizes with every topping imaginable and even some you never thought of before. Chopped onions are free. The one room holds twenty tables, but if you want to hear quiet local music while dining on pizza and sandwiches, Colatina has a bar upstairs that's open till late. Ask for the live concert series schedule for shows, which are held about three times a month, on Thursday or Friday evenings. For reservations, call (802) 222–9008.

Colatina's main dining room is open from 5:00 to about 9:00 P.M. seven days a week. Write to Colatina Exit, Main Street, Bradford 05033, or call (802) 222–9008.

If you're an antiques buff, you already know Vermont is filled with lots of shops and malls that offer some items you'd shake your head at, while others will cause you to take out your wallet and ask how much.

He Sure Pulled the Wool over Their Eyes

*O*ne of the better-known residents of Corinth, west of Bradford, was Horace McDuffee, who lived here in the late 1800s; he had a graduate degree in engineering from Dartmouth and compensated for his small stature by wearing many layers of overalls. Another Corinthian was Daniel Flagg, who loved animals so much that he didn't wear shoes, because they were made out of leather; he wouldn't ride a horse; and he invented the cowcatcher because he felt sorry for the cows who were speared when trains came roaring through the valley. And Orson Clement, still another Corinth native, raised sheep to such an extent that he stored the wool anywhere he could on his 600-acre farm: in the barn, the house, the granary basement, the stables. Clement was the equivalent of the man who saved every piece of string to make into a big ball. He never sold any of his wool until he was forced to do so by the federal government, which needed wool for uniforms during World War I. Even then, Clement managed to keep a sizable cache for himself that wasn't discovered until his death.

Happily, the owners of many antiques shops have pooled their resources to produce brochures and directories that point out all of the antiques shops and malls within a particular region. At the junction of Routes 5 and 25 in Bradford opposite the Hungry Bear is the rustic collaborative **Bradford 4 Corners Antiques.** Here some vendors have shops with storefronts, while others just set up their tables in the parking lot. Then there's the auctioneer in the large hall in between all of the other shops who conducts auctions every Friday at 6:00 P.M. and Monday at 6:30 P.M. sharp. The auctioneer is Ernie Stevens, and you can reach him at (802) 222–5113 or (603) 989–5809 for more information on the auctions, or write to him at Bradford 05033. But the best way to go antiquing in Bradford is to just show up.

Boston University alumni may be surprised to learn that their alma mater began just north of Bradford, in the tiny town of Newbury. Originating in 1836 as a school for the classical education of Methodist clergy, the Newbury Biblical Institute (as it was first called) was in a four-story brick building overlooking Newbury's common, next to the white Methodist Church, which was also part of the school. In 1846 the institute moved to Concord, New Hampshire, then to Boston in 1849, when it was renamed Boston University. A 1913 fire destroyed the original brick building, but the white **Old Village Church** still stands, recently restored by the Newbury Women's Club.

The Southern Connecticut River Valley

The southern Connecticut River valley is variously well populated, sparsely populated, mountainous, and flat in spots and offers a large selection of shops, numerous visitor attractions, a beautiful landscape, and a diversity of dining establishments.

With Route 4 serving as the only major east-west corridor from White River to points west—like Killington—the southern Connecticut River valley also gets more than its fair share of traffic. Every few years an article is proposed at the March town meeting in Woodstock—the town that most benefits from an increase in automobile and foot traffic—urging for a plan to widen Route 4 from a two-lane to a four-lane highway or to create a bypass to divert traffic around the town that parallels the Ottauquechee River. The townspeople and local business leaders make lots of noise, as almost everyone is opposed to the plan, except for the consultants and engineers from New York and Boston who have been paid to consider the benefits; the plan is defeated; and things die down for a while. At least until the next town meeting.

By contrast, Route 5 runs north-south, paralleling the Connecticut River, and receives a very light amount of traffic. I–91 runs alongside Route 5, and in these days of supersonic jet travel most people—Vermonters and tourists—choose to drive on the interstate, where a heavy foot pushing 65 miles per hour will get you where you want to go a lot faster than the 25- to 50-miles-per-hour speed zones through the attractive small towns along Route 5.

But sometimes it pays to slow down and smell the roses—or the pine forests that line the old state route. The southern Connecticut River valley is worth a leisurely inspection.

Woodstock

Route 4, between White River Junction and Woodstock, is one of the busiest highways in Vermont. It passes through Quechee, home of condos and glassblowers, and past many motels for about 10 miles until it reaches the town of Woodstock.

Woodstock has been called variously the Quintessential Vermont Village, the Most Photographed Town in the State, the Town That Time Forgot, and the state's most pernicious speed trap. At certain times of the year, the population quadruples with tourists, though its year-round population has hovered around the 3,000 mark since 1880. Given its proximity to Killington, its location on Route 4, and, yes, its quaintness, Woodstock is Tourist City.

In the midst of all this traffic, however, there is indeed a place that tourists rarely venture into, in part because *The Wasp* doesn't resemble the type of place most tourists come to Woodstock to ooh and aah over. Over the years, the owners have eschewed a sign and OPEN flag to identify the place, but now they've hung the sign.

The Wasp is a tiny, ten-stool diner that's been in town forever. No matter when you go, there's always a microcosm of Woodstock locals occupying—or waiting to occupy—one of the ten stools. Elegant Woodstock matrons who are lifetime members of the DAR, construction workers, and loggers, all sit side by side. It's the type of place where locals come in at 6:30 A.M. to reserve a piece of pie for lunch several hours later.

The Wasp is on Route 4, just east of the village. It looks like a dingy old modular home with green shutters, and it sits perpendicular to the road. The menu is just as dated: peanut butter and bacon, a hamburger at prices that will make you wonder if you've time traveled back to the 1960s.

Open from 6:00 A.M. to 2:00 P.M. Monday through Saturday, The Wasp is located at 67 Pleasant Street, Woodstock 05091. Call (802) 457–9805 to find out what the day's special pies are.

In addition to its great wealth, the Rockefeller family is well known for its deep commitment to conservation, an interest that first took shape in Woodstock. At the *Marsh-Billings-Rockefeller National Historic Park,* visitors can discover how the ideas of the first American conservationist, George Perkins Marsh, were put into action, first by rail king Frederick Billings and later by the Rockefellers. Tours include themes of gardening, forestry, and their relationship to conservation. The park is open Memorial Day through October, daily from 10:00 A.M. to 4:00 P.M. Admission is $6.00; $3.00 for ages five to fifteen and seniors. Call for reservations if possible. 54 Elm Street, Woodstock 05091; (802) 457–3368.

While there are motels all over Woodstock, the personal atmosphere of a B&B seems to better fit the town's genteel aura. *Canterbury House* has eight handsomely furnished guest rooms. Our favorite has a private entrance, a fireplace, and a big Victorian bathtub to sink into after a day's skiing at Suicide Six or hiking on the Appalachian Trail, which crosses

The Movable Bridge

Lincoln Bridge used to be in the middle of Woodstock, where the Billings Bridge is now. But in an 1869 flood the entire structure was washed some distance downstream, where it came to rest, intact, on an island. Charles Lincoln's bridge had also been washed away by the flood, but it was completely destroyed. Lincoln waited for a heavy winter with a hard freeze and plenty of snow and hauled the bridge up Route 4 on a sled. It's been at its present location, through hail and high water, since 1877.

Its ability to withstand being ripped from its moorings and carried by floodwaters is a testimony to its design, patented by T. W. Pratt in 1844. Its vertical posts and crossed iron rods were to become the prototype for hundreds of steel railroad bridges built with the growth of the railroads, but this one is the only remaining original covered bridge of this design.

just north of town. Rates range from $100 to $175, and guests must be over seventeen years old. Breakfasts are sumptuous, and the location is so convenient that you can walk everywhere—even to Billing Farm Museum. Canterbury House is at 43 Pleasant Street, Woodstock 05091; (802) 457–3077 or (800) 390–3077; www.thecanterbury house.com.

A few miles west of Woodstock, you'll come to the **Lincoln Inn,** beside the Lincoln Covered Bridge. Along with its cozy, comfortable guest rooms, the inn has an outstanding dining room, under the watchful eye of its Swiss chef/owner, Kurt Hildbrand. His presentations are works of art—no matter how often you order your favorite dish it will never look the same. Begin with the pheasant sausage and crisp sweet potato chips. Our shrimp in phyllo came one evening with a carrot slice carved into the shape of a fish sitting on top of it; the duckling in dark red cherries had a similar carved duck perched on it—little touches that tell us the chef's having some fun out there in the kitchen. But he's obviously paying close attention to the flavors, too, pairing rainbow trout with a creamy pistachio sauce and veal medallions with melted brie and shiitake mushrooms. Of course, you may not find any of these dishes on the menu, which changes often, but that's what keeps us (and a lot of other people) coming back. No matter how full you are, finish off with three scoops of different flavors of the chef's own sorbets, including mango, mandarin, and blueberry. They'll brew a fresh pot of decaf even if you're the last table left in the dining room (which we often are). Entrees range from $15 to $25, with more than half under $15; rooms are $125, or $175 during foliage, and include a three-course breakfast with your choice of entree. On Route 4, West Woodstock 05091; (802) 457– 3312; www. lincolninn.com.

Kedron Valley Inn is about the same distance south of town, and also has an excellent restaurant with an innovative chef. Rooms are well decorated with the owner's collection of antique needlework. More exam-

A Stop for Freedom

*T*he Kedron Valley Inn has an interesting history and is one of only a handful of places in the state that can be documented as a stop on the Underground Railroad. The nature of the endeavor—which was illegal—made it important not to keep any written records, so although many homes are thought to have been involved, only a few can be identified for certain. The building, which sits in front of the main inn and is now an annex with more guest rooms, was once a general store, and its owner was very active in helping escaping slaves. One of the guest rooms (and our favorite, not just for its history) occupies two floors, and the stairway between the two was once concealed in a closet. The room above was completely out of sight, an excellent hiding place. General stores made good stations in the Underground Railroad because no one took any special notice when large boxes were loaded and unloaded there.

ples, including some very fine old quilts, decorate public areas, each quilt labeled with its history. The inn has a beach on its private swimming pond. Rooms are $130 to $272, or with dinner (a bargain for such an outstanding dining room) $201 to $342. The inn is on Route 106, South Woodstock 05071; (802) 457–1473 or (800) 836–1193.

Suicide Six sounds fiercer than it is. One of the smaller of the state's ski areas, it is well-designed for families and offers adult-and-child ski clinics on weekends, when parents can learn to help their children become better skiers and pick up a few tips themselves. Although the elevation is not as high as many other areas, Suicide Six has an evenly divided mix of beginner, intermediate, and expert terrain. It is under the same ownership as the Woodstock Inn, and the inn offers a number of attractive packages that combine lodging and lift tickets. The ski area is on Stagecoach Road, South Pomfret 05067; (802) 457–6661, (800) 448– 7900, snow conditions (802) 457–6666; www. woodstockinn.com.

Hartland–Windsor

O n Route 5 south out of White River Junction, you'll find a relatively large amount of industry in the form of farms, factories, computer consulting companies, and other businesses. This part of the road is relatively industrial, but farms suddenly appear, with motels, campgrounds, and private homes also strewn about. This state highway is a winding, downhill road.

One of the real joys of summer and fall travel is the chance to find beautiful gardens at their peak. In Hartland we found **Talbot's Herb and Perennial Farm,** where you can see collections of herbs and perennials in attractively arranged show gardens. In addition to many of the more common perennials, there's a good selection of unusual varieties. Patty and David Talbot have developed an excellent reputation for the informative and practical gardening classes they hold in their propagation greenhouse. Much of each class is spent in hands-on activity, and students leave with plants and cuttings and divisions they have made themselves. The only drawback is that you must sign up for the whole series, which covers landscaping, garden design, old-fashioned roses, herbs, perennials, and many other subjects. Talbot's is 3 miles south of Quechee on the Hartland-Quechee Road, Hartland 05048, and is open Tuesday through Sunday from 9:00 A.M. to 5:00 P.M. spring through October; (802) 436–2085.

Route 5 plays tag with parallel I–91, weaving over and under it at various points. As you drive into Hartland proper, Routes 5 and 12 merge. Head north on Route 12 for 2 miles; you'll come into Hartland Four Corners and **Skunk Hollow Tavern,** a neighborhood pub and restaurant with good prices and food, a place where the menu is written on a large slate and where darts fly on Friday nights.

The second floor at Skunk Hollow is more formally decorated, but the same menu is served. The downstairs pub fills up most weekends by 6:00 P.M., since the tavern is a favorite local hangout.

Skunk Hollow Tavern is in Hartland Four Corners 05049; call (802) 436–2139—reservations are strongly recommended. Skunk Hollow is open Wednesday through Sunday from 5:00 P.M. until closing, and Sunday brunch is served from 11:00 A.M. to 2:00 P.M. There is live music Wednesday through Friday evenings.

A few miles south on Route 5 is Windsor. A short distance north of town is **Harpoon Brewery,** which offers tastings and tours, the latter at 11:00 A.M. and 1:00 and 3:00 P.M. Tuesday through Saturday. Lunch is served from 10:00 A.M. to 6:00 P.M. on the same days in their beer garden. You can get samplers of their ales to taste with your grilled panini sandwiches. 336 Ruth Carney Drive, Windsor 05089; www.harpoon brewery.com.

Route 5 is also the main street of Windsor, and you'll pass between rows of well-kept brick houses and distinguished business blocks, built when Windsor was a major player in the precision tool industry.

Just south of the intersection with Route 44 is a huge brick building, the **American Precision Museum,** on Route 5. The museum is a tribute to a bygone era when automated machines were a wonder to behold. Behemoth milling machines, lathes, steam engines, and generators fill an entire room, looking every bit the dinosaurs they are today.

Many of the machines here were invented by Vermonters who, far too stubborn to ask for help from the outside world, had to find a way to do the tasks themselves. It seems strange to see all these machines placed together like some Industrial Revolution graveyard. Glass showcases contain salesman's samples, planes, and levels, some with the original instruction booklets. Other display cases hold the modern calculator of 1903, a cylindrical slide rule, plastic toy molds, and early-model pencil sharpeners.

That's a Lot of Baaaaaaa

*In 1838 a herd of 18,000 sheep passed over the **Cornish Windsor Covered Bridge,** a predecessor of the one that spans the Connecticut between the two towns today. Three presidents—Hayes, Wilson, and Theodore Roosevelt—have crossed the present bridge, which was built in 1866 after the earlier bridge was swept away in a flood. The bridge is the longest covered bridge still in use in the United States, at 449 feet, 5 inches. No one recorded just how many sheep fit onto the bridge at one time, nor what it sounded like in there as they crossed.*

Cases display miniature models of lathes, presses, band saws, and shapers, scaled to a sixteenth of their true size. They actually run—press a button and the gears spin, just like the real thing. They're built by John Aschauer, a former toolmaker who spent twenty-seven years making these miniature machines. He used his memory to re-create them.

The museum is open daily from Memorial Day through November 1 from 10:00 A.M. to 5:00 P.M. The admission fee is $5.00 for adults and $3.50 for children. American Precision Museum, 196 South Main Street, Windsor 05089; (802) 674–5781.

Also downtown the **Vermont Witch Hazel Co. and General Store** features, as you would expect, witch hazel personal cleansing products such as soaps, cleansing gel, and distilled witch hazel. Derived from a shrub that grows primarily in the Northeast, witch hazel is reputed to reduce inflammation and pain, soothe rough and raw skin, clean the complexion, and reduce itching and swelling of insect bites. The general store has a large selection of Vermont-made handcrafts and Vermont products that include maple syrup, jams, horseradish, honey, and ice cream toppings. They are open Tuesday through Saturday 10 A.M. to 5 P.M. 113 Main Street, Windsor 05089.

In the 1900 former Boston & Main Depot, with its many years of paint removed to expose beautiful pine ceilings, is the family-run **Windsor Station Restaurant.** Entrees, priced from $11 to $15, include several veal dishes, chicken Kiev, roast duckling, and other continental dishes along with Mama's Pasta, a melange of seafood, white beans, and vermicelli. The restaurant is open from 5:30 to 9:00 P.M. Tuesday through Sunday; Depot Avenue, Windsor 05089; (802) 674–2052.

High on a hill overlooking the town stands a mansion built in 1901 during Windsor's glory days, which has been restored as **Juniper Hill Inn**. In the summer, its gardens are lovely, and you can enjoy them from a terrace with valley views for a backdrop. Fine paneling gives the large public rooms elegance, but they are still very comfortable, with big windows and well-chosen antiques. Guest rooms are also bright and large, with fireplaces. Dinner is served by reservation in the candlelit dining room Tuesday through Saturday, and they'll bring breakfast to your room if you ask. Rates range from $115 to $185. North of town on Route 5, look for Juniper Hill Road (R.R. 1 Box 79), Windsor 05089; (802) 674–5273 or (800) 359–2541; www.juniperhill.com.

Many areas once known only as ski mountains now offer attractions that make them into year-round facilities. One of these is **Ascutney Mountain Resort** on 3,144-foot Mount Ascutney. In winter the northwest slopes are a busy ski mountain, especially good for families. A good alternative to the mega-mountains elsewhere in the state, Ascutney is a place where the kids can ski on their own, with slope-side lodging and entertainment facilities.

Like other resort owners, the operators reasoned that all these facilities were just as good in the summer, with a little change in focus. In summer you can enjoy the Sports and Fitness Center, indoor and outdoor pools, miniature golf, hiking trails, and racquetball and tennis courts with a resident pro. For traveling families there's also a summer day camp with activities for kids, ranging from art to nature excursions. Special packages allow you to arrange canoeing trips on the Connecticut River or to golf at the Crown Point Country Club in Springfield or the Woodstock Country Club in Woodstock. To reach Ascutney, leave I–91 at exit 8 in Weathersfield and take Route 5 north. Take Route 44A (and Route 44) toward Brownsville; the entrance road will be on the left, well marked by signs. Ascutney Mountain Resort, Brownsville 05037; (800) 243–0011; ascutney.com.

Springfield–Chester

Route 5 heading south from Windsor into Springfield is a winding road with more farms and Wilgus State Park, where in some spots the forest is so thick it almost forms a canopy that blots out the summer sun. Just past the park, rows and rows of corn line both sides of the road from late spring into September. Between Windsor and Springfield lies the town of Weathersfield. As you pass through Weathersfield Bow, where the peninsula juts out sharply to the left, the identity of the land seems to meld with that of New Hampshire, which is visible most of the time from Route 5. Sometimes it seems as if you can wade across the river.

Route 11 leads from Route 5 to Springfield, a hard-living type of old mill town with more than its fair share of boarded-up brick buildings. There are many towns in the United States named Springfield. All of them were named after Springfield, Massachusetts, and the Springfield in Vermont holds the distinction of being the first such town to be named after the original.

The *Eureka Schoolhouse,* located on Route 11 just west of I–91, is the oldest schoolhouse still standing in Vermont. It was used continually from 1785 until 1900 and was reconstructed in 1968 on its current spot.

Inside, the schoolhouse is still set up as though a group of children will walk through at any minute, with desks and slates and quill pens and inkwells. But in a nod to current realities, such modern amenities as a fire extinguisher, telephone, and space heater are inside, too. Smell the old wood siding; the building smells as if it's seen a lot. Each of the old wooden shakes on the roof seems to have a personality of its own, as no two adjacent shakes point in the same direction. The schoolhouse isn't open to the public, but feel free to walk around and look.

To the left of the schoolhouse is an old *covered bridge.* It's the last covered bridge in existence in the town of Springfield. Like the schoolhouse, and like many other historical buildings in Vermont, it was moved from its original spot and reassembled on this site.

The *Springfield Art and Historical Society* has memorabilia of early Springfield, and its *Miller Art Center* houses a collection of dolls and information on Joel Ellis, America's first doll manufacturer. Born in Barnard, Vermont, in 1830, he was an inventor and manufacturer who started out making baby buggies and tops and at the age of twenty-eight started a factory for the manufacture of wooden dolls. He took out a patent on his system for the assembly of movable joints. The Miller

Center is free and open mid-March to the end of October Tuesday through Friday from 10:00 A.M. to 4:00 P.M. and Saturday from 2:00 to 5:00 P.M. It's located at 9 Elm Street, Springfield 05156; (902) 885–2415.

For a feeling of upper-crust and intellectual Vermont of the nineteenth century, stay at **Hartness House.** James Hartness's fortune was based upon his invention of the turret lathe, and he held over 120 other patents. With this fortune he built his mansion, Hartness House, beautifully preserved today as a 41-room inn. The gracious public rooms are paneled in oak, and antiques furnish rooms throughout the inn. Special midweek and weekend package rates are available.

From the dining room you can look out over the valley as you enjoy a dinner of pork chops stuffed with sweet and hot sausage, or a cumin-dusted Statler chicken breast. Rack of lamb and filet mignon are also on the menu, where entrees cost $15 to $20.

Hartness's avocation was astronomy, so while you are there ask to see his 600-power, 10-inch lens turret equatorial telescope. It is housed in an unusual structure, which is home to the Stellafane Society, an organization of amateur astronomers. 30 Orchard Street, Springfield 05156; (802) 885–2115, (800) 732–4789; www.hartnesshouse.com.

Springfield is also home to **Wellwood Orchards,** where from early September to November you can either pick your own apples or buy them from the stand. Tour the orchards on a wagon ride, and before picking let the kids enjoy the petting zoo. Among the apple varieties are Macoun, McIntosh, Empire, Cortland, and Red Delicious; there are also a few old-fashioned varieties. The shop has pies, cider, maple syrup and candies, pumpkins, and squash. The farm is 3 miles out Valley Street at 529 Wellwood Orchard Road, Springfield 05156; (802) 263–5200.

Route 11 leads to Chester, 8 miles to the west. Although it bears a few similarities to its more affluent and gentrified neighbor to the south—the town of Grafton—Chester is a good spot for visitors who want to get off the beaten path from Grafton.

Chester has lots of big, beautifully restored Victorian houses along both sides of the narrow green skirting its main street. Look for the cemetery across from the row of stores and hotels; the hulking stone building that fronts the street has an inscription that reads PUBLIC TOMB 1850. Just alongside the tomb is a cannon and a Civil War monument.

Look for School Street, a block off the green, and **Rose Arbour Tea Room & Gift Shop.** This is an old-fashioned kind of tea shop—you thought nobody made finger sandwiches and served fresh berries with clotted cream anymore?—that takes its tea seriously. While cream teas with scones are available anytime, for the full traditional afternoon tea ($17.50) you'll need to give the owner forty-eight hours notice, so she can prepare the special treats that bring her customers from all over southern Vermont—although the scones are enough to bring us back.

Classical music plays throughout lunch, which may include real English scones, a light herbal chicken salad, or an authentic ploughman's plate, with hearty cheddar, homemade bread, and an apple.

The tearoom is open from 11:00 A.M. to 5:00 P.M. Tuesday through Saturday November through June and every day July through October.

Upstairs at Rose Arbour are two bed-and-breakfast suites, furnished with four-poster beds, old samplers, and feather duvets. One of these is a large suite with a kitchen; the other sleeps four people. Double guest rooms cost $85, and a three-room suite is $240. When you're not sleeping upstairs or relaxing on the screened second-floor porch, you can play croquet or admire the herb gardens out back.

Write to Rose Arbour, School and Canal Streets, Chester 05143; (802) 875–4767.

If you look at your road maps and atlases, you'll probably see that some of them are published by the National Survey in Chester, Vermont. In addition to revising and publishing maps, the National Survey has a retail outlet next to the Rose Arbour on School Street, the **National Survey Charthouse.**

If you come in winter, you'll probably be interested in the Vermont Department of Highways Snow Removal Map from 1931, encased in plastic. The road system in the state was fairly well established then, although even many main thoroughfares were dirt roads, and the same roads that were primary roads years ago are still main roads today.

The charthouse has a wide selection of topographical maps dating from 1900 for Ohio, New York, Vermont, Delaware, North Carolina, and a few other states. Old foldout road maps from the 1930s and 1940s are here, as are the Victory Vacations book series from Consolidated Tours. These tour guides set the standard for the automobile vacations that began after World War II and continue today. It's interesting to see how many destinations and businesses mentioned in these guides are still around.

The charthouse is open Monday through Friday from 8:30 A.M. to 4:00 P.M. and Saturday from 10:00 A.M. to 4:00 P.M. The National Survey Charthouse is on School Street, Chester 05143; (802) 875–2121; www.natlsurvey.com.

Fine homes, mostly Victorian, line the main street of Chester, which is also Route 11. Just out of the village in Proctorsville is **Baba à Louis Bakery,** best known outside the area for the popular cookbook *Baba à Louis Bread Book,* featuring the chef's best bread and pastry recipes. Breads and cookies are for sale, along with light lunches, in this glistening high-ceilinged bake shop, where you can buy the book, meet the author, and even get his floury autograph.

Seven miles later, on the north side of the road, you'll see a striking brick building with the word SIMONSVILLE printed over its third-story outdoor porch. You've found **Rowell's Inn,** an exquisite original stagecoach stop that is furnished throughout with antiques and plenty of rockers.

The two guest rooms up on the third floor once served—together—as the inn's ballroom and are particularly impressive, with high vaulted ceilings, clawfoot tubs, and heated towel racks.

Four-course dinners are served to guests on weekends by reservation and may feature entrees such as rack of lamb and chicken breast Tuscany, filled with prosciutto and provolone and accompanied by a delicate wine sauce. The house special dessert is caramel-fudge pecan pie. After dessert, you may be glad you took our advice and asked for the third-floor room; the walk up the steep second flight of stairs will help work off the caramel. B&B rates are $120 to $175; add $25 per person for dinner.

Rowell's Inn, 1834 Simonsville Road (Route 11) Andover 05143; (802) 875–3658, (800) 728–0842; www.rowellsinn.com.

The **Inn at High View** is about as far off the beaten path as you can get,

Say Cheese

*A*s interest in cooking and fine dining has blossomed, so has interest in Vermont's fine farm-made cheeses. Sometime referred to as farmhouse cheese, these excellent specialty cheeses are made in small lots. One producer is Vermont Shepherd, founded by sheep farmers in 1990 who had to deal with an excess of ewe's milk after spring lambing. When demand exceeded their production capacity, they enlisted other sheep farmers, who now make cheese that is aged in the Vermont Shepherd caves. Other farms to look for are Vermont Butter and Cheese Company, Orb Weaver Farm, Shelburne Farm, and Grafton Village Cheese. The Vermont Cheese Council Web site features a virtual tour of the cheese farms; www.vtcheese.com.

at the top of a hill that offers views as far as Mount Monadnock in New Hampshire. A riot of color surrounds it, with brilliant flowers that seem to tumble down its hillside in a never-ending series of gardens. The rooms are nicely furnished, and on Saturday evenings you can make reservations for the excellent Italian dinners, which cost about $30, depending on the menu. This is not only a bargain, but it saves driving back from Chester or elsewhere after dinner. On clear evenings, you'll want to spend some time after dinner just looking at the stars; the inn is so far from any city that no lights interfere, and you can see more stars than you ever thought existed. Room rates are $130 to $175. In the spacious family suites, which sleep five and six respectively, additional people are $20 each. The owners will give you personalized directions when you reserve. The inn is at 753 East Hill Road, Andover 05143; (802) 875–2724; www.innathighview.com.

If you leave Chester on Route 103 to head back to Route 5 and the Connecticut River, you'll see **Putney Pasta** on the right, easily spotted by its clever sign depicting a batch of fresh pasta emerging from the fettuccini cutter. Here you can buy prototypes, closeouts, overruns, and pastas in their developmental stages that the rest of the world never gets to taste. And you can buy these (all frozen) at well below supermarket prices. You'll see the pastas in grocery stores, and you've probably tasted them in good restaurants, since Putney Pasta supplies chefs with designer pastas to match particular dishes they create. Expect to find as many as forty different flavors and styles, from chewy potato gnocchi, ravioli (maybe filled with smoked salmon), and tortellini to key lime-jalepeño and roasted sweet red pepper noodles. If you didn't bring your cooler to

Mountain Lions in Vermont?

*C*atamount *is the name given to the eastern native puma by Vermonters. Also known as the mountain lion, this cat is capable of 40-foot leaps and incredible speeds over short distances. The animals were thought to be extinct in Vermont since early in the twentieth century, victims of a bounty imposed to protect domestic sheep and cattle.*

Recently residents of Townshend, Grafton, and Newfane have reported sighting that have raised hopes that there is still a viable population. If you happen to see a big golden brownish cat, 4 to 6 feet long with a 4-foot tail, take a picture of it, then call Vermont Fish and Game. They'll probably tell you it's a bobcat, but you'll know the truth. For more information contact the Eastern Puma Research Network in Baltimore, (410) 254–2517.

carry them home, you can buy a small insulated box. Putney Pasta is open from 10:00 A.M. to 6:00 P.M. every day (with senior specials on Tuesdays). P.O. Box 445, Route 103, Putney 05143; (802) 875–4500; www.putneypasta.com.

If you head out of Chester on Route 35 South, you'll soon enter the village of Grafton, a very tourist-oriented town. Bypass the main village and head west on Route 121. Once you leave the village, the road turns to dirt. The **Grafton Swimming Pond** is a mile up the road on the left. Even on a hot Saturday afternoon in August, you may find the pond deserted. A field surrounds the pond, which is close to the road, and there's a portable toilet so you can spend the whole day at the pond. The pond has docks and a roped-off area for wading but no lifeguards.

Before leaving town, stop at **Grafton Village Cheese,** on Route 35 at the edge of the village. You can see parts of the cheese-making process here, as well as sample the product and buy some to take home. P.O. Box 87, Townshend Road, Grafton 05146; (802) 843–2221, (800) 472–3866; www.graftonvillagecheese.com.

Next to the cheese "factory" is a covered footbridge, part of Grafton's walking trail system.

Route 35 continues south through the town of Athens. As with Route 121 in Grafton, it's common in Vermont to have numbered main state roads turn to dirt in certain areas. Route 35 is dirt for a few miles, then turns back to blacktop.

In summertime pick-your-own and porchside farm stands abound throughout the state. There's usually at least one in each town. Also keep a lookout for the ingenious scarecrows people construct to fend off intruders.

Route 35 meets up with Route 30 in Townshend, sitting around its postcard-picture common. The Townshend Corner Store serves breakfast and lunch with old-fashioned counter service. North on Route 30 is the **Townshend Lake Dam** over the West River, operated by the U.S. Army Corps of Engineers. The dam was built between 1958 and 1961 to better control flooding of the West River. The dam is 1,000 feet long and 133 feet tall and has a capacity of almost eleven billion gallons of water.

If you drive across the top of the dam, you'll get a strange, vertiginous feeling. There are lots of paths to explore. On weekends the parking lot may be almost full with mostly Vermont plates, but it is usually relatively quiet: no loud radios and just the clink of horseshoes and the sound of people's voices.

The recreational facilities at the dam include picnic tables, horseshoes, boating and swimming areas, volleyball, and several trails, all with a view of the dam. The dam is part of Townshend State Park, which has a total of 856 acres and thirty-four camping sites. Call (802) 365–7500 for more information or write to Townshend Lake Dam and State Park, Route 30, Townshend 05353.

Scott Bridge, which you can see from Route 30, not far from the dam, is the longest wooden span in Vermont. (Remember the one in Windsor is not wholly in Vermont.) Strategically placed concrete blocks prohibit cars from crossing, but you can walk across it. Although it'll feel a little rickety, you'll be distracted by the initials and philosophies carved into the trusses and sides of the bridge by generations of local teenagers. Scott Bridge is 277 feet long and was built in 1870.

Bellows Falls–Putney

A s you travel south on Route 5, Springfield melds into Rockingham and the town of Bellows Falls, which is actually a village within the town of Rockingham—as is Saxtons River, farther west. Perhaps this habit of having what seems like towns inside of other towns is the most puzzling of all New England's idiosyncracies.

Waste Not, Want Not to the End

H etty Green, popularly known as "the Witch of Wall Street," was born in Bellows Falls in 1834. She was regarded as the richest woman in America and probably the cheapest, too.

As a young woman and heir to a New Bedford whaling fortune, she had flirted with New York society and danced with the Prince of Wales. She also multiplied her net worth by acquiring her aunt's sizable fortune and by marrying a third, belonging to a Bellows Falls native. She threw him out after he failed to take her advice in business. Her son lost a leg because she was too stingy to take him to a doctor for a kneecap injury; when she finally did, years later, it was under an assumed name so she could put him in the hospital's charity ward. By the time of her death in 1916, she had amassed a total of about $100 million, but when she had to travel to New York on business, she still stayed in a dollar-a-night rooming house in Brooklyn.

On Route 5 in Rockingham you'll spot *Leslie's,* an informal restaurant with a New American menu based on fresh produce from their own extensive gardens. They make their own pasta, then serve it in interesting combinations of meat, seafood, and vegetables. Many of the dishes are low-fat and heart-healthy as well as delicious. Dinner is served from 5:00 to 9:00 P.M. Wednesday through Sunday. Entrees range from $15 to $20. It's close to the interstate highway junction on Route 5; (802) 463–4929.

Bear left as you head south on Route 5 to enter the town of Bellows Falls for a cross-section of modern-day Vermont history: The *Miss Bellows Falls Diner* is housed in one of the original Worcester dining cars from the 1920s and 1930s and offers standard diner fare at diner prices. It's at 90 Rockingham Street 05101, just north of the main square; (802) 463–9800.

It would be a shame to pass through here without seeing the falls, just to your left at the square and visible from the tall stone bridge that leads to New Hampshire. Upstream are the dammed falls and another iron bridge, but the best views are of this lower section. These are a raging torrent of froth in the spring, but impressive anytime, not so much for their height as for the depth of the gorge and the amount of water compressed between the narrow rock walls. In case you're interested in geology, this is about the only place where you can actually see the seam in the rocks where the two tectonic plates meet—New Hampshire is actually a piece of Africa left off when that plate moved away. If it had taken all of itself, you'd be standing on the Atlantic shore here, and Vermont wouldn't be the only New England state without a coastline.

The first bridge to span the Connecticut River was built from Bellows Falls across to Walpole, New Hampshire. The falls for which the town was named also was the site of the first canal begun in the country, with construction started in 1792.

If you are in the area on Thursday evening, check with *Oona's Restaurant,* on the Square in Bellows Falls 05101, which offers live Thursday night country-western, bluegrass, and blues at 8:30 P.M. The suggested donation is $7.00, most of which goes to the players, the rest to pay for posters and mailers; (802) 463–3252 for information, (802) 463–9830 for the restaurant.

Be sure to see the huge (32 by 40 feet) wall mural painted by local artists Bonnie Turner and Cliff Clear. It's on Westminster Street and depicts the town square at the turn of the nineteenth century. Many of the same buildings are still there.

In its long history, the town of Westminster, south of Bellows Falls, has been variously part of New Hampshire, Massachusetts, New York, and Vermont, depending on what year you're looking at.

The town was first granted as part of Massachusetts and was known as Number One in 1735. The main village of Westminster lies on Route 5, which was originally constructed as the King's Highway and was built wide to allow for military training sessions by pre–Revolutionary War soldiers.

Westminster was in flux for the twelve years between 1740 and 1752, when the northern boundary of Massachusetts was determined to be farther south, and New Hampshire Governor Benning Wentworth regranted the land to New Hampshirites. In 1772, however, New York got into the act by locating a county courthouse in the town. Westminster officially became part of Vermont along with the rest of the state in 1777, when the Vermont government proclaimed itself to be a free and independent republic.

Things in town have been pretty quiet since Vermont decided to join the United States in 1791. The only time things really heat up in Westminster is when the *Westminster MG Car Museum* opens each Columbus Day weekend for its annual rally.

The museum is the world's largest private exhibit of a single model of car, with twenty-seven different models of MGs on display. Write to the Westminster MG Car Museum, Route 5, Westminster 05158, or call (802) 722–3708 for more information on this museum, which opens only once a year.

From Westminster you can take an unnumbered road west to the village named (not surprisingly) Westminster West, where you will find one of Vermont's many homegrown businesses. *Tile Works of Westminster West* makes original and unique decorative tiles and home accessories, which range from fish-shaped toothbrush holders and soap dishes to towel racks. Their designs are all inspired by the sea and fish, with some very attractive wall plaques of specific species. Depictions are very realistic, and the glazes make the surface of each fish shimmer as though it had just jumped from a Vermont stream into the sunlight. The work is moderately priced, with many items in the $25 range. Be sure to ask for a business card—you'll see why when you see the card. The open sign is always on the studio door, even if no one is there, so feel free to enter. The mailing address is RFD 3, Box 728, Putney 05346; (802) 387–6661.

Another back road will take you straight into Putney and a slice of life almost frozen in time from the 1960s, when Putney was hippie heaven.

As you roam its back roads, you'll still see, mixed in with the trust-fund farms, metamorphosed homes that grew out of the back-to-the-land homesteads of escapees from the draft and the modern world itself. Communes thrived, and while those days have gone, they have left a mellowing mark on Putney that makes it a nice place to spend some time and a haven for artists and craftspeople.

From the *Putney Hearth Bakery and Coffee House* adjoining *Heartstone Books,* you can take your coffee and pastry out onto the long porch of the Putney Tavern Building and watch the easy comings and goings in the center of town. The cafe is open from 7:00 A.M. to 5:00 P.M. Monday through Saturday and from 8:00 A.M. to 3:00 P.M. Sunday; you can browse for new or good previously read books daily from 10:00 A.M. to 7:00 P.M. Main Street, Putney 05346; (802) 387–2100.

As the heart of Vermont's back-to-the-land movement, Putney is an appropriate home for an outstanding natural-fiber spinning mill. *Green Mountain Spinnery* processes local wool into knitting and weaving yarns, which you can purchase at their shop. On the first and third Tuesdays of the month, tours of the mill are given, and you can see how the entire process takes place. The mill shop is open Monday through Friday 9:00 A.M. to 5:30 P.M., Saturday 10:00 A.M. to 5:30 P.M., and Sunday noon to 4:00 P.M. Look for it off Route 5 in Putney, at the end of the exit 4 ramp from I–91, opposite Putney Inn, Putney 05346; (892) 387–4528; e-mail: spinnery@sover.net; www.spinnery.com.

Putney Mountain, the 1,600-foot elevation that rises west of town, has a 360-degree unobstructed view of the valley, the river, and the surrounding hills and mountains. It's an easy walk via a trail that begins near the Putney School, a private school on West Hill. At the summit you can sit and watch hawks soaring on the thermals.

Brattleboro

rattleboro is a small, bustling city that incorporates the best of urban, rural, and even suburban characteristics. It is influenced by the presence both of the Brattleboro Retreat, a highly respected drug and alcohol rehabilitation center and the largest employer in town, and of the Experiment in International Living, an exchange program that trains students to live and serve in the Peace Corps overseas. Many of the men and women who came to Vermont in the 1960s to live in communes ended their journey as soon as they crossed over the Massachusetts border into Vermont, and so the town still has a New Age flavor, as evidenced by the posters on telephone poles that advertise shiatsu, peace meetings, and Brazilian dance lessons.

Downtown Brattleboro—or "Brat," as locals refer to it—is the old section, with relics of factories and hotels from the booming railroad days. Restaurants, shops, and cultural events abound here. Drive a few miles out of town, and once you're up in the hills you'll feel as if you're miles away from Main Street. But when you head west on Route 9 or south on Route 5, all the accoutrements of suburbia are there, from fast-food restaurants to motels and supermarkets.

Petria Mitchell is a Brattleboro artist who works in an unusual medium for these times: scrimshaw. She favors engraving animal and nature scenes on real ivory from prehistoric mammoth and walrus tusks, not from elephants and rhinos recently poached in Kenya.

Petria will custom-design everything from a knife handle to a piece of jewelry, but her work is most striking in the form of a single display piece. Since the ivory she works with can be up to 40,000 years old, the surface can be somewhat stained and mottled. That quality adds to the overall feeling of the piece, fooling you into believing that the scrimshaw was created on a long-ago ocean voyage by some wizened, grizzly sailor.

Petria's studio is located at 127 Main Street, Brattleboro 05301; her hours can be erratic, so call ahead at (802) 257–4021 to be sure the studio is open.

Many Brattleboro residents consider the only place in town to meet to be *The Common Ground,* a health food restaurant and clearinghouse for anything and everything that's alternative in town—or in the area. The Common Ground is one of the few businesses in Vermont that is solely worker-owned.

You'll look long and hard to find a place that's more laid-back; no servers take your order—you choose from a list written on the board at the counter, then find a seat at one of the mismatched tables, helping yourself to a cup of tea (you can blend your own), a glass of cider, or a bowl of soup on the way. Somewhat (sometimes very somewhat) later, either someone will bring you your food, or you'll go back to the counter and find it yourself. When you've eaten and finished your conversation—or your book—you can go back to the counter and pay for your meal.

This relaxed air isn't for everyone, and The Common Ground almost lost its footing recently, falling back to Thursday-through-Sunday hours only.

But that, like everything else at The Common Ground, could change, too, so you'll have to check for yourself. The restaurant is up a steep flight of stairs, at 25 Elliot Street, Brattleboro 05301; (802) 257–0855.

A motel right on Brattleboro's most beaten path is an unlikely spot for genuine Indian cuisine, but that's what you'll find at **Dhaba.** Here, inside the Quality Inn, the owners cook their naan in a fully traditional tandoori oven. Unlike many Indian restaurants, where you expect the same menu of facsimile curries, Dhaba offers the real thing. The samosas are crisp and freshly made. Vegetarian and meat choices abound, with spicy and mild dishes to suit any tolerance level. There are several varieties of mango shakes. Service and ambience are very pleasant, with an attentive staff that welcomes families and never forgets a face. Even friends who don't normally choose Indian food are glad they joined us at Dhaba, 1380 Putney Road (Route 5 North), Brattleboro 05301; (802) 254–8701, ext. 274.

Still on the Asian end of Brattleboro's culinary spectrum, **Anon's Thai Cuisine** offers selections from the traditional pad thai and chicken satay to basil calamari and our personal favorite, a salad roll with cilantro, Thai noodles, mint, and carrots with a homemade peanut sauce. The restaurant also has a full takeout menu, and you can find Anon's mobile version on Saturdays in summer at the Brattleboro Farmers Market (it's easy to tell which stand is theirs—it's the one with the long line). Anon's restaurant is hidden off Canal Street, which is Route 5, close to exit 1 from I–91 at 4 Fairground Road, Brattleboro 05301; (802) 257–1376.

Brattleboro is well supplied with restaurants and cafes, including **Peter Haven's,** right across Elliot Street. There are only ten tables, so you should make reservations on weekends to sample the deceptively simple-sounding menu. Appetizers include gravlax, escargot with garlic butter and Dijon mustard, and smoked filet of trout. For entrees, sea scallops are sautéed with roasted red peppers and crabmeat in a delicate cream sauce, and boneless breast of duck may be roasted with a sauce of sour cherries, black currants, and port wine. For dessert, we head straight for the lemon tart with strawberry sauce. Entrees range from $18 to $22. Dinner is served Tuesday through Saturday from 6:00 P.M. The restaurant is closed for two weeks each at the end of March, the beginning of July, and the end of November. Peter Havens is at 32 Elliot Street, Brattleboro 05301; (802) 257–3333.

Farther up Elliot Street is the outstanding but tiny **T. J. Buckley's,** with an eclectic menu of only four items, which change daily. Everything is strictly fresh (the chef often shops from local farmers at the biweekly farmers' market) and flawlessly prepared. It's worth every penny of the $25 for a main course. The restaurant has such a following that you'd better make reservations if you hope for a table. Credit cards aren't accepted, but you can pay by personal check. This is one book you can't judge by its cover—it's located in a 1927 Worcester diner at 132 Elliot Street, Brattleboro 05301; (802) 257–4922.

You can shop from the same local farmers on Saturday at the **Brattleboro Farmers' Market,** on Route 9 just west of town. Like so much else in Brattleboro, this is a local institution, where you will find both old favorite vegetables and the trendiest new varieties. Big truck farms join small homestead farmers here; one stand sells nothing but Asian vegetables and greens. In the spring you can buy plants for your own garden, and all summer you'll find a smattering of crafts (including stunning dried-flower wreaths) and farm-related products, such as herb vinegars, fruit jams, fresh-baked breads, cheese, maple syrup, and organic honey.

Many people go just for lunch and the live music that's often playing on the shaded lawn inside the circle of stands. Several vendors sell only prepared foods, which you can eat at picnic tables or carry off for dinner later. These usually include Japanese udon noodles, Lebanese dolmas and other dishes, and authentic Mexican and Thai foods. There's a booth with great coffee and tea and freshly baked breakfast goodies and cookies. What you won't find are burgers and fries or hot dogs. At every booth you'll find at least one big smile; it's the friendliest group of people you'll meet anywhere. Open Saturday, May through October, from 9:00 A.M. to 2:00 P.M. A smaller version is held in front of the Merchants Bank on Main Street from 10:00 A.M. to 2:00 P.M. every Wednesday, and the group holds a craft fair just before Christmas (see Events in the Connecticut River Valley chapter).

The **Old Creamery Bridge** is close to the Brattleboro Farmers Market. Named for the Brattleboro Creamery, which once stood on the far side, it was built in 1879 and has ever since provided an easy route from the west end of Brattleboro to downtown. In 1917 a footbridge was added to one side, allowing pedestrians to cross Whetstone Brook without fighting traffic. This is the last remaining of the four covered bridges that once carried traffic in Brattleboro.

Just west of the farmers' market grove on Route 9 is West Brattleboro, an attractive enclave of distinguished old homes and a tiny business center with several places to eat. At the far edge of these is **Max's,** an intimate restaurant with a menu that is both sophisticated and varied. The staff is well versed on the dishes, and service treads a fine line by being proper without being stiff. On the spring menu you may find wild mushroom soup, rich and earthy, almost chewy, with finely chopped fungi. The goat-cheese crespelle is equally memorable, served in an asparagus vinaigrette with a hint of sesame, and tiny free-range quail is boned, laquered in soy, and served over white polenta.

Unlike many chefs, who seem to put all their creativity into the appetizer menu, the talented owner of Max's keeps up the momentum throughout dinner. The risotto is rich and creamy, generously laced with salmon and shellfish. Salmon is encrusted in pistachio nuts, served over a green onion risotto cake and flavored with lemongrass and Thai curry. Lamb chops are tiny, delicate, and perfectly cooked, served with mild whipped turnips and broccoli rabe. Baby greens—tender pea shoots, beet sprouts only 2 inches long—are custom grown on local farms. They add a crisp, fresh tang to garnishes and salads, which may combine juicy pears with blue cheese and walnuts in a lemon dressing.

The wine list is extensive, even to carefully chosen dessert wines. While dessert may seem impossible after such a feast, the pace of dinner here is so well-timed that even the five-course tasting dinner (served on weeknights only) does not seem overwhelming. A chocolate cloud cake is dark and soufflé-like, fruit sorbets are crisply flavored, and banana spring rolls—banana wrapped in phyllo and baked—are a nice finale. Entrees range from $14 to $24, with most under $20. Max's is open for dinner from 5:30 P.M., Wednesday through Sunday, on Route 9, Brattleboro 05301; (802) 254–7747.

Farther along, *Chelsea Royal Diner* is also on Route 9, just before the road heads over Hogback Mountain (or, if you're headed east, just as you see the first straight, flat stretch of road you've encountered since Wilmington). The menu is a slightly updated version of traditional diner food, with liver and onions, macaroni and cheese, and meat loaf along with slightly more sophisticated fare. Wednesday through Saturday you'll find a few Mexican-style dishes, too. Prices are strictly of the old diner tradition, with most entrees around $6.00. Be sure to check out the specials board, which may offer an all-you-can-eat catfish fry with hush puppies and other irresistible deals. Chelsea Royal Diner, Route 9, West Brattleboro 05301; (802) 254–8399.

The *Bonnyvale Environmental Education Center (BEEC)* sponsors programs in schools and for the public throughout the area. It offers a busy schedule of outdoor activities, usually hikes and walks accompanied by astronomers, geologists, zoologists, botanists, and other experts to examine some phase of the natural world. Most of the trips are free but require advance registration. The Sunday morning A.M. Ambles, also free, don't require registration; just show up at 8:30 A.M. each Sunday at the appointed place. Past ambles, which last about two hours, have explored Putney Mountain, West River, and Hamilton Falls, a rare patch of old-growth forest, and Mount Olga. To get a complete schedule with the meeting places, contact BEEC, Brattleboro 05301; (802) 257–5785.

On Memorial Day weekend, **Morris dancers** hop and prance on nearly every open space in town. The annual Morris Ale is held on this weekend each year at nearby Marlboro College, but the dancers perform all over the area, with the greatest concentration of them in Brattleboro on Saturday. After individual groups have danced all over town, they gather for a massed show on Elliot Street at 5:00 P.M. These lively, good-humored dance troupes travel from all over the East for this event.

Two Brattleboro B&Bs are striking examples of the enthusiasm of the 1920s and 1930s for revival architectural styles. Each is located conveniently on a major route into town, but within walking distance of the center.

Approaching town from the north on Route 5, just after you cross West River at its junction with the Connecticut, is an eye-catching French château. Its name, which was also its address in the days before Brattleboro changed its street numbers to accommodate 911 identification, is the **40 Putney Road Bed & Breakfast.** Inside, the double-thick brick walls are well-decorated rooms awash with thoughtful amenities, such as ironing boards, bathrobes, hair dryers, small refrigerators, queen-size beds, and

Jumping Off a Mountain

*D*ownhill skiing was still a novelty when Fred Harris started the annual Harris Hill Ski Jump meet in Brattleboro in 1923. As an undergraduate, he had helped start the annual Winter Carnival at Dartmouth College in Hanover, New Hampshire, in 1911. Some of the world's best ski jumpers have competed here, including Torger Tokle, his brother Art Tokle, Art Devlin, Hugh Barber, and Vladimir Glyvka. The contests, which take place in three-hour segments on each of two days, usually include present and future Olympians and World Cup contenders. The date may vary, but the event is usually held on Presidents' Day weekend. It's an exciting show, even for the spectators, who cheer the contestants by ringing cowbells. If you don't have one to bring, you can buy a bell there. Applauding with mittened hands isn't very effective, hence the bells.

modems. Most rooms have couches or love seats, and all have modern private baths. A tiny private pub downstairs has beer and wine for guests, as well as light dishes for those who decide not to sample Brattleboro's ample restaurant offerings. Breakfast is served from a menu—so you can choose your own style—in a sun-filled dining room or under the awning on the terrace, which overlooks a garden with fountains. Rooms run from $120 to $180 for two. Incongruously, 40 Putney Road Bed & Breakfast is at 192 Putney Road, Brattleboro 05301; (802) 254–6268 or (800) 941–2413; fax (802) 258–2673; www.putney. net/40putneyrd/.

The other building is just as striking a sight as you enter town on Route 9 from the west, a large half-timbered and brick English Tudor home, **The Tudor.** Its large guest rooms all overlook the garden, a well-groomed yard with paths and fountain. Two of the rooms have working fireplaces, and all have original beautifully tiled private baths. Rooms are air-conditioned, with cable TV and telephones. A full or continental breakfast is served in a gracious paneled dining room. Both the dining room and the large guest living room, where you can relax in front of the fireplace, overlook the garden. Rates are $135 to $150 for two. The Tudor is at 300 Western Avenue, Brattleboro 05301; (802) 257–4983 or (800) 232–6392; fax (802) 258–2632; www.thetudor.com.

Hey, It's a Live One!

*Y*ou never know what you'll find happening in Brattleboro. One Saturday in May, my daughter and I were driving into town to have lunch at The Common Ground, and as we came past the small park at Wells Fountain, we noticed a group of young people dressed in white, jingling across the street with bells on their legs. "Morris dancers!" we both said at once, and I quickly found a parking space in front of the library.

We followed them to the park and sat down on the lawn to wait for the dancing. They also sat down, in little groups on the granite steps and on the lawn, and quickly became engaged in animated conversations. Assuming that they were waiting for someone or something, we waited. And waited. Finally, a dancer about my daughter's age noticed her, as young men tend to, and wandered casually toward us and engaged us in conversation. When he learned that we'd come to watch the dance, he looked startled, then quickly called to the others, "Hey, we've got a real audience!" and they all jumped up and took their places to begin.

—Barbara Radcliffe Rogers

Bogey in a Blizzard

*R*udyard Kipling liked Vermont best in the winter, possibly because fewer people tried his patience then by invading his treasured privacy. Sir Arthur Conan Doyle, a frequent guest at Naulakha, gave Kipling a pair of skis, on which he loved to tour the eleven-acre property. He was an early golf enthusiast and is credited by the U.S. Golf Association with inventing winter golf. He painted golf balls red and created holes by sinking tin cans into the snow.

Rudyard Kipling, whose *Jungle Book* you might expect to have been written during languid and steamy afternoons of the Raj, somewhere in the India it portrayed, was actually written just over the Brattleboro town line in **Dummerston.** So were *Captains Courageous* and some of the *Just So Stories.* Just as you enter Brattleboro on Route 5 from the north, assuming that you avoid being sideswiped by a truck as you share the new and ineffective roundabout at the junction with Route 9, turn west (right) on Black Mountain Round and head uphill. There's no mistaking the shingled "cottage," which Kipling referred to as a ship, sailing along the hillside to your left.

You can't take a tour of **Naulakha,** but you can stay there by advance reservation. The house, restored even to the shingled roof, just as Kipling had it built, belongs to Landmark Trust, a British preservation society that restores historic homes in Britain. The group extended its territory to acquire this property because of its connection with British literature. Inside, the home gleams with polished wood; many of the furnishings belonged to the Kiplings. It's entirely self-catering and is big enough for eight people, for three-night minimum stays. For information about the house, call (802) 257–5840 or (800) 848–3747. To make reservations, contact the Landmark Trust, Shottesbrooke, Maidenhead, Berkshire, UK SL6 3SW; (01144–628) 825–925.

**MORE PLACES TO STAY
IN THE CONNECTICUT
RIVER VALLEY**

(ALL AREA CODES 802)

NORWICH (05055)
The Inn at Norwich,
Main Street, is a vintage
village inn updated and
with a good, reasonably
priced dining room;
649–1143.

WOODSTOCK (05091)
*Woodstock Inn and
Resort,* 14 the Green,
05091. With a pool, alpine
and Nordic skiing, golf
course, and indoor sports
facilities, the inn is a complete resort in the center of
the village; 457–1100 or
(800) 448–7900;
www.woodstockinn.com.

CHESTER (05143)
*The Inn at
Cranberry Farm,*
61 Williams River Road,
was built in 1992. The
eleven-room inn centers
around a room with a 30-
foot-high cathedral ceiling
and was formerly known as
Madrigal Inn. Rates include
a full breakfast, and there is
hiking right out the door.
They hold occasional quilt-
ing weekends;
(800) 854–2208,
(800) 463–1339; www.
cranberryfarminn.com.

Inn Victoria, on the Green,
is a carefully restored Victorian home, thoughtfully
translated into lodgings;
875–4288 or (800)
732–4288.

PUTNEY (05346)
The Putney Inn,
Depot Road (at exit 4 of
Interstate 91), has large,
well-decorated rooms,
each with its own outside
entrance; 387–5517.

To Learn More in Connecticut River Valley

Brattleboro Chamber of Commerce,
182 Main Street, Brattleboro 05301;
(802) 254–4565;
www/brattleboro.com.

Woodstock Area Chamber of Commerce,
18 Central Street, P.O. Box 486, Woodstock 05091;
(802) 457–3555.

MORE PLACES TO EAT IN THE CONNECTICUT RIVER VALLEY

(ALL AREA CODES 802)

PUTNEY (05346)

The Putney Inn,
Depot Road (at exit 4 of Interstate 91), has a highly acclaimed and creative chef favorite New England dishes and ingredients with artistic flair; 387–5517.

BRATTLEBORO (05301)

Walker's Restaurant,
132 Main Street, serves a fairly predictable selection of well-prepared favorites, from quiche or chili to steaks and seafood. There's an excellent selection of beers; 254–6046.

Sarkis Market,
50 Elliot Street, is a Lebanese cafe that serves authentic Middle Eastern dishes; 258–4906.

Southwest Vermont

The southwestern corner of Vermont seems at times cut off from the rest of the state, largely because no interstate highway is within 40 miles of the far reaches of the area. The Green Mountains separate it from eastern Vermont, and Pownal, a town that is as far away from Montpelier, the state capital, as you can get, seems to have more in common with the bordering states of New York and Massachusetts than it does with the rest of its own state.

The landscape here is one of rolling hills and mountains, alternating with wide, flat, fertile valleys. The region is also historically rich, since it served as an early gateway to settlement in the rest of Vermont.

Although at one time or another all of Vermont has fallen to some kind of border dispute with neighboring states—and one foreign country—the southwest corner seems to have seen more than its share of fights over where Vermont ends and Massachusetts and New York begin—and even where New Hampshire ends.

The remote *Tri-State Monument* that marks the exact spot where Vermont, New York, and Massachusetts converge is buried deep in the woods at the southwest corner of the town of Pownal, almost 2 miles from the end of the nearest dead-end road. The granite marker is 8 feet tall and 14 inches square and has four sides, three of them marked with the initials of the state it faces. The final boundary was settled in 1812, but the marker wasn't erected until 1896.

Easy Come, Easy Go?

The most illustrious native of Pownal was born in North Pownal in 1834. "Jubilee" Jim Fisk has been variously described as a railroad magnate, a Wall Street genius, and a playboy. Fisk took over the Erie Railroad and gambled in the gold market against another notorious New Yorker of the time, Jay Gould. Fisk's other accomplishments included purchasing an opera house, spending his fortune as quickly as he made it, and being murdered in a love triangle in what was then the Broadway Central Hotel in 1872.

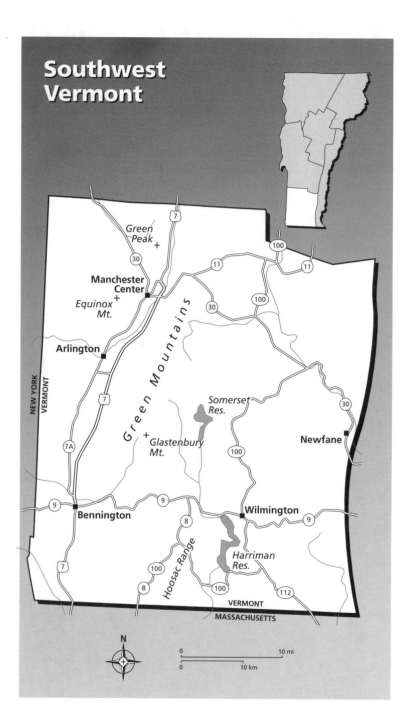

Southwest Vermont

Green Peak

7

30

Manchester Center

Equinox Mt.

Arlington

NEW YORK

VERMONT

7

7A

Green Mountains

100

11

11

30

100

Somerset Res.

Glastenbury Mt.

100

30

Newfane

9

9

Bennington

8

Hoosac Range

100

Wilmington

9

Harriman Res.

8

100

112

VERMONT

MASSACHUSETTS

7

N

0   10 mi

0   10 km

AUTHORS' TOP HIGHLIGHTS

Equinox Skyline Drive

Canoeing the Batten Kill

Magic Mountain Ski Area

*Bromley Ski Area
and Alpine Slide*

*Robert Todd Lincoln's
Hildene*

Bennington

ennington, in fact, is where it all began. It
was the first town west of the Connecticut
River to be chartered by New Hampshire royal
governor Benning Wentworth. The charter was
drawn up in 1749, when New York and New
Hampshire both claimed the land.

During the American Revolution, the Battle of
Bennington in 1777, fought in lands from Cambridge, New York, to a
point about 5 miles west of Bennington in Vermont, turned the tide
against the British and caused the British leader John Burgoyne to
rethink his strategy in the war. Colonial militia, under the command of
General John Stark, discovering General Burgoyne's plans, fought and
destroyed British and Hessian forward elements of his army, leading to
Burgoyne's retreat. The battle ended British plans to defeat the colonies
by splitting them in half and made the final American victory possible.

After the battle—which is immortalized by the 306-foot-high ***Bennington Battle Monument,*** visible from most parts of town—Burgoyne

How Vermont Began

*olonial boundaries were
determined by royal grants made in
London and bore little relationship to
land surveys or geographical landmarks. These resulting vague boundaries led to inevitable disputes
between colonies, particularly Massachusetts, which claimed areas around
Brattleboro, and New York and New
Hampshire, which contested all of the
area covered by Vermont. To royal
governors, the granting of townships
was an important source of income,
and the governors of both New Hampshire and New York granted townships
that often overlay one another, causing
violent disputes over title.*

*The Allen brothers, Ira and Ethan, both
highly independent landowners under*

*New Hampshire grants, became ardent
champions in defense of the New
Hampshire grants against the attempts
of New York to enforce its grants. Nei-
ther state was able to enforce its
authority, however, and the residents
finally established the Republic of Vermont. During the Revolution, this new
republic even flirted with seeking a separate peace with the British.*

*After the war, New Hampshire and
New York continued their tug-of-war
over the Green Mountains, and Con-
gress repeatedly failed to accept the
Vermonters' application to join the
Union. It wasn't until Vermont paid
New York $30,000 to give up all claims
that Vermont was admitted to the
Union as the fourteenth state in 1791.*

wrote a letter describing Vermonters as "the most active and rebellious race on the continent." The monument, by the way, was built over the course of four years and dedicated in 1891 by President Benjamin Harrison. When an elevator was installed, a few Vermonters balked, believing that if the Green Mountain Boys could prove their valor by fighting the British, then it would be a small task by comparison to walk up the 412 stairs that make up the climb to the top. To visit the site of the actual battle, you'll have to travel into New York, following Route 67A (Northside Drive) to North Bennington, then Route 67 across the state line to the battlefield, about 5 miles from the center of North Bennington.

The late fiction writer Shirley Jackson, author of *The Haunting of Hill House* and the famous short story "The Lottery," was a resident of Bennington. Jackson's husband taught at Bennington College, and she, formerly from upstate New York, incorporated into her fiction many of her feelings about small-town life in Bennington.

Bennington is home to one of the state's fish hatcheries, the **Vermont State Fish Culture Station.** This is a fascinating place, especially for kids, who will be intrigued by the sight of thousands of trout massing in the tanks. From Route 9 on the east side of town go south on South Stream Road. The hatchery is open daily from 8:00 A.M. to 3:30 P.M. (802) 447–2844.

On one of Bennington's back streets is the **Bennington Potters Yard,** a factory store featuring high-priced pottery dinnerware you also see in swank gift and kitchenware shops. Here you'll find full range of dinnerware and accessories, along with seconds at lower prices. On the grounds is a shop with fine glassware and a restaurant. At the intersection of East Main Street (Route 9) and North Street in the center of town, take North Street north 3 blocks and turn right onto County

The Molly Stark Trail

*I*t's ironic that Route 9, the only year-round route across the southern part of Vermont, should be named for a New Hampshire woman. Even more ironic, perhaps, is the fact that it is named not for the heroic leader of the Battle of Bennington, but for the wife he rode home to after the battle. On a simple stone in the cemetery behind the white church in West Bennington, you'll find the carved inscription of General Stark's famous words, which he uttered before the decisive battle: "Boys, yonder are the redcoats, and they are ours, or this night Molly Stark sleeps a widow."

WORTH SEEING

Park-McCullough House and Gardens,
Off Route 67A, North Bennington; (802) 442–5441.

Norman Rockwell Exhibition, *Route 7A, Arlington; (802) 375–6423.*

Weston Playhouse, *On the Green, Weston; (802) 824–5288.*

Adams Farm, *15 Higley Hill, Wilmington; (802) 464–3762.*

Street. The Potter's Yard is at 324 County Street, Bennington 05201; (802) 447–7531.

On Route 7, 1 mile north of the junction with Route 9, is the ***Blue Benn Diner,*** a local institution offering everything from burgers and lasagna to tofu. The jukebox is equally eclectic, and the clientele ranges from Bennington College students to construction workers.

The lines and colors inside are sharp, with neon reflecting off the smooth chrome surfaces of the display cases and milk machine. Despite its '50s diner look and atmosphere, the Blue Benn serves an updated version of comfort foods, with several Mexican favorites along with the meat loaf.

The Blue Benn is open Monday and Tuesday 6:00 A.M. to 5:00 P.M., Wednesday through Friday 6:00 A.M. to 8:00 P.M., Saturday 6:00 A.M. to 4:00 P.M., and Sunday 7:00 A.M. to 4:00 P.M. It's on Route 7, Bennington 05201; (802) 442–8977.

The menu is always inviting at the casual ***Alldays and Onions,*** where you can get hefty sandwiches at lunch, stacked onto tasty whole grain breads. Vegetarians will be comfortable here, with several good choices. The dinner menu offers both traditional and innovative dishes; unfortunately, the service at dinner often lags behind the cuisine, but you may forgive all after one of the chocolate desserts. Alldays and Onions is open from 7:30 A.M. to 4:00 P.M. Monday through Saturday and for dinner from 6:00 to 9:00 P.M. on Friday and Saturday in the winter and Wednesday through Saturday the rest of the year. It's located at 519 East Main Street, Bennington 05201; (802) 447–0043.

The offices of ***Hemmings Motor News*** are on Route 9 west of town. *Hemmings Motor News,* in case you're not a fancier of old cars, advertises everything from the Volkswagen Thing to Model A Fords, from parts to entire cars and even fan clubs.

This is where it's all put together. A small store in the building sells books on every kind of old car there is, and if you want to sneak a peek at upcoming issues, you can take a tour through the production and subscription departments during the publisher's regular hours. Back issues, *Hemmings* sweatshirts, fifteen-year subscription pins— they're all here. Vintage vehicles are on display, and the shop sells tools, toys, and models.

Antique automobile at *Hemmings Motor News*, Bennington

Write to *Hemmings Motor News*, Route 9, Bennington 05201, or call (802) 442–3101. The *Hemmings* shop is open from 7:00 A.M. to 10:00 P.M. daily.

The ***Bennington Interpretive Center/Images from the Past*** is run by interpretive historian Tordis Ilg Isselhardt, an expert on local and New England history. The center is a combination of Isselhardt's expertise in the form of walking tours and slide shows—which she designs for many tour groups—and a small shop where she sells postcards, old photos, T-shirts, cards, and posters. All the items evoke the past of Bennington, Vermont, and the United States.

Isselhardt says that her main task in interpreting history for people is to help them orient themselves in time and space about Bennington and its history, which will then enable them to see the current period in the context of a long continuum of people and events.

She accomplishes this task through the use of a variety of reprints from negatives of photos by the late Robert L. Weichert, who took hundreds of photos of old, craggy Vermonters who wear their entire life histories on their faces.

The center's hours vary, because Isselhardt is frequently out guiding groups on walking tours through the town; catch her in by chance or by appointment. Write to the Bennington Interpretive Center/Images from the Past, 155 West Main Street, Bennington 05201, or call (802) 442–3204.

Off Route 9 west of Bennington is the ***Bennington Center for the Arts.*** The permanent collection includes Native American pottery, nature art, kachinas, and Navajo rugs. Four galleries host permanent and touring exhibits. The center is open May through October, Tuesday through Sunday from 11:00 A.M. to 5:00 P.M. It's located at Gypsy Lane, Bennington 05201; (802) 442–7158.

The nearby **Bennington Museum** has long been a favorite for admirers of Grandma Moses, one of the state's best known primitive folk artists. The museum's extensive collection of her work, memorabilia, and schoolhouse studio are part of a new Grandma Moses Family Heritage Gallery. A new addition has also added more space for displaying the museum's collections of fine art, Bennington pottery, furniture, toys and colonial and Civil War–period artifacts. The outstanding collections of American glassware and early-to-Victorian quilts have a bit more elbow room now. Even if you saw this museum a few years ago, it is definitely worth another stop. It is on Route 9 west of Bennington and is open June through the end of October daily 9:00 A.M. to 6:00 P.M., November through May 9:00 A.M. to 5:00 P.M. Admission is $6.00 adults, seniors and students $5.00, under 12 free. 75 Main Street, Bennington 05201; (802) 447-1571, www.benningtonmuseum.com.

Green Mountains South

Not long out of Bennington, Route 9 East begins to climb, then enters the **Green Mountain National Forest.** The forest's western border begins just outside Bennington and stretches eastward to the town of Wilmington, a good 20 miles away. This part of the forest is one of the largest, most uninterrupted tracts in the state, and its untamed look proves it. The roadside signs with a moose silhouette are not there to look quaint, but as a warning to drivers, especially at night and around dawn and twilight hours.

On the right is **Greenwood Lodge,** an American Youth Hostel facility that is rustic yet homey and welcoming. Many people stay here for its remoteness and for its access to Prospect Mountain and the Long Trail; the location provides opportunities for short hikes and walks as well as serving as a jumping-off point for hiking the entire Long Trail end to end.

Greenwood Lodge consists of two dormitories and five private rooms, sleeping a total of fifty people; twenty tent sites are also scattered throughout the hostel's 120 acres. The lodge is open July through Labor Day. For information and reservations, write to Greenwood Lodge, Route 9 East, Bennington 05201, or call (802) 442–2547.

Woodford, by the way, is the highest town in Vermont, at an elevation of 2,215 feet. But with just 314 people, it ranks among towns having the smallest populations.

After its steep ascent, Route 9 drops into Wilmington, where civilization (some might question that word applied to such commerical density) begins in a big way, with a gauntlet of shops, eateries, and lodgings.

From the center of Wilmington, head south on Route 100 for 8 miles into Jacksonville and Route 112. In the southern end of the village is the **North River Winery,** located in a farmhouse built in 1850. Apples grown at Dwight Miller's Orchards north in Dummerston are handpressed, and the juice is made into unique wines.

In the back are nine fermenting tanks. The larger ones hold 2,500 gallons, which translates into 12,000 bottles or 1,000 cases. The smaller tanks hold 820 gallons, or a mere 3,600 bottles or 320 cases. North River's offerings run from a tangy crisp Green Mountain Apple to Vermont Pear,

South Central MOOver

*W*ilmington is Vermont's definition of the beaten path, so we have not discussed it here. But, the area around it is not as crowded and is worth exploring, which you can do by bus. Area towns have formed the Deerfield Valley Transit Association, which serves the area, including Wardsboro, Readsboro, Dover, Whitingham, and Wilmington, with buses painted in black and white cow spots that would make Gateway jealous. Call (802) 464–8487 for schedules or visit their Web site at www.moover.com.

which resembles a slightly sweet pinot grigio. The Vermont Harvest Apple, flavored with cinnamon and a touch of maple syrup, can be served hot or cold.

The winery is open daily from 10:00 A.M. until 5:00 P.M. Tours of the winery and tastings are free. Write to the North River Winery, Route 112, Jacksonville 05342, or call (802) 368–7557.

Although Lake Champlain is probably the best-known body of water in the state, locals and visitors know that one of the most dramatic is the *Harriman Reservoir* west of Wilmington. And you can do more than just gaze at it, because the *Green Mountain Flagship Company* conducts narrated excursions in the form of ninety-minute cruises several times each day from May 1 until late October. Captain Richard Joyce welcomes visitors aboard the MV *Mt. Mills,* a pontoon boat. Part of the fascination of the trip are his stories of the village of Mountain Mills, which was destroyed in the creation of the lake. He uses music and sound effects to spice up the narration, which centers on the history of the reservoir and the surrounding mountains, where logging was once the premier occupation.

For more information call the Green Mountain Flagship Company at (802) 464–2975.

Not far from the top of Hogback, about 4 miles east of Wilmington, is the motel-style *Horizon Inn.* Its contemporary rooms are attractive and well kept, and the staff couldn't be more accommodating. All rooms have coffeemakers, and rates are from $80 to $115. The Horizon Inn is at P.O. Box 817, Wilmington 05363; (802) 464–2131; fax (802) 464–8302; www. horizon@sover.net.

Mt. Mills on Harriman Reservoir, Wilmington

But They Didn't Build Condos

Wardsboro, north of Stratton, holds the distinction of being the last town in Vermont that New Hampshire governor Benning Wentworth chartered, in 1764. The Vermont government officially granted the town's charter in 1780, when Vermont was its own republic, to a resident of nearby Newfane, Vermont— William Ward—along with sixty-two others. Although few chose to live and settle on their land grants, many people throughout southern New England wanted their own piece of Vermont even back then.

If you follow the curiously named Screw Auger Road north from Route 9 in Marlboro, you'll come to South Newfane, a tiny village greatly overshadowed by the grand buildings of better-known Newfane. But it's an address well known to gardeners. Over the past decade, day lilies have become an important part of home landscaping, and much of this increased popularity, at least in New England, is due to **Olallie Day Lily Gardens.** The display plantings show an amazing variety of lilies in a riot of shades. There's also a shop with books, gifts, and tools for the gardener. To get to South Newfane from Brattleboro, take Route 30 north about 8.5 miles along the West River, then take a marked road left about 3.5 miles to Williamsville and South Newfane. Olallie Day Lily Gardens is open 10:00 A.M. to 5:00 P.M. Wednesday to Monday spring through mid-September. 129 Augur Hole Road, South Newfane 05351; (802) 348–6614; www.daylilygarden.com.

Route 9 climbs again, this time to the top of Hogback Mountain, where, along with a sweeping view, you'll find the **Living History Association Museum.** The museum stages frequent reenactments, re-creating battles, fairs, and other events of long ago. The aim is to bring history to life in a way that textbooks could never do. The museum is still growing but is filled with interesting displays on American history, especially early military history. For a schedule of events, write to P.O. Box 1389, Wilmington 05363, or call (802) 464–5569.

If you follow Route 100 north from Wilmington, the commercial atmosphere is repeated when you approach Mount Snow, named not for its winter covering of white, but for the Snow family, which once owned all this land.

Although most people know about Mount Snow and its ski slopes, a less crowded time to visit is in summer. Many ski areas in Vermont open up their lifts for scenic gondola rides in the warm weather, but Mount Snow goes one better: The resort runs a **Mountain Bike School** that takes place every weekend.

Participants are housed in local inns on Friday and Saturday night, then spend all day Saturday and Sunday morning on the grassy slopes, learning rudimentary mountain-biking skills and safety techniques or, for the more advanced biker, more challenging maneuvers.

Write to the Mountain Bike School at Mount Snow, West Dover 05356, or call (802) 464–7788 or (800) 451–4211 for more information.

A new addition to the ski area is the free *Snowseum,* located at the base of Mount Snow. It has an interactive display on the history of skiing in the United States starting in the 1880s and covering the sport through the present day; (802) 464–1100, ext 4603.

The town of Stratton, which is not to be confused with Stratton Mountain the ski area, is to the west of Route 100. You can reach Stratton the town by making a left in the town of West Wardsboro and driving about 4 miles into a tiny village. Stratton Mountain ski area is accessed by continuing north on Route 100, then heading west on Route 30 into the village of Bondville.

As you drive through the town of Stratton from West Wardsboro, continue on for 3 more miles until you reach the *Grout Pond Recreation Area,* a splendid, almost-unknown, 1,600-acre reserve with camping, boating, and swimming on seventy-nine-acre Grout Pond.

It's a peaceful, unspoiled area that contrasts sharply to the developed ski area in the northeast corner of the town. The overlapping Long Trail and Appalachian Trail pass nearby, and there are miles of hiking trails on old logging roads within the boundaries of the area. You might even see a few old cellar holes on the trails.

For more information, call (802) 362–2307, or write to Grout Pond Recreation Area, West Wardsboro 05360.

Green Mountains North

Route 100 weaves back and forth among the mountains as it makes its way north, connecting so many of Vermont's ski areas—from Mount Snow to Stowe and even Jay Peak—that it's known as the Skier's Highway.

In addition to the famed skiing, there are two other outdoor activities near Stratton Mountain. *Zoar Outdoor* runs a few white-water rafting trips on the class III and IV rapids of the West River. The trip starts with a strenuous walk down a rockbound trail to the river, just below the Ball Mountain Dam, and goes all the way south to the takeout at Townsend Dam. Along the way there is a picnic and swim along the

Glastenbury was once a thriving township with a population peak of fifty in 1834. The charcoal kilns in the town were located near the Bennington and Glastenbury Railroad, which was built after the Civil War ended. A hotel, houses, and a trolley line soon followed, but the bust came as quickly as the boom. Today you can find cellar holes that run along the Appalachian Trail in an area that has become a ghost town. The town was officially unorganized back in 1937 after one member of the only family remaining served in every town office, from supervisor and fire warden to town representative in the state legislature.

river, and the trip finishes with a chicken barbecue. There are only a few trip dates each year, usually in April and September, so arrangements should be made early. The cost is about $84, and a package with lodging and breakfast is $112. Why go all the way to the Grand Canyon? Zoar Outdoor, P.O. Box 245, Charlemont, MA 01339, (800) 532–7483; www.zoaroutdoor.com.

Close by, at **Sun Bowl Ranch** on Stratton Mountain, you can explore the mountain trails on horseback or enjoy the countryside on a wagon ride. From mid-June to mid-October there are one- and two-hour horse rides for $27 and $50, respectively. For $55 you can saddle up for a ninety-minute ride, with a picnic lunch. Hayrides in a real wagon drawn by two big Belgian draft horses are $15 adults, $10 for children under twelve. Rides run from 9:00 A.M. to 5:00 P.M. traveling over backwoods roads and ski trails. During the winter, from Christmastime (or Thanksgiving, if snow allows) through mid-March, there are sleigh rides on Friday, Saturday, Sunday, and Monday holidays. The cost of $17 for adults and $12 for children includes a bonfire and hot cocoa. An overnight package ($150) includes a three-hour ride, dinner, lodging, and breakfast. Reservations are strongly recommended. Write the ranch, Stratton Mountain 05155, or call (802) 297–9210 Friday through Sunday from noon to 8:00 P.M.; (800) 787–2886 all other times; www.sunbowlranch.com.

Weston receives more than its fair share of visitors, due primarily to the **Vermont Country Store,** a step-back-in-time general store that offers goods in cracker barrels and penny candy amid the aura of an antique, wood-burning potbellied stove. Although you'll find a lot of moose T-shirts and cow-spotted socks designed for tourists, the overriding mission here is to provide those useful things you might have thought weren't made anymore. You'll also find good warm, sensible clothing and quality kitchen utensils. The Vermont Country Store is open Monday through Saturday from 9:00 A.M. to 5:00 P.M.; P.O. Box 3000, Manchester 05255; (802) 824–3184; www.vermontcountrystore.com.

Weston was once part of the town of Andover, but because the severe winter made traveling over Markham and Terrible Mountains the only way to get from Andover to West Town—as the western part of Andover was called in those early times—West Town became its own town, Weston, in 1799.

The *Farrar-Mansur House,* a colonial tavern facing the attractive village green, is Weston's historical museum, showing furnishings, clothing, household implements, and firearms from the town's past. Next to it is a water mill, also part of the museum. Both are open Saturday and Sunday from 1:30 P.M. to 4:30 P.M., June through mid-October, plus Wednesday through Friday in July and August. Write to the Farrar-Mansur House, Weston 05161.

As you head north out of the town of Weston, where Route 100 and Route 155 meet is a beautiful place called the *Weston Priory.* This monastery of Benedictine monks welcome the public to its services every day. The gift shop carries books and crafts, many of which are made overseas and in northern New England.

A variety of Nativity scenes are on display from September through Christmas. One scene, from Spain, is made from terra-cotta and lacquered cloth; another is made of hand-carved wood from a Mexican monastery; still another has soapstone sheep from Kenya. Colorful hand-painted and -carved wooden ornaments and Christmas decorations from El Salvador cover a wall of the shop, which is a serene place, in keeping with the overall tone of the priory's grounds.

The Weston monks are well known for their liturgical choral music, which is available on tape and CD at the shop. The art gallery downstairs displays the work of both Weston monks and brothers from around the world. Prayer services are open to the public four times a day in one of two chapels, depending on the season. Walking paths invite strolling throughout the grounds.

For more information, write to the Weston Priory, Route 155, Weston 05161, or call (802) 824–5409. The public is welcome at daily services, but the times of the liturgies vary with the season, so call ahead.

If you're in the area in late September, be sure to visit the *Peru Fair,* a wonderful example of a traditional country fair held during the peak of foliage season. Many residents plan all year for the event, much to the benefit of locals and visitors. The weekend-long fair has music, lots of food, arts and crafts, games, and an old-fashioned pig roast.

Before the mega-resorts hit the Green Mountains, *Magic Mountain* was known as a skier's mountain, one of those special places where people kept returning because of the variety and challenge of the runs.

A Town by Any Name

Peru is the town where the movie Baby Boom, *starring Diane Keaton, was filmed. For filming of the movie, the WELCOME TO PERU signs were changed to WELCOME TO HADLEYVILLE, the name of the fictional town in the movie. But back in 1761, the signs would have read WELCOME TO BROMLEY, the original name of the town. Residents changed the name to Peru in 1804, because they felt it was more affluent-sounding. Apparently, the name Bromley conveyed the attitude of a slumlord and thus slowed economic growth. After the name was changed to Peru, the fortunes of the town began to look up—a situation that continues today in this quiet town of about 300 people.*

In 1991, when the last ticket was sold, the only snowmaking was done by nature. Trees began to grow on the slopes, and no one expected to ski them again, but astute skiers who tired of long lines and snow bunnies helped the resort come back to life during the 1997–1998 season.

Most of the thirty-five trails have been cleared, and 87 percent of the mountain has snowmaking coverage. Vertical drop at Magic is 1,600 feet, and the longest run is Wizard, an intermediate to expert slope (read that high-intermediate, with sections of heart-stopping expert), a bit over a mile and a half long. In fact, every trail, from beginner to expert, has at least one section that will challenge the skills of that level skier. Some of the double diamonds verge on extreme. Because it doesn't have the glitter or a Swiss-style village at its base, Magic tends to be less crowded than other places, and during the week you practically have it to yourself.

You'll also find a tube park with plenty of lanes, an all-terrain park, and a half tube for boarders. Rates are in the low $40 range weekends and under $35 weekdays. Seniors are well respected here, with free skiing after age seventy. Everyone gets a bargain on Tuesday and Sunday afternoons, with rates at $20. The lodge has full services, including rentals. Lodging is available at the Trailside Condominiums at Magic (802–824–5620). You'll find Magic on Route 11, P.O. Box 536, Londonderry 05148-0536; (802) 824–5645; fax (802) 824–5199.

On the Magic Mountain approach road, and within skiing distance of the base lodge, ***Dostal's*** is a longtime tradition for many travelers in this part of the state, in all seasons. It's Austrian, from the architecture to the menu and the warmth of the friendly staff. In the summer you can enjoy the large outdoor pool and excellent hiking and walking trails on Magic Mountain. The owners will arrange with an outfitter in Ludlow to bring canoes and kayaks. The motel-style rooms are attractive, nicely furnished, and fresh. Meals in the wood-paneled dining room include Wiener schnitzel, beef Stroganoff, mahimahi, and roast garlic and cheese ravioli.

Rooms are available with or without dinner; doubles in summer are $56 weekdays, $62 weekends, and in winter $69 weekdays and $109 weekends without meals. MAP prices are about $60 per person weekdays, $80 on weekends, and there are special package rates, particularly in the winter. Dostal's, R.D. 1, Box 31, Londonderry 05148; (802) 824–6700 or (800) 255–5373; fax (802) 824–6701; www.dostals.com.

Another well-equipped but down-to-earth ski area is a few miles farther down Route 11 at **Bromley Mountain,** only 6 miles from Manchester. Bromley was one of the earliest Vermont ski areas, founded in the late 1930s by Fred Pabst, who started the brewery. It was always a pioneering area: In 1947 Pabst was the first to contour the slopes, and he pioneered grooming by being the first in the state to roll snow to keep it packed. Bromley was also one of the first to install snowmaking machinery and has recently expanded its snowmaking to cover nearly all its trails. Of the thirty-nine trails, 36 percent are rated beginner, 35 percent intermediate, and the balance expert. For the skier of average to low-expert ability there is plenty of challenging terrain. The vertical drop is 1,334 feet, and the longest trail, suitable for an advanced beginner or intermediate, is about $2^1/_2$ miles long. The variety of ability levels makes this a nice area for families, and even during holiday periods lift lines are rarely more than a five- or ten-minute wait.

At the rental shop you can try out demo parabolics during the first and last hours of the day. If you don't like the conditions during the first hour after you buy your ticket, you'll be given a pass for another day.

Ho Hum, Another Quiet Week of Magic Mountain

*T*he new owners came along just in time, according to Dan Roupp, the man in charge of trails and snow-making. "On the upper half of the mountain, 7- and 8-foot saplings were growing under the lifts and in the middle of trails," he says. Dan and his crew went for supper at a local restaurant shortly after they'd begun clearing, and a group of local men told Dan that he could never get the trees cut off the ledges under the black chairlift in time to open the season. Dan's not the sort you say that to. The next day Dan and his crew took their all-terrain vehicles as high up the lift line as they could go, then went on foot to cut the trees from the steep path. Often they were hanging by one hand while using a chain saw with the other. A week later they went to supper again at the same place, and when they entered were asked, "When're you going to start on the black lift line?"

"Oh hell," Dan replied. "We decided to take it easy, so we finished that last week."

Summers at Bromley also offer thrills on the mountain, on the ²/₃-mile *Alpine Slide,* the longest alpine ride in the United States. Bromley Mountain, Box 1130, Manchester Center, 05255-1130; (802) 824–5522.

The Batten Kill Valley

As you travel up the Batten Kill Valley, you'll see the Taconics on the west and the Green Mountains on the east, divided by a valley that grows wider and flatter as you go north. These are fertile farmlands with rich alluvial soil, and in the north you will see large farms along the valley floor. Route 7 is a limited-access highway in some places, but the quieter Routes 7A and 30 provide an alternative.

The town of Arlington is best known for its famous citizen Norman Rockwell, who painted things as he saw them right here in Arlington. There's a museum devoted to Rockwell's art.

Another fascinating look at Vermont's people can be found in the *Dr. George A. Russell Collection of Vermontiana,* near the schools on East Arlington Road. Doc Russell was one of the subjects Rockwell painted, specifically for his *Country Doctor* portrait. The collection is considered one of the largest anywhere devoted to Vermont history and ephemera; the doctor collected the materials his entire life. When he died, he left the entire collection to the town of Arlington. The collection, which is really a library, not a museum of artifacts, is open on

Friends Forever

In 1946, when an eleven-year-old classmate died of cancer, a group of Burlington girls raised $48 to buy a painting from Norman Rockwell to hang in the school as a memorial to her. Rockwell donated the painting The Babysitter, and the girls spent the money on a brass plaque to put on it. Class after class graduated, and the painting was, at some point, removed and stored in the boiler room. When the painting was found recently and

appraised at $300,000, the school board decided to sell it and put the money toward the school budget.

But old friendships die hard in Vermont, and the classmates once again assembled and vowed to raise the money to buy the painting back from the school. They then donated it to the art gallery at the University of Vermont, this time as a permanent memorial.

Tuesdays and by appointment if a volunteer is available; call (802) 375–6307 for more information, or write to the Dr. George A. Russell Collection of Vermontiana, Arlington 05250.

There is no better way to see the Batten Kill Valley than from the river itself, which you can do with **Battenkill Canoe, Ltd.** The river rises on the west side of the Green Mountains and flows down through Arlington before leaving Vermont, finally emptying into the Hudson River in New York. It offers some of the nicest, most scenic water travel experiences in the state. The stream is nonthreatening and passes through fields and forests, under covered bridges, and through tiny settlements. Battenkill Canoe offers equipment rentals or whole packages, including drop-off and pickup. Ask about the On the Batten Kill day trip or the two to five-day Canoe Inn to Inn packages. Make arrangements with Battenkill Canoe at 6328 Vermont Route 7A, Arlington 05250; (802) 362–2800 or (800) 421–5268; www.battenkill.com.

Travelers who remember the East Arlington Cafe, near the covered bridge in East Arlington, may be distressed to find it's no longer there. But chef David Ingison is still in town, at his new **Arlington South Side Cafe and Restaurant,** where he still serves those wonderful crab cakes. The new restaurant is larger, both in the dining room and the kitchen, which allows him to expand the menu along with the seating. Plans call for the opening of a casual cafe that will also serve breakfast. As before, the chef has concentrated his wine list on those that offer high value at very reasonable prices. Entrees range from $10 to $18 and include salad or soup courses. The restaurant is open Tuesday through Saturday 11:30 A.M. to 2:30 P.M. and 5:30 to 9:00 P.M. at 2802 Route 7A, Arlington 05250; (802) 357–9900.

If Arlington's Norman Rockwell connection fascinates you, reserve a room in his former home there, now the **Inn on Covered Bridge Green.** Rooms in the main house are nicely decorated, all with private baths, and some overlook the village green and church. Each is different in size, shape, and decor, but all have queen- or king-size beds, often four-poster. Two separate buildings are now guest cottages; one, formerly Rockwell's studio, has housekeeping facilities. Rates vary but run between $100 and $200 a night. The inn is on River Road at Covered Bridge Road, Arlington 05250; (802) 375–9489 or (800) 726–9480; www.coveredbridgegreen.com.

Mount Equinox, a long mountain that lies almost parallel to Route 7A, rises to more than 3,800 feet. It is the highest peak in the Taconic Range, which is, admittedly, not known for its high elevations. But Equinox has some splendid views from the top, which you can reach by car via *Mount Equinox Skyline Drive.* During foliage season the views are breathtaking—even native Vermonters make the trip this time of year. The road continues up the mountain for 5.2 miles, and your car will thank you for keeping an even speed of about 25 miles per hour on the ascent. Even with automatic transmission, you should descend in low gear.

This toll road is accessed from Route 7A between Arlington and Manchester Village and is open from May through foliage season and on into November, as long as the weather permits. Early snow or ice storms will end the season. A fee of about $6.00 is charged for the car, plus $2.00 more for each passenger. Mount Equinox Skyline Drive, Route 7A, Manchester 05254; (802) 362–1114.

Manchester has a deeply split personality: Manchester Village and Manchester Center. The former is a gracious village with marble sidewalks and beautifully maintained homes—many of which are closer to mansions—lining the main square. Just a short way north, Manchester Center is a series of factory outlet malls—albeit in nicely designed buildings for the most part—where you can buy everything from designer clothes to kitchenware.

One of the most elegant of the mansions in Manchester Village was owned by the law partner of Robert Todd Lincoln, whose own mansion, Hildene, sits nearby. The *Inn at Ormsby Hill* is a class act, furnished in antiques and carefully chosen reproductions. Rooms are designed with panache—doors over the double whirlpool bath open for a view of the fireplace—and decorated with flawless good taste. And speaking of taste, the full-course breakfast (served in a magnificent dining room) even has dessert. You'll need to reserve *well* ahead for the tower room, a three-story suite with a view of the world. Rates are from $190 to $310. The inn is on Route 7A, 1842 Main Street, Manchester 05255; (802) 362–1163 or (800) 670–2841; www.ormsbyhill.com.

Behind the inn is *Hildene,* the country mansion of Robert Todd Lincoln, son of the president and himself president of the Pullman railcar company. Built in the opening years of the twentieth century, this sumptuous building is a fine example of a period country home of a wealthy business magnate. Many of the furnishings came from Mrs. Lincoln's family, and there are personal items of the president, such as his famous stovepipe hat. On the landing of the grand staircase, a thousand-pipe 1908 Aeolian organ works again after a 1980 restoration. The elegant Queen Anne–furnished dining room and the wood-paneled parlor face each other across a broad carpeted hallway. Outside, stunning formal gardens over-looking the valley have been restored, re-creating many of the original plantings, and an ongoing project is restoring the kitchen gardens.

In the winter Hildene's grounds are traversed by twenty-one groomed cross-country trails, with facilities for all levels, a warming hut, a ski rental shop, and refreshments in a carriage barn. Annually after Christmas the house has Candlelight Tours with horse-drawn wagons or sleighs to bring guests through the snow to the front door. Approaching the house aglow in the snow-covered landscape is a magical sight. The schedule of events is worth checking at any time of year, since there are many treats, from pops concerts to garden parties, antiques shows to fairs. Hildene is off Route 7A, Manchester Village 05255; (802) 362–1788; www.hildene.org.

Although Manchester was chartered in 1761, the town didn't earn its bustling, upper-crust reputation until the mid-1800s, when it was promoted as a mineral springs vacation destination. The geology of Vermont consists of bedrock made up of granite and sedimentary rocks such as limestone, shale, and sandstone. This means that the groundwater contains a higher level of minerals than water where the rock is less porous.

During the second half of the nineteenth century, many urbanites were drawn to small Vermont towns for "spa vacations"—back then the phrase had a meaning very different from today's version. Somewhere along the line in the mid-nineteenth century, physicians and other health promoters claimed that regular partaking of this water would restore health to pasty-faced city people and even prolong life. Germany was then in the forefront of this "taking of the waters," and the practice spread to the United States.

Thus tourism in Vermont was born. Some Vermonters—most of whom never drank this mineral water, which was usually full of sulfuric deposits and smelled like rotten eggs—began to push the waters to out-of-staters. The popular belief was that the worse it smelled and tasted, the better it was for you. Some enterprising Vermonters even bottled the water and shipped it to Boston and New York for sale. Of course, proximity to a railroad line—rails were also being aggressively laid at the time—didn't hurt sales.

This influx of wealthy summer visitors inspired the expansion of the Marsh Tavern, which had stood in the middle of town since 1769, into a hotel, where guests could, for an extra fee, improve their health with Equinox Sparkling Water. Soon the hotel's columned facade was the centerpiece of the village.

In 1883 Charles Orvis, founder of the fly-fishing business, bought a "cottage" next to his brother's hotel, The Equinox, which had been in the Orvis family since mid-century. He opened C. F. Orvis Company in the brick bank building next door, where he manufactured split-bamboo fishing rods and artificial flies.

His home, which stands facing the classic white-spired church in Manchester Village, is now the *Orvis Inn,* and his legacy of fly-fishing lives on in the inn's restrained fisherman's-club decor. Old photographs of fishing camps share wall space in the public and guest rooms with beautifully framed fishing lures. The suites in this very upscale lodging include full-sized kitchens, gas fireplaces, phones, and televisions and a blend of custom-built furniture and antiques. Guests enjoy all the services of The Equinox, plus their own concierge, a continental breakfast, and a complimentary bar adjoining the billiard room downstairs. Rates for these suites are much higher than rooms in the Equinox's main building. Historic Route 7A, P.O. Box 46, Manchester Village 05254; (800) 362–4747; www.charlesorvisinn.com.

Devotees of fishing can complete the pilgrimage by visiting the *American Museum of Fly Fishing* next door to the Orvis Inn, open Monday through Friday from 10:00 A.M. until 4:00 P.M. P.O. Box 42, Manchester 05254; (802) 362–3300, www.amff.com, and the *Orvis* store, a bit north of the museum on Route 7A, Manchester 05254; (802) 362–3750; www. orvis.com.

Although *The Equinox* is far better known than its smaller neighbor, it has some unique and little-known experiences in store for its guests. It is located at 3567 Main Street, Manchester Village, 05254; (800) 362–4747; www.equinoxresort.com.

Those who want to get way off the beaten path can learn new skills in off-road driving at the *Land Rover Driving School,* one of only two off-road driving schools in the United States. A specially built 80-acre course offers a variety of terrain, including steep climbs and drop-offs and sharp side tilts on tracks through the woods. Longer programs, from two to eight hours in duration, include expeditions on the slopes of Mount Equinox over logging roads and private trails.

The emphasis is on safety for both passengers and vehicles, skilled handling, and treading softly on the land. While lessons are not inexpensive, the principles learned in even the hour-long course are useful in driving conventional vehicles in difficult situations. Their programs are open to the public as well as guests of The Equinox. The Land Rover Driving

School is on Union Street, Manchester Village 05254; (802) 362–5685.

Also unique in New England (and rare in the United States) is the **British School of Falconry** at The Equinox. While you may have seen raptors and read about them at the Raptor Center in Woodstock, here you get to see them up close and actually work with them, under the close observation of a falconry expert, of course. The school is the first of its kind in the United States and was started in 1995 by Steve and Emma Ford, Scots who started teaching falconry in 1982.

While a lesson here will not make you into a certified falconer, you will learn about raptors and how they hunt. You also get a chance to see an African Tawney eagle, a Lanner hawk and Harris hawks, all used for hunting. Once, each level of royalty had its own assigned species. Bob Waite, our certified falconer and instructor, explained the uses for different species and explained that the Harris is the best for most purposes because it is the calmest. We also learned that those funny little helmets they put on the birds are to keep them calm in transit; when they can't see they don't worry.

All equipment, including warm jackets and boots, if necessary, is provided, and participants in the short lesson learn how to hold a falcon on their gauntleted hand, how to "cast" or release the bird into flight, and how to signal for the bird's return. It is a great thrill to see these magnificent birds in flight, but to see them do so at close quarters and to have them alight on your hand is a rare experience.

The school has a number of programs available. The introductory lesson, which lasts about forty-five minutes, costs about $85. But there are also Hawk Walks ($145), during which you get the full lesson and also have the pleasure of seeing a free-flying hawk following behind you, landing in the branches of trees, and coming when you call. This program is about an hour and a half long. In the school's hunting program, guests actually hunt with the birds and specially trained hunting dogs and see how, for more than 4,000 years, man and bird have worked together. The hunt is about three and a half hours long, including transit time ($299). The school is at 1550 River Road, Manchester Village 05254; (802) 362–4780, fax (802) 362–4817, E-mail: falconry@ equinoxresort.com.

Opposite The Equinox, in a building that once housed its staff, are several shops, most of which emphasize fine arts and crafts. *Claire Murray,* widely known for her beautiful hooked rug designs, has a showroom and shop here. The stunning array of hooked rugs shown and sold here includes patterns from traditional geometrics to scenics and seasonal designs. Part of the second floor has been opened, creating a bright showroom with a mezzanine. They also handle kits, needlepoint, and throws and give lessons in winter, when the shop is not as busy. Open daily 10:00 A.M. to 5:00 P.M., Route 7A opposite The Equinox, Manchester Village, 05254; (802) 362–3334.

The Vermont State Craft Center (central office: 888–388–3177) also has a notable presence in Manchester Village in the shops opposite The Equinox. The shops, called *Frog Hollow,* show a potpourri of work by some of Vermont's finest craftsmen. Here you will find exquisite hand-blown art glass and tableware, fine pottery, jewelry, furniture, artwork in several media, the eclectic "found" sculpture of Bill Heise (see Burlington, page 5), and other work. This is as much a multimedia gallery as a shop, in essence a museum of contemporary arts where you can buy the items exhibited. Route 7A, Manchester Village, 05254; (802) 362–3321, www.froghollow.org.

Mount Equinox rises steeply behind the Equinox Resort in Manchester Village, and the land along this western slope is part of the Equinox Preservation Trust, which works with a consortium of other conservation and environmental organizations to protect and preserve the fragile lands on the mountain. While preserving the land, they also operate and maintain a large series of trails used for hiking, skiing, and horseback riding. Trails lead to ponds and the upper slopes of the mountain. One series of trails will take you across the lower slopes of the mountain to the Southern Vermont Art Center (see below).

The terrain of the mountain is quite varied and contains many rare species of plants. Among these is the very rare yellow lady slipper, a member of the orchid family. The rare protected environments of Table Rock and Deer Knoll are accessible only on tours led by naturalists

Free, but Valuable

*A*s you travel through the state, look for the Vermont Country Sampler, *a small newspaper that you can pick up free in tourist information centers, restaurants, and many other places. It features articles on historical subjects, along with features on local* places you might not otherwise find. Seasonal activities and events are well covered, too, both in articles and in a calendar of events in each issue. In planning your trip, send for a free sample copy by mail, Vermont Country Sampler, P.O. Box 226, Danby 05739.

from the Vermont Institute of Natural Science (VINS), which maintains an office at the Equinox Resort in Manchester. Call for a schedule of their programs, (802) 362–4374. Their programs focus on learning about the mountain's rare habitats.

There are two trailheads, giving access to several trails, most of which are short. Although individual trails can be as short as ½ mile, they do link together to create longer hiking opportunities. The Pond Road trailhead is at the end of Pond Road, the street south of the Equinox Resort. From here, a nice, easy trail rounds Equinox Pond to Bower Spring and the Mountain Bluff Trail (⁸/₁₀ miles). To get to the Red Gate trailhead, take Seminary Road on the north side of the Equinox Resort to West Union Street, following it to the trailhead. The longest trail is the Blue Trail (2 ⁸/₁₀ miles), which starts at the Red Gate and climbs upward along an old roadway, leading to a narrow, steep trail to the summit and lookout rock. From this ledge are sweeping views of New York, New Hampshire, and Vermont.

Look for a map of the preserve and its trails in a brochure entitled *Equinox Preservation Trust,* which you will find at the Tourist Information Office, at the Equinox Resort, and in brochure racks in most of the businesses in Manchester Village and Manchester Center. Equinox Preservation Trust, (802) 362–4700, VINS (802) 362–4374.

Manchester Depot is a tiny corner of Manchester Center, only a block off Route 11/30 but almost completely hidden. Locals know it for its charming architecture and for a clutch of shops that face Elm Street. At the intersection of Elm Street and Highland Avenue is a collection of wonderful old nineteenth-century storefronts that have not been defiled by modernization and are well worth the visit.

Al Ducci's Italian Pantry is at that intersection and itself is worth the side trip. Once inside, it's like being transported to Boston's North End, with the same tangy smells, friendly service with a touch of wise guy, and products you didn't think could be found this far from a city. In the cold cases you'll find a nice selection of salads, links of their own premises-made sausages, and chunks of their own mozzarella, made daily. They have really good made-to-order sandwiches that run about $5.00 and a list of their own special sandwiches such as a veggie combo (roasted eggplant, roasted peppers, fresh mozzarella, tomato, and basil), a prosciutto sandwich (with fresh mozzarella, roasted peppers, and fresh basil) and chicken cutlet with roasted peppers, fresh mozzarella, and fresh basil. These are served on your choice of white Italian, sourdough, semolina, focaccia or multigrain breads (we suggest the focaccia). Get your sandwiches to take out or to eat in the dining room next door, a bright little room with a molded tin ceiling and red checkered cloths on the tables. Al Ducci's is at 133 Elm Street at Highland Avenue, Manchester Center, 05255; (802) 362–4449, fax 362–0640.

Next door to the dining room, in another old-fashioned storefront, are the combined shops of *Maiden Lane at Le Depot* and *Judy Pascal, Antiques and Interiors.* Maiden Lane has women's clothing and vintage dresses and linens (they also do dressmaking), and Judy Pascal has an interesting mix of country furnishings, vintage textiles, and antique household accessories. The mix works well, and the shop is a pleasure to browse through. They are both on Elm Street next to Al Ducci's, Manchester Center, 05255. (802) 363–2004.

A good choice for breakfast and lunch in this neighborhood is the *Lion's Share Bakery and Coffee Roasters.* They have a very good selection of breakfast breads, Danishes, muffins, scones, and cinnamon buns and at lunchtime sell fresh-made sandwiches on their own freshly baked breads. They also have homemade soups. The corner of Center Hill and Elm Streets in Manchester Center; (802) 366–8272, E-mail: jstalcup@ourhouse.net.

Manchester has an abundance of places to eat, from bakeries, cafes, and pubs to elegant dining rooms. *Marsh Tavern* is our favorite, with a varied and seasonally changing menu that ranges from New England crab cakes and chicken pot pie to hazelnut-crusted trout and char-broiled filet mignon. Ingredients are impeccably fresh, with a preponderance coming from local farms and suppliers. The chef works closely with the Vermont Fresh Network to feature the finest locally grown ingredients. For example, on the tavern's lunch menu, a croissant is served with sliced sirloin, Major Farm's Shepherd cheese, and sautéed mushrooms. Flavors and textures seem to play with each other on the plate, as in the New England bouillabaisse, a blend of lobster, shrimp, scallops, and clams served in a delectable lobster broth with fennel and fresh tomato. The single-malt mousse cake is an unexpected specialty on the dessert list. Dinner entrees are mostly between $16 and $23. The Tavern is at the Equinox, Route 7A in Manchester Village, 05254; (802) 362–4700, (800) 362–4747.

In a former tollhouse perched between the winding road and a rushing little brook in a ravine is *Mistral's,* where classical French flavors and techniques are skillfully updated. For openers there is a tapenade of black olives, capers, and a touch of anchovy served with thin crisps of bread. Their *pâté maison* is a triumph of flavor and texture, moist and lean with a tenderness that is almost crumbly, and a serving that is large enough to share. Entrees, which include bread, Salad Mistral (a mesclun of tender young greens), and vegetables, range from fish and seafood to chicken, duck, sweetbreads and beef, and specials. The signature dish of this chef-owned restaurant is the Norwegian salmon cannelloni, a pair of rolled salmon filets, stuffed cannelloni-style with a mixture of lobster and finely diced shallots and vegetables, in a light pink beurre blanc. The service is exceptional, always there when needed but almost invisible. Among their enticing desserts is the signature Coup Mistral: coffee ice cream rolled in toasted hazelnuts with hot fudge and Fra Angelica.

The restaurant takes full advantage of its setting, with more than half of the tables along the wall of windows overlooking the dancing brook. The ravine is floodlighted at night, and although it is lovely at any time of year, we like it best in winter, when the brilliant white of snow and ice contrast with the transparent darkness of rushing water and deep greens of the overhanging conifers. Although they do virtually no advertising, Mistral is a top choice among knowledgeable locals, so a reservation is advisable even on weeknights. Entrees run $22 to $30. They are open Thursday through Tuesday for dinner from 6:00 P.M. Take Routes 11/30 east from Manchester, look for a sign on the left (north) side of the road. Toll Gate Road, Manchester Center 05255; (802) 362–1779.

Also highly thought of for the excellence of its dining is **Bistro Henry,** outside of town on Route 11. The appetizer menu tempts with offerings such as grilled shrimp with mango lime sauce or Alsatian onion tart. Entrees might include chicken breast stuffed with walnuts, herbs, and Boursin cheese or sweetbreads with bacon and shallot sauce. Lamb shanks, not commonly found on menus, are braised in merlot. Entrees include a salad, bread, and vegetables.

Henry's welcomes families and has a separate children's menu. Another good thing is that Dina's Vermont Baking Company is also on the premises, offering pastries, cakes, and other temptations such as Grand Marnier brûlée, pear and blueberry crisp, tangerine cheesecake, and sorbets. The team that owns the two enterprises is Henry and Dina Bronson, and they don't allow baseball caps or cell phones in the dining room—both rules we applaud. They are open 5:00 to 9:00 P.M. Tuesday through Saturday. During summer they also open Sundays. They close for about a month in mid-April to mid-May, so call during those months to be sure they are open. 1178 Routes 11/30, Manchester Center 05255, (802) 362–4982, www.bistrohenry.com.

At the other end of the spectrum is **Mrs. Murphy's Donuts,** an unassuming luncheonette on Routes 11/30 that sells the best doughnuts in Vermont. They're deep-fried, crunchy, and doused with powdered sugar. Mrs. Murphy's also offers special flavored coffees—one that's featured occasionally is Kahlúa creme coffee—and muffins. In addition to the traditional blueberry, bran, and apple raisin, there are pumpkin raisin, peanut, and red raspberry muffins. And, of course, they're all baked fresh daily. Mrs. Murphy's also offers soup, cereal, and egg breakfast sandwiches—but just *try* ignoring those doughnuts.

Open from 4:30 A.M. until 6:00 P.M., Mrs. Murphy's Donuts is at 374 Depot Street, opposite Friendly's, Manchester Center 05255; call (802) 362–1874 to learn the coffee of the day.

The **Southern Vermont Arts Center** on West Road in Manchester (05254) is a respite from the bustle down below in the town. The art starts from the second you enter the grounds and continues all the way up the beautiful, gradually ascending drive to the main estate, the Yester House. The grounds at the top of the hill are nicely landscaped and highlighted by more sculptures. The Boswell Botany Trail leads from the 1917 mansion into the woods, where you will find more than 100 varieties of native wildflowers and ferns. Many of these are rare species, such as the showy orchids and yellow lady's slipper. The woodland flowers are at their best bloom in the spring.

Inside space is used for constantly changing exhibits of art and for performances that may include chamber music, dance, or vocal music. Recent renovations have expanded the exhibit space and added a sparkling little cafe that serves luncheons and desserts. Admission is charged to the galleries, but the grounds are free. The center is open from the middle of May through October, Tuesday through Saturday 10:00 A.M. to 5:00 P.M. and on Sunday from noon until 5:00 P.M.

For a schedule of seasonal events, contact the Southern Vermont Arts Center, West Road, Manchester Village 05254, or call (802) 362–1405; www.svac.org.

Anyone rushing along Route 7 north of Manchester will probably miss the small sign that points travelers to Danby, a beautiful little town that once was the prosperous center of an active marble quarrying industry. It sits on a hillside, a quarter mile off the main road. The author Pearl S. Buck, who spent much of her life in China and wrote *The Good Earth,* spent her last years here, devoting much of her renowned energy trying to breathe life back into the town as the marble industry collapsed. Its nineteenth-century beauty has been saved, without the embellishments of more modern times, probably because no one had the money to modernize it.

The energetic new owners of *The Silas Griffith Inn* have modernized it where it matters, while preserving and restoring all the mansion's wealth of architectural and decorative detail. Each of the twenty-one redecorated rooms in the Victorian main house and its carriage shed has a gas fireplace and private bath, as well as new beds, most of which are queen-size. The first thing you will notice as you enter the house from its wide veranda are the floors: They not only sparkle in their newly refinished glory, but the wood is rare red birch, curly red birch in the dining room. Intricately embossed tin ceilings, original fireplaces faced in brass, bronze, and copper, crown moldings, and a stunning oval pocket door are among the details you'll admire here. Outdoors is a heated swimming pool and a six-person heated whirl-pool tub built into the elegant gazebo. Summer rates begin at $139, and winter at $129. The inn serves dinner to guests by reservation on holiday and some summer weekends. The Silas Griffith Inn is on Main Street, Danby 05739; (802) 293–5567, (800) 545–1509, www. silasgriffith.com.

While in town check out the *Danby Antiques Center,* also on Main Street. You'll find a broad and eclectic selection of nice items ranging from bric-a-brac to furniture.

Mountain View Ranch is run by horse-lovers Letitia and John Sisters. From mid-October through mid-June you can take horseback rides for just about any length of time you choose, through the woods and fields of this mountainous rural countryside. The 2.5-hour ride is a tour of local farms and costs about $55. A one-hour ride is about $30. In the autumn and spring the ranch is open just about every day, but for winter riding, the hours are 9:00 A.M. to 4:00 P.M. Monday through Thursday. Get the directions when you reserve; Mountain View Ranch, 502 Easy Street, Danby 05739. (802) 293–5837. Rides are also offered at Sun Bowl Ranch, Stratton Mountain (see page 144).

Directly across Route 7 from Danby is Mount Tabor, a town that lies at the foot of the Green Mountain range. Mount Tabor was called Griffith between 1891 and 1905 because local lumber proprietor Silas Griffith owned so much land in town. People sending mail to the town, used the name Griffith instead of Mount Tabor.

In 1905 marble quarrying overtook logging as the town's top industry, and the town regained its previous name. Today the *marble quarry* is still in operation in Mount Tabor.

At the crossroads on Route 7, take the road on the right that runs to the **White Rocks National Recreation Area.** The Long Trail passes through this forest, and there are many trails and picnic areas that run through the towns of Mount Tabor and Wallingford, the next town north. You can view the White Rocks without taking a strenuous, 3-mile hike by taking the second right going north in the center of Wallingford. Continue down this road for almost 3 miles until you come to the White Rocks picnic area. Then look up. The center peak, at 2,680 feet, is the highest of the three White Rocks mountains. A combination of limestone and quartz accounts for the mountains' name.

The Mettawee Valley

I f you choose to drive north out of Manchester on Route 30, you'll soon come into the town of Dorset. So many artists, woodworkers, quilters, and other craftsworkers have set up shops in their homes along Route 30 that you could spend an entire day visiting them all.

Like Manchester, Dorset is genteel country, and you pass fenced-off estates lining both sides of Route 30. Dorset's population numbers half that of Manchester, with many more summer residents. In fact, the first summerhouse in Dorset was built in 1868, setting the tone for the future.

The **Dorset Playhouse** features performances by professional actors-in-residence in the summer and showcases community theater in the winter. There's also a local writer's colony in town that draws authors from all over the world. For more information, contact American Theatre Works, Inc., P.O. Box 510, Dorset 05251; (802) 867–2223; e-mail: theatre@sover.net.

Some of the houses in the village were rescued from Massachusetts when whole towns were flooded to create the Quabbin Reservoir. They were taken apart and brought to Dorset for reconstruction, a project financed by a local philanthropist not only to save the fine old homes but also to provide work for local men during the Depression.

Mount Aeolus, which rises directly behind the village, was the site of Vermont's first commercial marble quarry and provided the stone for the columns and facing of the New York Public Library. About twenty-five quarries once employed hundreds in extracting, cutting, and shipping the marble, and you can still see one of them beside Route 30, just north of its intersection with West Road.

If you follow a little-used road called Dorset West Road, you'll find the **Marble West Inn,** an eight-room inn with a gas fireplace and baby grand piano in the common area. The old house has the aura of the grand style, but is casual enough to be really comfortable.

The grounds of the inn have two ponds to loll by, and a view of Mount Aeolus looms across the road. When you're relaxed and want to explore the inn itself, you'll notice that this 1840 Greek Revival house—which was owned by one family until 1985—has stenciling in the main foyer, marble steps and fireplace mantels, and polished wood everywhere. The stenciling was done by Adele Bishop, who literally wrote the book on wall stenciling.

June and Wayne Erla are the innkeepers, and the fact that Wayne taught himself to cook and took countless culinary classes becomes evident when you sit down to breakfast. If you gather a minimum of six people, you can book one of Wayne's five-course dinners; these feature local products in season and homemade stocks.

Write to the Marble West Inn, Dorset West Road, Dorset 05251, or call (802) 867–4155 or (800) 453–7629 for more information.

North of Dorset the towns of Rupert and Pawlet are on the Mettawee River, which follows Route 30. Follow Route 315 West off Route 30 once you cross over the border of Rupert from Dorset. Look for the historical marker that designates the site of *Vermont's First and Only Mint.* Back when Vermont was an independent republic, resident Reuben Harmon received government permission to operate the Green Mountain State's only mint, where he worked with copper coins.

Harmon's first coin had the saying "Vermontensium Res Publica, 1786" pressed into it, with a mountain sunrise and a plow on the front of the coin and a radiated eye with thirteen stars on the back.

Continue on Route 315 West until you come on the *Merck Forest and Farmland Center,* a massive, 2,700-acre land preserve where a family can spend the entire day outdoors enjoying nature and farm life. There are hiking trails, a visitors center, and a barn filled with horses, chickens, and other farm animals. You can watch and learn about a variety of farm chores, from boiling down maple syrup to breaking in horses. Camping is available in cabins on the land, and the center serves as an active community resource, with a summer day camp for children and a series of nature and farming workshops for adults. The center is open daily from 8:00 A.M. to 4:30 P.M.

For a schedule of events, write to the Merck Forest and Farmland Center, Route 315, Rupert 05768, or call (802) 394–7836; www.merckforest.org.

From the village of Rupert, west of the Merck Center, Route 153 heads north into West Pawlet. Contrary to current appearances, West Pawlet was a bustling outpost back in 1850; it was, in fact, considered one of the ten most populous employment centers in the state. You will see why as you leave the village heading north and cross the slate quarry and its slag piles. That explains the slate roofs on so many of the town's buildings.

Pawlet on Route 30 is home to the **Pawlet Potter,** a.k.a. Marion Waldo McChesney. McChesney favors frog and seascape subjects, with oceanic color schemes brought out in her gently shaped pots and vessels. Look at the aqua plate that has frogs molded onto it; they're swimming and chasing flies and look like they're about to leap off the plate. She calls this style "Road Kill Impressionism."

McChesney's studio is in Wickham House, built in 1810. The building was almost destroyed by a fire in 1976, but Marion and her husband, Lee, rebuilt the structure, which now serves as her shop and studio.

The Pawlet Potter is off Route 30, Pawlet 05761; call (802) 325–3100. The shop is usually open Monday through Saturday, 10:00 A.M. to 5:00 P.M. McChesney, however, is not always there. When she is, watch her throw pots on the wheel.

Down the road is **Valley Woodworking,** run by Jim Boyd. Boyd moved up to Vermont in the late 1980s from Rhode Island, and specifically to Rupert because there are a lot of craftspeople in this part of the state, and he wanted support from his peers. Jim does a lot of custom work, as well as refinishing, repair, and reproduction work. He says he's been doing this kind of work "forever." He graduated from the Rhode Island School of Design.

Jim sells a unique piece of furniture made from solid oak that serves as an ironing board, a chair, and a step stool. It is based on a colonial antique. Jim has a few on hand—ask him to demonstrate one for you. And a massive, true-reproduction china cabinet is a creation he built entirely with hand tools, using mortises and pegs; the cabinet is complete with plate and spoon racks built into the shelves. Along with detailed reproductions, Jim builds custom kitchen cabinets.

He welcomes visitors and spends most days working in the barn workshop, so you'll probably catch him in. Write to Valley Woodworking, Route 30, North Rupert 05761; (802) 325–3910.

MORE PLACES TO STAY IN SOUTHWEST VERMONT

(ALL AREA CODES 802)

BENNINGTON (05201)
Molly Stark Inn,
1067 East Main Street, is a country Victorian home with handmade quilts and big old-fashion bathtubs. Rates are $70 to $125; 442–9631; (800) 356–3076; www.mollystarkinn.com.

WILMINGTON (05363)
Nutmeg Inn, Route 9, is a cozy New England classic, with wood-burning fireplaces. A full country breakfast is offered; 464–3351.

ARLINGTON (05250)
Arlington Inn, Route 7A, is an elegant Greek Revival mansion with antiques and an excellent dining room. Rates are $90 to $230; 375–6532 or (800) 443–9442; www.arlingtoninn.com.

SANDGATE (05250)
Green River Inn, Sandgate Road. An attractive fourteen-room inn close to Manchester and Arlington, on a quiet dead-end road. Some rooms have whirlpool tubs, and some have fireplaces. Breakfast included and prix fixe dinner (about $25) is available by reservation; (888) 648–2212, (802) 375–2272, www.greenriverinn.com.

DORSET (05251)
Inn at West View Farm, Route 30, has comfortable rooms with a relaxed country atmosphere; 867–5715.

Barrows House, Main Street, has rooms in nine buildings spread over its extensive property, making it a favorite for families. Rates are $135 to $215 B&B, $180 to $275 MAP. 867–4455 or (800) 639–1620, www.barrowshouse.com.

WESTON (05161)
Colonial House Inn and Motel, Route 100, combines a homey B&B with motel units. Serves home-style meals; (802) 824–6286.

To Learn More in Southwest Vermont

For more information on the mountain area, contact the Mount Snow/Haystack Regional Chamber of Commerce, P.O. Box 3, Page House, Main Street, Wilmington 05363; (802) 464–8092.

You can reach the Bennington Chamber of Commerce at (802) 447–3311, (800) 229–0252.

The Manchester area has its own Web site: *www.manchestervermont.com,* where you can learn about events, see the views, and vie for prizes.

OFF THE BEATEN PATH

**MORE PLACES TO EAT IN
SOUTHWEST VERMONT**

(ALL AREA CODES 802)

DORSET (05251)
Inn at West View Farm,
Route 30, has a menu filled
with consistently sparkling
choices, accenting locally
grown ingredients;
867–5715.

**MANCHESTER CENTER
(05255)**
Candeleros, Main Street, is
the most popular Tex-Mex
restaurant in the region,
with a good selection of
Hispanic dishes and New
England regional foods at
lunch and dinner.
362–0836.

PAWLET (05761)
Mach's Brick Oven Bakery
serves lunch and snacks
and sells fresh-baked
breads and pastries;
325–6113.

WESTON (05161)
Village Sandwich Shop is
open daily summer and fall
from 10:00 A.M. to 4:00 P.M.,
serving sandwiches and
pastries; 824–5477.

Middle West Vermont

ithin the area that stretches from the northern segment of the Green Mountain National Forest to the lower Champlain Valley and the New York border is almost everything that's considered typically Vermont. Here are snow-covered ski trails, the Long Trail for hiking, wide flat valleys painted green by farmland and dotted with red barns, dirt roads winding through woods and over mountains, country inns, lakes, small tidy brick downtowns, and white-clapboarded villages set around the tall spires of their meetinghouses.

But there is more than the postcard image to this part of the state, and you don't even have to leave its main roads to find it. Although some of the state's best-known slopes bring skiers pouring in during the winter, and the year-round resorts that cluster at their bases are filled in the summer, much of this part of Vermont remains—or at least seems—largely untouched, the legacy of the national forest lands that form its eastern third.

To the west are the lower, but often still rolling lands that stretch to Lake Champlain, as it narrows and finally seems more like a very wide river. Wetlands here provide migration and nesting grounds for a wide range of bird life, and smaller lakes provide swimming and boating, without being overrun by tourists.

Ludlow and Points North

udlow is a sizable town whose population doubles in winter. Ludlow is in Vermont's heavy snow zone—100 to 120 inches of the white fluffy stuff is not unusual. During the Great Depression, when the New Deal was trying to find ways to revive the economy, the Civilian Conservation Corps was formed to give jobs to young people and to stimulate use of natural resources. One of the areas chosen for the newfangled idea of skiing was *Okemo Mountain* in Ludlow. The snowfall and the natural contours of the mountain combined over the following half century to make Okemo one of the state's best, state-of-the-art facilities, but with a minimum of glitz.

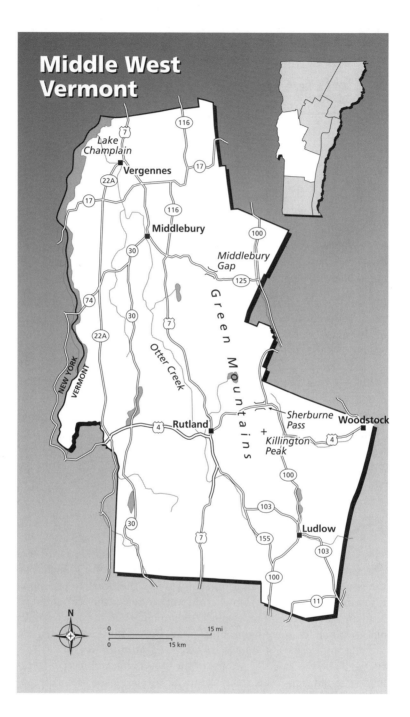

Middle West
Vermont

Lake
Champlain

■ Vergennes

Middlebury

Middlebury
Gap

Green Mountains

Otter Creek

NEW YORK

VERMONT

■ Rutland

Sherburne
Pass

Woodstock ■

Killington
Peak

■ Ludlow

N

0   15 mi

0   15 km

MIDDLE WEST VERMONT

AUTHORS' TOP HIGHLIGHTS

*President Calvin Coolidge
State Historic Site*

*Green Mountain
National Forest*

Texas Falls

Mount Independence

M/V Carillon

Chimney Point

Okemo has trails on two mountains, an impressive vertical drop, and an easy trail from the top over the Mountain Road that lets even relatively inexperienced skiers enjoy the breathtaking view to the north and east. One reason the area has become popular is the multitude of challenging intermediate slopes and a good selection of expert runs on the upper part of the mountain. Broader, gentler slopes near the two lift lines from the base lodge to the Winterplace Condos provide excellent training areas for beginners. Okemo has a Snowboard Zone with specially constructed challenges for snowboarders in The Park, The Pipe, and The Pull, along with its own tuning and demo center.

Okemo has all the services you would expect, including condos scattered along the slopes that are available through their lodging office (800–786–5366) and several restaurants and lounges in and about the huge main lodge.

Specials include a Sunday afternoon rate for skiers from Vermont and New Hampshire. If you buy a three-day or longer ticket you can use it at Stratton Mountain for one day during your stay. Okemo's "Try Before You Buy" policy allows you to try the conditions free, from lift opening at 8:00 A.M. until ticket sales begin at 9:00 on weekends, and from 9:00 to 10:00 A.M. on weekdays. This is a good family area, with good variety and tremendous lift capacity on fast-moving chairs. At night there is a special nightclub for teens. Okemo is just off Route 103 in Ludlow 05149; (802) 228–4041; snow line (802) 228–5222; okemo@ludl.tds.net;www.okemo.com.

The *Fletcher Farm School* is located on Route 103 near the Cavendish-Ludlow town line to the south. Numerous outbuildings—barns, cabins, and motel rooms—serve as accommodations for visitors and guests who want to spend two weeks painting, weaving, folk dancing, and engaging in other arts and crafts activities. The school is owned by the Society of Vermont Craftsmen, which also runs a small arts-and-crafts store on the premises during summer, selling items made by guests at the farm. A single reasonable price includes lodging, three family-style meals a day, lessons, and studio and practice space.

The Fletcher Farm School offers classes from June through October. For the current year's schedule, write to Fletcher Farm School, R.R. 1, Box 1041, Ludlow 05149, or call (802) 228–8770.

From Route 103 in Ludlow, turn onto Buttermilk Falls Road at the VFW building and go to the end of the road to see **Buttermilk Falls**.

The water rushes hard even in a dry autumn, and it completely drowns out the sound of heavy traffic on nearby Route 103. A couple of big flat rocks in the river are perfect for sunning and picnicking. And along the road are other footpaths leading down to the river. There are two good spots, one at the very end of the road and the other a few tenths of a mile before the end. A path leads to the falls from Buttermilk Falls Road, about 1.3 miles from its intersection with Route 103 in town.

In the town of Ludlow, the **Black River Academy Historical Museum** sits in a stately old brick building perched above the main road on High Street. Each room has a different theme: the President's Room, the Rotary Room, the Grange Room, and the Coolidge Room—this last being named for Calvin Coolidge, who graduated from the academy when it was a renowned private school back in the late 1800s. The building itself was constructed in 1889 and today sits next to a former schoolhouse, the old District School No. 1, which now serves as Ludlow's senior center and community center.

The museum—a truly fascinating place—is open Wednesday through Sunday from noon to 4:00 P.M. from Memorial Day through Labor Day and only on weekends from noon to 4:00 P.M. from Labor Day through Columbus Day weekend. Write to the Black River Academy Historical Museum, High Street, Ludlow 05149, or call (802) 228–5050 for more information. Admission is free, but donations are encouraged.

The **Crowley Cheese Factory** is the antithesis of the mammoth Cabot Cheese Factory located in the town bearing its name, just north of Montpelier. Just past the Crowley Cheese Store on Route 103 is a sign

Try This at Home

*I*n case you grow fond of the traditional Vermont ingredients, such as maple and cheddar cheese, while traveling here, or if you enjoy the flavors of the updated New England cooking styles you encounter here, look to the new omnibus of New England cuisine, The New England Cookbook, *by Brooke*

Dojny (The Harvard Common Press, *$16.95 paper, $29.95 hardcover). In its more than 350 recipes, you'll find very traditional dishes in their original forms and as interpreted by the throng of chefs trained in such bastions of creative cuisine as Vermont's own New England Culinary Institute.*

reading HEALDVILLE ROAD. Two miles down is an old, weather-beaten house where up to a ton of cheese is made every day, by hand.

The store out on Route 103 sells the cheese, as well as maple syrup and gift items, but if you want to see the cheese being made, go the extra 2 miles. You are unlikely to find them making cheese, however, in November or December. The factory is open from 8:00 A.M. to 4:00 P.M. on weekdays, while the gift shop on Route 103 is open from 10:00 A.M. to 5:30 P.M. daily from June through December. January through May it's open the same hours Friday through Monday. For information, write to the Crowley Cheese Factory, Healdville 05147; (802) 259–2340.

As you head back to Route 103, you'll see that this is a good foliage road; Sawyer Rocks, a huge outcropping, is straight ahead, dotted with trees that in autumn are brilliant in their color.

On Route 100 north of Ludlow is Echo Lake. This is a summer camp area owing to the three major lakes running alongside the road: Lake Rescue, Echo Lake, and Amherst Lake.

Echo Lake Inn is one of only five inns in Vermont from the 1800s that were built as inns (many large homes from that century have been converted to inns), an imposing structure with a long rocker-studded porch. The new owner, while completing a thorough modernization of its facilities (including safety features), feels strongly about keeping its character, with rooms of varying sizes and prices, an individually chosen mix of antiques and newer furnishings in the guest rooms, and the general ambience of a venerable inn. Those who prefer a bit more privacy can choose the detached condo units, with fully equipped kitchens, TVs, cable, stereos, and microwave ovens.

Although these condos have everything you need to prepare your own meals, many condo guests still opt for a meal at the inn, long known for its outstanding dining room. The menu is always tempting, with dishes such as fresh scallion pasta shells stuffed with lobster, shrimp, and scallops; rainbow trout with sun-dried tomatoes, artichoke hearts, and pignoli; veal medallions and portobello mushrooms marsala; and grilled Angus sirloin with red pepper coulis and horseradish cream. So many choices, so little time. Entrees range from $17

ANNUAL EVENTS IN MIDDLE WEST VERMONT

Early June: Town-wide yard sale, Main Street, Poultney; (802) 287–9111

Early July: Independence Day Celebration, Brandon, with Vermont's largest parade, on the Saturday nearest July 4; (802) 247-6401.

Mid-July: Summer Festival on the Green, Middlebury, a week of performing arts; (802) 388–0216.

Early September: Vermont State Fair, Fairgrounds, Rutland; (802) 775–5200.

Early December: Christmas in Middlebury, with artisan open houses, a festival of wreaths and music; (802) 388–4126.

The Sound of Silent Cal

Stories, many of them apocryphal, abound illustrating the taciturn nature of the Vermonter known as Silent Cal. One of them involved a society matron who was introduced to President Coolidge at a particularly tedious garden party in Washington. "Oh, Mr. President," she gushed, "I have a bet with a friend that I can make you say more than two words!"

"You lose," he replied.

to $25. The inn also serves both breakfast and lunch to the public as well as to guests.

Winter room rates range from $119 to $279, and summer from $99 to $209, including breakfast. Expect higher rates on holiday weekends, and ask about special packages and off-season discounts. All inn guests have access to a swimming pool, lighted tennis courts, and a private lake dock with canoes. Contact the Echo Lake Inn, P.O. Box 154, Ludlow 05149, or call (802) 228–8602 or (800) 356–6844 for more information.

From Route 100A in Plymouth to Route 103 in Ludlow, Route 100 is known as the Calvin Coolidge Memorial Highway. Coolidge was one of two American presidents born in Vermont.

Coolidge was born in Plymouth Notch on July 4, 1872. His position as governor of Massachusetts led him to a spot on the ballot as running mate to Warren G. Harding in the presidential race of 1920. On August 3, 1923, while Coolidge was in Plymouth helping his father get in the hay, President Harding died in California. The presidential oath of office was administered to Calvin by lamplight over the family kitchen table at 2:47 A.M. When John Coolidge, the father of the new president, was later asked why he thought he was authorized to administer the presidential oath, his reply was characteristically Coolidge: "I didn't know I couldn't," he said.

Today the hillside farm is the ***President Calvin Coolidge State Historic Site,*** with the homestead where he grew up furnished exactly as it was in 1923 (the president's son gave the house to the state). The farm's cheese factory still produces cheese, and its original equipment is shown, along with other farm implements and horse-drawn vehicles, in the Wilder Barn. The Wilder House, once a tavern and the childhood home of Calvin's mother, Victoria, is now a small restaurant where you can have traditional dishes such as chowder and chicken pot pie.

The site is open from 9:30 A.M. to 5:00 P.M. every day from Memorial Day through Columbus Day. Admission is $5.00 for adults; children under twelve get in free. Coolidge State Historic Site, P.O.B. 247 (clever number, that—the hour of his presidential oath), Plymouth Notch 05050; (802) 672–3773.

Past Lake Rescue and just before you reach Echo Lake as you're heading north on Route 100, take a right. About a mile up the steep, winding

MIDDLE WEST VERMONT

road is the **Plymouth Kingdom Cemetery,** where several Revolutionary War soldiers are buried. In the cemetery old slate markers stand in back of VFW markers and flags. The cemetery is surrounded by a split-rail fence, and stone steps lead up to the cemetery. Kingdom Brook rushes by on the other side of the road.

Back on this pastoral road is a pleasant drive, with rolling land, estates, and ponds. A mile up from the cemetery, there's a boat access area to Colby Pond.

To experience Vermont's out-of-doors without sacrificing luxury, consider a stay at **Hawk Inn & Mountain Resort,** right on Route 100 in the Black River valley. The low-to-the-land buildings are contemporary, with large, comfortable rooms and public spaces built to please upscale young families. It is open all year and has a wealth of recreational facilities including an indoor pool, sauna, hiking trails, ice-skating, sledding, snowshoeing, and cross-country skiing. They also can arrange horseback riding or boating on Lake Amherst, and in the winter they offer sleigh rides. The dining room, which is open to the public, is stylish and cozy, with views onto the well-landscaped grounds. The menu is New American, and dishes are well-prepared; appetizers are often ample enough for an entree. As you might expect in a place catering to this clientele, the wine list is quite good. Reservations are wise, especially in ski season. Hawk Inn & Mountain Resort, Route 100, Plymouth 05050; (800) 685–HAWK; www.hawkresort.com.

North on Route 100 a short distance is **Bear Creek Mountain Club,** a unique concept for skiers. This private ski club sits on its own mountain, with a 1,300-foot vertical drop and fifteen trails covering 51 acres. Plans are afoot to expand the number of lifts and trails. Nonmembers can ski ($50 a day, $30 half day from 1:30 P.M.), but only 450 people can ski per day. Members, of course, have priority. The difference in skiing here is the sense that you have the whole mountain to yourself. The clubhouse at the base has an excellent dining room, which is open to the public. Bear Creek Mountain Club, Route 100, Plymouth 05056; (802) 672–4242, e-mail: thecreek@vermontel.com; www.bearcreekclub.com.

Route 4 leaves Route 100 in West Bridgewater, heading through Bridgewater Corners and on east to Woodstock. A short distance from the

Worth Seeing

Vermont State Craft Center, Frog Hollow, 1 Mill Street, Middlebury; (802) 388–3177.

UVM Morgan Horse Farm, 2.5 miles from downtown Middlebury, at 74 Battell Drive (Route 23), Weybridge; (802) 388–2011.

Vermont Marble Exhibit, 62 Main Street, Proctor; (802) 459–2300.

New England Maple Museum, Route 7, Pittsford; (802) 483–9414.

intersection, on Route 4, you'll come to ***Blanche and Bill's Pancake House***. There's usually a wait in the twenty-four-seat restaurant, but it's worth it. Blanche personally takes your order and then goes back and cooks it. Signs of menu items predominate here, as do specials named for local people and landmarks, from radio stations to taxicabs. Lunch is served, but breakfast all day' is the main attraction.

And we're talking real country, lumberjack-size breakfasts. The blueberry pancakes come heaped with blueberries and syrup on top, while the French toast arrives with cinnamon sugar liberally sprinkled over the fat slices of bread. Eggs and waffles are also on the breakfast menu, with burgers and grilled sandwiches the mainstay of lunch. Blanche and Bill's Pancake House is open Wednesday through Sunday from 7:00 A.M. to 2:00 P.M. and is closed Monday and Tuesday. It has no telephone. It's on Route 4, Bridgewater Corners 05035.

If it's lunchtime, or if you've a mind to sample some Vermont brew, keep going until you reach the three grain silos that mark the ***Long Trail Brewing Company***. We like the philosophy of its founder and owner: Since beer is 95 percent water, it shouldn't have to be imported. Everything at the brewery is made in Vermont, from the brewing equipment to the woodstove and heavy wooden tables in the beer hall/pub. A sampler of six different ales costs about $5.00, and you can savor and compare them at the bar, at a table inside, or on a deck overlooking the river. Through a glass wall you can see the giant gleaming vats and the business part of the brewery. Good, sturdy goes-great-with-beer food is served, too—bratwurst steamed in Hit the Trail Ale, chili, ale and cheddar soup, or soft pretzels, made on the premises with Long Trail beer. The visitors center is open daily from 11:00 A.M. to 6:00 P.M., with food served from 11:00 A.M. to 6:00 P.M. It's on Route 4, east of Route 100, in Bridgewater Corners 05035; (802) 672–5011; www.longtrail.com.

You can take Route 100A here, then cut back southwest through Plymouth (passing the Coolidge homestead) and come out on Route 100, making a tidy little loop—a nice afternoon's excursion from the Echo Lake Inn or from the Lincoln Inn on Route 4 west of Woodstock (see the Woodstock section of the Connecticut River Valley chapter).

As you're heading back for Route 100, Killington Mountain looms so large that at times it looks like you're going to drive right into it. Killington, the second highest peak in the state, is where Vermont purportedly received its name. A minister from Connecticut was traveling on horseback through the area in 1763, and when he reached the top of Killington—all

4,241 feet of it—the Reverend Sam Peters was said to have called the land *verd mont,* French for "green mountain."

Under the shoulder of the mountain, on the west side of Route 4/100 is a modest-looking restaurant with a lot to brag about. *Hemingway's* has been praised by just about every food publication in the country, and its chefs have been awarded, lauded, and invited to cook at the James Beard Foundation in New York. But despite all this attention, they continue to serve uncompromisingly good dinners to a full house almost every night. Each dinner is complete with three courses, hors d'oeuvres, and coffee. The first course might be lobster soup with roasted corn or scallops and crab cakes with mango, followed by an entree of pan-roasted squab with rabbit tortellini or Thai glazed venison—there will be about nine entrees to choose from. Hemingway's is open Wednesday through Sunday, and occasional other days as well, for dinner only. Route 100, Killington 05482; (802) 422–3886. You can browse the current menu at www.hemingwaysrestaurant.com.

Though it's easy, from the many restaurants to the ski facilities and other activities, to get the feeling that the watchword around Killington is *indulgence,* there is one place you can go in the area where the focus is on fitness and self-preservation. *Jimmy LeSage's New Life Fitness Vacations* is located at the Inn of the Six Mountains, and although the participants at Jimmy's spa may be surrounded by people who are hell-bent on cramming as much as possible into their time at Killington, the New Lifers find it doesn't matter: They're having a great time anyway.

From May through October Jimmy offers a variety of fitness weeks and weekends that combine just the right amount of healthfulness and pampering, from low-calorie meals that are nonetheless satisfying to a good dose of massages and leisurely walks, on which you can

A Step Forward to the Past

*J*ust in time for the twenty-first century, one Vermont town returned to the name that it abandoned at the turn of the nineteenth century. Like Constantinople, you can't go back to Sherburne, Vermont, anymore. In April 1999 its citizens voted to return the name of the town to Killington, to match the mountain that dominates the area and the ski slopes and resorts that give it its fame. This won't confuse very many people, since nearly everyone has been calling it Killington all this time anyway.

appreciate the activity for its sensual pleasures and not for the exact number of calories you've just burned. That's not Jimmy's focus.

For more information, write to Jimmy LeSage, New Life Fitness Vacations, P.O. Box 395, Killington 05751, or call (802) 422–4302 or (800) 228–4676.

In Stockbridge on Route 100, you'll see a sign that reads THE ROCK SHOP. And that's just what it is: a shop for rock fans—the hard kind, not the musical kind. Randy and Marilyn Gibson run the **Riverknoll Rock Shop,** where you can find cheap jewelry, rock scavenging and mining knickknacks, books, crystals, and prospecting equipment, all in one room off the side of a house.

If you like, they can also teach you how to cut gems—or will do it for you—and how to restring beads and pearls. They can also tell you where the best places to pan for gold are in the area.

The shop is open most days and weekends but it is wise to call ahead. You have to walk through the Gibsons' kitchen to get to the shop. Riverknoll Rock Shop, Route 100, Stockbridge 05772; (802) 746–8198.

North of Stockbridge on Route 100, the town of Rochester, which abuts the Green Mountain National Forest, has always seen a lot of activity, although the businesses have changed their stripes over the years. The White River Valley Railroad once coursed through the town, logging and mining and dairy farming being the primary industries in former times.

Today Rochester has a tidy village green, a cafe, and several shops, including one that rents bicycles. It also has a working guest farm, **Liberty Hill Farm,** located just off Route 100. When you first step out of your car, you'll be greeted by the ubiquitous sign of a dairy farm: the smell of manure. When you step into the house, you'll find the welcoming aroma of fresh-baked something or other, and your stomach juices will gurgle in anticipation of what is to be that night's dinner.

That "innkeeper" Beth Kennett prepares everything from scratch is indicative of the farm as a whole: Liberty Hill is a thriving, old-fashioned dairy farm, a rare chance to step into an increasingly rare way of life for a few days.

In the mid-1980s, when the price of milk plummeted, to keep the tradition of dairy farming going, the Kennetts opened their home to guests.

The farm is also a cacophony of sounds: roosters sub for alarm clocks, tractors putt-putt by the house, cows moo, Lassie barks. Chickens, ducks, turkeys, rabbits, assorted barn cats, and, of course, the Holsteins are never out of earshot. Stirred up all into one stew, they provide a gentle humming all day long that lulls you to sleep at nightfall.

Then there's the food. Casseroles, baskets, and pans filled with everything homemade are passed and repassed while tales of fishing, milking, and antiquing whirl around the breakfast and dinner table.

The farm is open year-round, and guests come for skiing, fishing, hiking, and canoeing and to work in the barn. If you like to feed calves, pitch hay, and tell the cows to "gwan" when it's time to go out for the night, you can keep busy all day and night. In fact, some high-ranking corporate executives have been known to get into their flannels and jeans and head for the barn at six each morning for a week and to claim that they want to trade places with Bob.

A night's stay at Liberty Hill Farm costs about $75 ($35 for children under twelve) and includes full breakfast and dinner. Liberty Hill Farm, 511 Liberty Hill Road, Rochester 05767; (802) 767–3926; www.liberty hillfarm.com.

Five miles north of Liberty Hill, at the junction of Routes 100 and 125, try the kielbasa grinder with peppers and onions at the *Vermont Home Bakery,* housed in the Old Hancock Hotel. A 6-foot-high wood carving of a tuxedoed raccoon carrying a pizza greets you at the door of this historic building that, since its beginnings in 1788, has served as a Revolutionary War–era tavern, a hippie crash pad, and a speakeasy.

The menu starts with breakfast dishes, served all day, of which a venison sausage breakfast is the most expensive at $5.99. A cob-smoked ham sandwich is $5.00, and most dinner entrees are under $10.00— including sole amandine, vegetable lasagna, linguini pesto, and shrimp scampi. It's an informal country store/bakery/lunchroom/restaurant with a tiny and appropriately named Unknown Obscure Little Bookshop, where you can get real bargains on some amazingly diverse new titles, including many published in Europe. The good-natured owners also have a couple of rooms for rent upstairs at $50 a night, but they are always occupied when we stop in (usually for the venison breakfast on our way over the gap to Middlebury to ski), so we haven't seen them. Open from 7:00 A.M to 8:00 P.M. Sunday through Thursday and until 9:00 P.M. on Friday and Saturday; Routes 100 and 125, Rochester 05767; (802) 767–4976.

In and around Middlebury

f you follow Route 125, it takes you over the Green Mountains, at Middlebury Gap, one of its few low spots (well, lower than most of the summits) with a road that's open all winter. As you begin to climb, look for a sign to **Texas Falls**, an easily accessed and lovely gorge, where the river compresses to rush through a narrow passage in the rocks, dropping through a steep chute before plummeting through the gorge and into a pool. After a June shower, it's a raging, swirling froth. The path leads down to a log bridge that spans the gorge and gives great views without ruining this woodland setting. It's one of the most accessible falls in the state, and one of the prettiest. The road sinews up (and up and up) until it reaches the height of land and begins to drop, more gently, onto the western side of the Green Mountains.

You know you're at a real "skier's mountain" when you find a can of Bag Balm on the ticket counter at a ski area. You'll also find smiles, families, college students, and laid-back skiers of all ages at **Middlebury Snow Bowl,** on uncrowded trails that work with the mountain's natural terrain. Gentle trails from the top are good for beginner and intermediate skiers, so you don't have to worry about getting on the wrong lift and finding yourself with nothing but black diamond trails to the bottom. Experts will get a workout on several trails, too. Although the official number of trails is thirty-two, Middlebury doesn't inflate the number by giving each segment of a trail a different name, as most other resorts do. If it followed the example of most Vermont ski areas, the count would be forty-eight.

Grooming is good, lift operators know the trails and can give you reliable advice on their conditions and challenge, and the chili in the lunchroom (which closes at 2:00 P.M.) is rich and meaty. What more is there to a day's skiing? Rentals, which feature up-to-date equipment, are fast and easy; lift tickets are well below the glitzy places, among the lowest in the state at $26 on weekdays and $32 on weekends. Seniors and students ski for about $6.00 less. For conditions or information, call (802) 388–4356. The address is Route 125, Ripton 05753.

The most unexpected feature is the library in the ski lodge, where you can seek quiet and a selection of books and magazines if you decide to leave the trails early or take a midday break. You'll find it well used during midterms, when Middlebury students hit the books and the slopes alternately.

Ripton is a tiny town that lies totally within the Green Mountain

National Forest but is one of the largest towns area-wise in Vermont, having 32,704 acres within its town lines. Its population, though, only numbers in the low hundreds.

Even though Robert Frost spent a good deal of his life in New Hampshire, Vermonters in this part of the state still like to think of him as one of their own, since he spent many of his last summers writing in his cabin in Ripton. In fact, you can visit the **Robert Frost Cabin,** nestled in the heart of the Green Mountains. When you see the environs in which Frost worked, you'll better understand his intense creativity.

To get to the cabin, turn off at the Robert Frost Wayside picnic area; take the unmarked dirt road to the immediate right of the area. Drive $\frac{1}{2}$ mile up the road, and you'll see the Homer Noble Farm, a white farmhouse. Park in the small lot, then walk up the trail 100 yards beyond the house. There's an opening to the left. The cabin is unmarked from the main road because locals want only those visitors who want to see it badly enough to ask for directions. Middlebury College owns the cabin and most of the land on both sides of Route 125 in this mountainous area. Although you can go only onto the porch and not in the cabin, inside it remains as Frost lived in it from 1939 to his death in 1963.

Also in Ripton you'll pass the Bread Loaf campus, maize-colored buildings that are home to the annual Bread Loaf summer writers' programs that Middlebury College maintains. There are lots of trails scattered throughout the forest, many with trailheads on Route 125.

Two miles west of the cabin on Route 125, pull into the parking lot of the Chipman Inn to read the sign that gives the rates of toll for the Center Turnpike, as Route 125 was previously called, the stagecoach road from Middlebury to Woodstock. The turnpike was chartered in 1800, and some of the tolls are as follows: man and horse, 8 cents; person on foot, 2 cents; and sleighs drawn by two oxen or horses, 12 cents, with each additional ox or horse costing 2 cents.

Sheep and swine could travel over the road for a half cent each if fewer than a dozen of them were traveling the road. More than twelve cost 3 cents a dozen. But no need to reach into your pocket; the road is now free, no matter how many sheep you have with you.

Guests enter the **Chipman Inn** through a unique front door with a fanlight and separate side windows, just one of the features of this well-restored 1828 building, whose trim and woodwork are noticeably similar to that of the Sheldon Museum in Middlebury. Guest rooms are simply and tastefully furnished, several with both double and single beds and all with private baths. Hearty breakfasts are included in the rates, which range from $110 to $135, and a five-course dinner can be reserved ahead. The menu might include Maryland crab cakes or chicken breast with apricots and currants. The Chipman Inn is on Route 125, Ripton 05766; (802) 388–2390 or (800) 890–2390; www.chipmaninn.com.

From Ripton, Forest Road 32 provides access from the south into the Moosalamoo wilderness area and two more delightful places to get away from it all: Judith's Garden Bed and Breakfast and Blueberry Hill Inn (see page 184).

Once you get to Middlebury proper, park your car and walk around the bustling village that serves an extended college campus. Middlebury was chartered early in the state's history, in 1761, and received its name because it was located halfway between the adjacent towns of Salisbury and New Haven.

The **Vermont Folklife Center** is in the Gamaliel Painter House, just off the green. The center encourages the promotion and development of folk traditions in Vermont and in other countries. It conducts special events in collaboration with its exhibits, which frequently involve children's art projects, from both Vermont and other places.

The gallery at the center is open Monday through Friday from 9:00 A.M. to 5:00 P.M. year-round and Saturday from noon to 4:00 P.M. from Memorial Day through mid-October. Admission is free. Write to the Vermont Folklife Center, Gamaliel Painter House, 2 Court Street, Middlebury 05753, or call (802) 388–4964.

The **Sheldon Museum**, in an 1829 marble-built merchant's home in the center of town, is the oldest community museum in the United States. Like the Fairbanks Museum, it was founded by a man who was a tireless collector, but his passion was for antiquities and local history. Ten rooms show one of the state's best collections of early furniture, decorative arts, paintings, and implements of daily living. The museum is open from 10:00 A.M. to 5:00 P.M. Monday through Saturday year-round. It is at 1 Park Street Middlebury 05753; (802) 388–2117.

Skiing is a way of life for students and faculty at Middlebury College, and the school has a **Ski Touring Center** at the Breadloaf Campus on Route 125, less than 2 miles west of the Snow Bowl. It also lights a downtown cross-country trail until 10:00 P.M. for those who want to take a bracing glide under the stars without driving up the mountain. To tour the downtown campus, which has some fine examples of architecture, pick up a map from the admissions office in the Emma Willard House on

South Main Street (Route 30), or join a tour there any weekday morning during the academic year (except during exams); (802) 443–3000.

Look for **Neil & Otto's Pizza Cellar,** literally in a cellar—of the Baptist church. Two friends from high school days, both in their early twenties, opened this pizzeria, where you can get a staggering variety of pizzas starting at $4.15 for a small cheese. You won't stagger out, however, because they have no beer license (it's in a church, remember), but they're open until 2:00 A.M., at 11 Merchant's Row, 05753; (802) 388–6774 or 388–6776.

For a quick lunch, especially if you are planning a picnic, head to **Baba's Market and Deli.** Their well-stocked deli has all the sandwich-makings you will need. They also have wood-fired pizza, a good selection of Middle Eastern and Greek specialties, and a good case of chilled salads. They open at 7:00 A.M. every day, closing at 10:30 P.M. weekdays and 11:00 P.M. on Friday and Saturday. Baba's is off Main Street, south of the river at 6 College Street, Middlebury 05753; (802) 388–6408.

Outside of town, in the most unlikely of places, you will find three fascinating businesses to visit. Look for Exchange Street, which runs through the middle of an industrial park on the north end of town. From Route 7 North, turn west onto Elm Street, just north of the Methodist church. Exchange Street is the next street on the right.

You will come first to **Vermont Soapworks,** makers of fine-grade handmade soaps and identified by a small sign at the roadside. Here are some of the mildest soaps made anywhere, the same ones you will find in the best gift and bath shops in Vermont (at much higher prices). The factory store has first quality soaps for sale, as well as seconds—those bars that were slightly unshapely when cut for wrapping. Herbs and flowers create the wonderful natural scents in the soaps. While there, notice the little "museum" of old soap packaging and advertising pieces, which you might miss; they are in a glass-topped case that doubles as the sales counter. Unfortunately, Vermont soapworks is no longer able to give individual tours. It is in an industrial building on the east side of the street, open Monday through Friday 8:00 A.M. to 4:00 P.M., Saturday 11:00 A.M. to 4:00 P.M.; 616 Exchange Street, Middlebury 05753; (802) 388–4302; www.vermontsoap.com.

A short distance from the soap factory, on the other side of the street, **Otter Creek Brewing** is one of the best small artisanal brewers in the state. Brews run from a light pale ale all the way to stouts, with many in between. Last time we were there, we found a very nice hickory smoked ale (they smoked the malt, not the ale). Case specials are available; you never know what good deals they may have. The brewery is open Monday through Saturday 10:00 A.M. to 6:00 P.M., with tours at 1:00, 3:00, and 5:00 P.M. It's at 783 Exchange Street, Middlebury 05753; (800) 473–0727, (802) 388–0727.

On the same side of the street, a few buildings farther along, is **Maple Landmark Woodcraft,** a real find if you have young kids in your life. This is a maker of high-quality small maple toys designed for toddlers. Little wooden engines with brightly colored cars run on grooved maple tracks that you can arrange into any configuration. Bright letters of the alphabet ride on flatcars, so you can personalize the train with the child's name. Other toys include wooden farm animals, wild animals, and old-fashioned cube-shaped blocks with deeply engraved alphabet letters. Look also for checkerboards, cribbage boards, domino sets, and other small cherry and maple gifts. Firsts and seconds are available, with seconds and discontinued items at half price. Call for their catalog or visit Monday through Saturday from 9:00 A.M. They close weekdays at 5:00 P.M., Saturday at 4:00 P.M. 1297 Exchange Street, Middlebury 05753; (800) 421–4223, (888) 388–0761; www.maplelandmark.com.

Four miles north of the town of Middlebury off Route 7 is the **Dog Team Tavern.** The tavern concentrates on traditional New England dishes like prime rib and chicken. Many Vermonters, however, never make it to dinner at the tavern and instead just breeze in and out for a tin of hot, fresh-baked sticky buns that are the best in the state.

While the tavern is a very popular place to eat, and you may not get a table right away, they offer you a menu to browse while you're waiting in the lobby, so you can order your dinner before you sit down.

The tavern serves dinner year-round from 5:00 to 9:00 P.M. Monday through Saturday and from noon to 9:00 P.M. Sunday, at 1338 Dog Team Road, New Haven 05472; (802) 388–7651.

Also a few minutes north of Middlebury on Route 7, on the way to Vergennes, is a restaurant that draws people even from Burlington just to have dinner. And for good reason. **Roland's Place** is in a former home and tavern built while George Washington was president and Middlebury and Vergennes were battling it out to determine which of them would be the capital of Vermont. In 1796 they were the two biggest towns in the state, and a spot about halfway between them was a perfect place for a tavern. Now they are two of the most attractive and historic towns in the state, and it's a perfect place for a fine restaurant owned by a French chef with a passion for fresh products grown and raised in Vermont and seafood from its New England neighbors.

Roland's menu, and his masterful presentation, should put his prices up there in the top range of Vermont restaurants, but we've never seen anything on the menu, except lobster, at more than $20.00; most entrees average around $18.00. Locally raised rabbit is served with tartiflette, a savory dish of Yukon gold potatoes with Canadian bacon, cheddar cheese, and cream; veal is sautéed with several varieties of wild mushrooms and served with wild rice and baby asparagus spears. Slices of tender pink duck breast are fanned vertically over mashed Yukon gold potatoes (which Roland was featuring on his menu long before these flavorsome tubers were available in grocery stores). Beside them a river of crisp-cooked snowpeas is bridged by half a ring of squash. Venison may be served with tender spaetzle, crisped just before serving. Each plate is garnished with fresh herbs that Roland and his wife, Lisa, grow in the garden behind the restaurant.

Don't even try to choose from among the appetizers—smoked Vermont emu, Roland's savory terrine, home-cured salmon with currant vinaigrette, grilled portobello mushrooms with goat cheese and colby polenta. Ask for a sampler plate to share, and try a little of each. When you see the size of it, you may rethink ordering an entree. In the winter, when Roland scales back his usual menu to eight or nine choices of appetizer, you may find a creamy sweet potato soup, a rich puree perfumed with clove with finely shredded raw sweet potatoes stirred in. Delicately smoked trout (smoked here) is paired with grilled portobello in a swirl of light sour cream.

While the primary focus here is on the food, Roland's has three cozy guest rooms upstairs, which he does not advertise. But if you ask, you can stay there, particularly nice in the winter when you can just toddle upstairs after dinner instead going outdoors. One room has a deep whirlpool bath in an alcove, and all have private baths. The next morning, breakfast is served in front of a glowing Franklin stove, and if you are lucky, Roland will start your day with a hearty wedge of quiche, each mouthful of which is infused with the flavor of smoked meat. The homefries are like none we have eaten elsewhere, subtly seasoned, soft inside and crispy on the outside.

The best quality dining bargain in Vermont may be the early-bird special for a full dinner between 5:00 and 6:00 P.M. Roland's is open daily year-round for lunch from 11:30 A.M. to 2:30 P.M. and for dinner from

5:00 to 9:00 P.M. Sunday brunch is served from 9:00 A.M. to 2:00 P.M. Roland's Place is on Route 7, New Haven 05472; (802) 453–6309.

Route 116, a north-south road connecting East Middlebury with the town of Bristol, is a lovely road to drive, with mountain views and attractive farmland, and Bristol is a small, but busy and attractive town. If you follow Route 116, which joins with Route 17 through town, until just shortly after the two separate again, you'll see a parking area for the **Bristol Memorial Forest Park**. One of Vermont's loveliest picnic sites, it has tables overlooking a gorge and paths along its brink with railings and bridges to give you the best and safest views of the entire gorge and its waterfalls.

If you follow Route 17, it will take you over the Appalachian Gap, with an elevation of 2,300 feet as it climbs over the sharp spine of the Green Mountains and drops into Waitsfield. An equally dramatic route over the mountains, on an unnumbered and less-used route, is across the **Lincoln Gap,** with a 2,400-foot elevation. Before Routes 116 and 17 diverge, take a road to the south marked LINCOLN, then follow signs to Warren. It is one of the state's most memorable drives, closed in winter because of the difficulties in keeping the road passable. When you see the pitch of the road, you'll know why the snowplows don't tackle it. As you leave Bristol, you can't miss seeing the **Lord's Prayer Rock,** a boulder on Route 17 on the eastern side of town that has the complete Lord's Prayer inscribed on it. A doctor from Buffalo who grew up in Bristol saw many loggers drag their loads and horses up the road, which back then was muddy most of the year. As a boy, he was offended by the laborers' language, so he paid a local stonecutter to chisel the complete Lord's Prayer into the rock.

If you're fascinated by tales of lost treasure, before you leave Bristol, ask directions to **Hell's Half Acre**. This was the site on a dirt road 2 miles south of town where, supposedly, a huge deposit of silver was buried. Many people have spent thousands of hours over the years trying to locate it, without luck. The story is a long one, involving foreign intrigue and revenge. Maybe you'll have more luck than the hordes before you.

West of Middlebury, also on Route 17 (which you can best reach from the center of town via Route 23), are the vast lowland marshes and waterways of the **Dead Creek Waterfowl Area.** This is birders' paradise, especially during spring and fall migrations, when thousands upon thousands of birds rest here during their journeys. Few sights in life can match that of a flock of snow geese filling the sky as they resume their trip. You can canoe here, except in the area south of Route

17 between the road and the dike, but be careful to stay well away from the shore between April and June, when birds are nesting.

At its southern end, Lake Champlain narrows to a small passage before broadening again to the south. Originally settled by the French as a part of New France, the point became known as Chimney Point for the blackened chimneys rising from the cellar holes of homes burned by the settlers as they fled the advancing British during the French and Indian War. The narrows made this spot a popular ferry crossing, and, of course, where there was a ferry there was a tavern to house and comfort travelers. *Chimney Point State Historic Site,* at the Champlain Bridge crossing of Routes 17 and 125, has its visitors center and museum in the eighteenth-century tavern on the banks of the lake. It has exhibits on the original native peoples and on the French settlers that were driven from this land. The site is open from Memorial Day through Columbus Day from 9:30 A.M. to 5:00 P.M. Wednesday through Sunday. It is at 7305 Route 125, Addison 05734; (802) 759–2412.

The Brandon Area

A total of five different routes, each with its diversions and inter-connecting side roads, lead from Middlebury to Brandon. The most direct is busy Route 7. More scenic are Route 30 to the west and Route 53 to the east around Lake Dunmore. Our favorites, of course, are the other two. Between Routes 30 and 7 is a sometimes-unpaved road through West Salisbury and Leicester Junction. And farthest to the east is the totally unpaved National Forest Road 32, which takes you through the thickly forested heart of Moosalamoo.

You won't find *Moosalamoo* on any map. It's an area defined by a unique partnership of landholders and groups with a passion for keeping the wildlands wild but accessible. Public Service, the Green Mountain National Forest, Branbury State Park, Middlebury College, the Green Mountain Club, the Audubon Society, the Vermont Institute for Natural Sciences, an association of snowmobilers, and a few inns are among the partners, and their purpose is to protect the unique natural environment, maintain trails for year-round use, and provide interpretive signs and materials for the people who use the area. Look for the black brochure with a moose silhouette, which contains a good map and more information about the area. While Moosalamoo has a lot of raw wilderness, it also has three numbered highways, homes, businesses, a boys' camp, two ski areas, and a lot of other human activity. That's the

When All Else Fails . . .

So suspicious of newly tilled gardens in remote areas were the narcotics agents in Vermont a few years ago, that when Judith first planted her extensive perennial beds, narc squad helicopters repeatedly circled overhead as she worked. "So close I could see the whites of their eyes," Judith recalls. "I got so tired of the pot-cops snooping over my delphiniums that I went out in the driveway and shook my fist at them." Evidently that scared them off, because they haven't been back since.

point of it—a coexistence that is to everyone's benefit, including the moose. For a schedule of free events, which may include guided hikes, garden tours, fishing lessons, or a falcon program, contact the Brandon Chamber of Commerce at their little white house on the green in Brandon; (802) 247–6401.

In the middle of Moosalamoo is one of the state's most remote B&Bs, owned by an engaging British lady who has created a remarkable (and extensive) perennial garden on a hillside with views to the Adirondacks. *Judith's Garden Bed & Breakfast* really is what many B&Bs try (and often fail) to be: a private home where you are a personal guest for a few nights. This doesn't mean that Judith and Dick are in your way, nor that you are expected to spend your evening being sociable if you don't want to. They're very astute at being there when you'd like to chat and not being there when you want to read a good book or be off hiking or skiing on the trails that leave from their backyard. This is the only B&B we've ever stayed in where they invite you to take fresh bread, cheese, fruit—even some muffins from breakfast—for your lunch. They'll help you make the sandwiches and give you bags to keep them in.

"So many people who stay here want to hike during the day," Judith explains, "that it seems silly for them to have to go all the way to Brandon for lunch foods." Like we say, it's just like staying with relatives in the country, except that Judith never asks you what you're going to be when you grow up. Plan to be there to watch the colors of the flowers brighten as the long sunsets' rays bathe them in that color-intensifying light that seems to make each blossom glow from within. Judith's Garden is on Forest Road 32 (the road between Goshen and Ripton), Goshen 05733; (802) 247–4707; e-mail: gardenbb@together.net.

Also in the Moosalamoo wilderness area, surrounded by national forest, is *Blueberry Hill Inn,* a handsome inn on a hilltop at an altitude of 1,600 feet. Some of the rooms are in the nineteenth-century farmhouse, and others in a carefully designed modern addition. This is the place for active outdoor lovers who want a pleasant place to relax at the end of the day.

The inn has beautiful gardens to explore, and 47 miles of trails lead through the nearby wilderness area, some connecting with the Cata-mount and Long Trails. The inn will provide shuttles for guests who want to walk segments of the Long Trail without doubling back. In winter it's a cross-country and snowshoe center, with equipment rentals and well-kept trails. As owner Tony describes it, "with 60 to 70 kilometers of different trail options available from the front door, there's no gerbil-cage skiing here."

After a hike, we especially like to grab a cookie (or two or three) from the jar in the large open kitchen and go out into the solarium to read a good book. The spacious and well-decorated guest rooms have private baths, and in each you will find a jar of the inn's own dreamy skin cream, made right here from extractions of calendula and chamomile petals and other herbs from the inn's gardens. Children are welcome at Blueberry Hill and are sure to enjoy the private garden of the owners' daughter.

Rates include breakfast, and Blueberry Hill Inn also serves dinner, carefully prepared and presented, but you must reserve a space. The chef uses only the freshest local produce in season, much of which comes from their own extensive organic gardens or from neighboring farms. Dinner might begin with a delicate salmon pâté or tangy chilled gazpacho and move on to a perfectly cooked and subtly herbed rack of lamb. Accompaniments are given the same attention as the main event; last time we were there, the couscous was prepared with mascarpone. Blueberries will be on the menu during the season, perhaps in a blueberry Napoleon. The inn has no license, and you are welcome to bring your own wine. Blueberry Hill is just the other side of nowhere, on Forest Road 32, Goshen 05733; (800) 448–0707, (802) 247–6735, E-mail: info@ blueberryinn.com; www.blueberryhillinn.com.

Take Your Pick

*P*laces to pick wild blueberries are usually closely guarded secrets, like the location of the best fishing holes. But in Moosalamoo there's one everybody knows about, since there are signs pointing it out and a parking lot for your car. It's located on Forest Road 27, a short distance to the east of Road 32, which are both north of Route 73, the road over the Brandon Gap. You are welcome to go there with your pail and pick away— or to just wander in for a handful or two eaten on the spot. They ripen in midsummer. You can tell if they are ready by the number of cars in the lot; if it's empty, there are probably no berries.

Route 73 leads east over Brandon Gap or west into the town of Brandon. This attractive town, filled with beautiful old homes, was first chartered in 1761 with the name Neshobe and is the birthplace of Stephen Douglas, Lincoln's adversary, and home to a whole slew of inventors, such as Quimby Backus, who invented one of the first electric heaters, and John Conant, who produced the first iron stoves in the state after bog iron was discovered in 1810.

This is only the beginning of Brandon's long and fascinating history, which includes its claim to a place in the Morgan horse hall of fame, as well as the story of the early industry of Vermont and the Underground Railroad.

Park Street, which was once a parade ground for the militia, is lined with fine Victorian homes, including the rambling *Moffett House Bed & Breakfast,* a relaxed place with a gregarious host. Beautifully decorated rooms range from $80 to $125 in high season and $70 to $110 in the off-season. It's at 60 Park Street, Brandon 05733; (802) 247–3843.

On the same street, in an elegant Arts and Crafts–period mansion, is the *Lilac Inn,* once the home of the Farr family, whose public and private benefactions are still appreciated by the people of Brandon. It was later owned by an architect, who made the house's transition from the home of a wealthy family to an inn so seamless that you wouldn't be surprised to find the formidable Mrs. Farr at the head of the breakfast table. Instead, you'll find breakfast served in a sunny room overlooking the landscaped grounds or outdoors in the summer.

And Take Your Attitude with You!

*W*hile traveling on Cape Breton Island in Nova Scotia a few summers ago, we were eating breakfast at our B&B with a woman who told us she was from Brandon, Vermont. We said how much we've enjoyed going there, and she replied rudely: "That's what's wrong with Brandon: The tourists are ruining it."

Since we'd never noticed that Brandon had very many tourists, we were a bit taken aback by this, but even more astonished when she went on to say that she often worked in the town's visitors center. As we drove away later, we pondered this, thinking of all the friendly and hospitable people we'd met in Brandon—especially in the little white house on the green that serves as the information office. We decided that the other people who worked there had taken up a collection to send her to Canada for a vacation and get her out of town!

—*Barbara Radcliffe Rogers and Stillman Rogers*

The inn is well known for its oak-paneled dining room, where a New American menu displays the skillful use of fresh ingredients. You may find pomegranate-glazed scallops, loin of venison robbed with coriander, or seared rabbit loin with sweet-corn flan. Entree prices range from $17 to $24. Rates for the bright, stylish rooms are from $135 to $210, including breakfast. The Lilac Inn sponsors frequent concerts, both outdoors on the terrace and in the salon, a perfect venue for chamber music. The Inn is at 53 Park Street, Brandon 05733; (802) 247–5463.

In Central Park, on Fridays from mid-June through mid-October, the Brandon Farmer's Market sells local produce, flowers, and herbs, as well as maple syrup, baked goods, jams, and jellies.

East of Brandon is Orwell and Lake Champlain, an area that played a significant role in the American Revolution. On the way you will pass through Sudbury, through which the earliest road passed, built in 1759. Its route is marked by the *Crown Point Military Road Monument,* located a short distance west of Route 30, at the point where it is joined by Route 73 from Brandon. A part of this original road is still passable to the north of the monument, but to the south it is little more than a trail in most places. The road was built to connect Lake Champlain to the Connecticut River. Modern roads have used the original route in many places.

The *Crown Point Road Association* is a group of dedicated enthusiasts whose purpose it is to research, locate, mark, and preserve the first major highway in the state. The road was built in 1759 by British general Jeffrey Amherst to supply his outpost at Crown Point during the wars with French Canada. During the Revolution it was expanded as the need to protect Fort Ticonderoga and Mount Independence became imperative. From spring through fall, the group conducts hikes over the known sections of the road. You are invited to bring lunch (and mosquito repellent). Contact the association c/o James Moore, 51 Eden Street, Proctor, VT 05765; (802) 459–2837.

Mount Independence, east of Orwell, is still in the active process of restoration, its historical significance having been largely ignored until the 1970s. Two hundred years earlier, Mount Independence was an important sister fort to Fort Ticonderoga, across the lake in New York, and the two were connected by a floating bridge. Garrisoned by about 2,500 soldiers, it had extensive earthworks. In July 1777 it was attacked, and the defending Continental troops finally abandoned it, retreating to Hubbardton where they managed to beat off an attacking troop of British soldiers, blunting General Burgoyne's drive to the south. These

Get Those Sheep off Grannie

*T*he town of Orwell maintains two cemeteries, one on Chipman Point overlooking Lake Champlain and the other off Route 73 on the road to Shoreham. The maintenance of these two cemeteries created a bit of a town feud in 1991, when a flock of seventeen sheep was placed in the cemeteries to graze and trim the grass.

Some townspeople thought it was a great idea; the town would save on gasoline and pay. The sheep also ate everything from poison ivy to wild grapevines—things regular lawn mowers usually miss—and their owner, Jean Beck, transported them back and forth between the two cemeteries for one month before protests

began from townspeople who didn't like the idea of sheep manure covering their loved ones' graves.

A group of ten residents volunteered to mow the cemeteries in place of the sheep, but selectboard chairman Ronald Huntley warned that the volunteers would be closely monitored to make sure they were doing their jobs. "If they don't maintain the cemeteries, the sheep go back in," he said.

So when you're in Orwell, stop by to see if the sheep or the human beings won. We're all betting on the sheep, especially since Orwell for many years served as the top sheep-raising town in the Champlain Valley.

two battles were precursors to the crucial Battle of Bennington.

You can learn more about this conflict at the museum and visitor center. There are four trails around the 400-acre site, from ¼ mile to 2½ miles in length, and in winter the trails are available for cross-country skiing. Trail maps with historical notes and descriptions are, or should be, available at the trailhead and, during the season, at the visitors center. The park remains an active archaeological site and has an ongoing program of investigation and restoration. The park is on Catfish Bay Road in Orwell 05760, and can be reached summers at (802) 948–2000. It's open daily from Memorial Day through Columbus Day from 9:30 A.M. to 5:00 P.M.

A great way to see Mount Independence and a lot of Lake Champlain is to take the M/V *Carillon,* which leaves from Teachout's Lakehouse Store and Wharf at Larrabee's Point, to the north in Shoreham. The 60-foot-long knife-bowed cruise boat was built in 1990 especially for this run. It is a replica of the sleek power yachts built for the wealthy from the 1920s through the 1950s, and, as was the custom, there's lots of shiny woodwork. The two-hour cruises leave at 11:00 A.M., 1:00 P.M., and 3:00 P.M. in July and August. If you want to see Mount Independence, take one of the two earlier cruises and get off, spend two hours exploring, and get back onto the next boat to continue the cruise. The boat does a figure eight between Larrabee's Point, Fort Ticonderoga, and Mount Independence. Fares for the two-hour cruise are $8.50 for adults and $4.50 for children three to twelve. Call for reservations and information at (802) 897–5331. Shoreham is on Route 22A; follow Route 74 west to Larrabee's Point.

Rutland and Its Environs

ituated as it is on a bed of marble, and close to the western border of the Vermont-New York line, the city of Rutland has at various times been known as Marble City and Gateway City. Today it is a thriving city that serves as a business and social magnet for the surrounding towns.

It was named for Rutland, Massachusetts; John Murray, of the Massachusetts Rutland, was the first grantee of the town, which was chartered in 1761. The first settler of Rutland was James Mead, of Manchester, Vermont, who came to town in 1770 with his wife and ten children. Mead built a log cabin and soon followed with a gristmill and a sawmill nearby, thereby cementing the active industry of Rutland that continues to this day.

Rutland's downtown has some interesting architecture—an art deco building on West Street just past the court house is not in good repair, but a fine example of an architectural period that's beginning to be more appreciated. Merchant's Row is lined with well-kept commercial buildings, and there is a neighborhood of excellent brick Victorian mansions and churches, along with the library, along Court and Center Streets, up the hill from the business district.

But on West Proctor Road is the city's most unusual building, *Wilson's Castle,* one of the few historic houses/museums open to the public where you can walk on rugs, sit on chairs, feel the texture of the old draperies, and take flash pictures. The admission fee, which includes a tour, is $6.00, but this is as close as you'll probably get to an American royal palace.

The estate consists of 150 acres and sixteen buildings. The castle was built in the mid-1800s, and its thirty-two rooms hold eighty-four stained-glass windows and thirteen fireplaces. The rooms contain everything from a Louis XVI crown jewel case to a Tiffany chandelier. The castle also boasts a library, a music room, a drawing room, an art gallery, and a veranda.

Wilson's Castle is open daily from 9:00 A.M. to 6:00 P.M. from late May

Louis XVI crown jewel case,
Wilson's Castle, Rutland

through mid-October. Follow the signs from Route 3. For more information, write to Wilson's Castle, West Proctor Road, Rutland 05701, or call (802) 773–3284.

Also on the north side of town, on busy Route 7, is *Seward's Family Restaurant,* a local dairy and restaurant with window and table service and a gourmet food shop that sells freshly brewed Green Mountain Coffee in thermoses that keep the coffee fresh and piping hot. Try the hazelnut cream coffee with a dollop of Seward's fresh milk—that is, if the thermos isn't empty.

The dairy is out back behind the restaurant, and you'll find the milk in most local supermarkets and general stores. The restaurant offers food as fresh as the dairy, along with sandwiches and soups, in a comfortable, homey atmosphere.

Seward's is open from 6:30 A.M. to 11:00 P.M. seven days a week in the summertime; it closes at 10:00 P.M. the rest of the year. Seward's Family Restaurant is at 244 North Main Street, Rutland 05701; call (802) 773–2738.

Just west of Rutland and Route 7 is Route 3, known as the Marble Valley Highway. Even if you are not fascinated by geology (as we admit we are), this area is interesting to visit because it is the heart of Vermont's marble industry. Each of the fifty states and some foreign countries have buildings made of Vermont marble. Two of the best known are the U.S. Supreme Court and the Jefferson Memorial, both in Washington, D.C. So versatile is this building stone that the Beinike Rare Book and Manuscript Library at Yale University in New Haven, Connecticut, has even used thin luminescent slabs of this marble as "windows" to let light in.

The *Vermont Marble Company,* headquartered in Proctor, not far from Wilson Castle, explores this stone in the *Vermont Marble Exhibit.* A visit starts with an eleven-minute film about the company

Pittsford was the home of Samuel Hopkins, who received the first patent in the United States, in 1790, signed by George Washington. It was for the making of pearl-ash, and upon this ingredient for soap making was founded Vermont's first main economic base.

and about the immigrant workers that labored here. Displays include a miniature marble chapel with a carved Last Supper and the Hall of Presidents. The latter has bas-relief busts of all U.S. presidents including George W. Bush, a work in progress. Visitors can watch the sculptor-in-residence as he releases a figure from its marble bonds.

The exhibit, displayed in seventeen rooms with a total of 27,000 square feet of space, looks at how marble was formed, explaining the evolution of the earth and the titanic energy of its crust as the plates move, collide, and create new continents. "Raymond" is an actual cast re-creation of the only articulated triceratops ever found. Plan on several hours to explore all the corners of this fascinating place.

Tickets for the exhibit are available at the site for $6.00 adults ($4.00 seniors, $3.00 ages fifteen to eighteen) or in advance at substantial savings: $4.00 adults ($2.75 seniors, $2.50 teens). The exhibit is open mid-May through the end of October, 9:00 A.M. to 5:30 P.M. daily, at 52 Main Street, Proctor 05765; (800) 427–1396, (802) 459–2300; www. vermont-marble.com.

A nice loop drive out of Rutland takes you into countryside far removed from the city's streets. Leave town on Route 4 East, which leads over the mountains toward Pico Peak and Killington. You will come to Mendon, and an unusual monument that thousands of people pass by every day without even knowing it's there. Once you cross the border into Mendon from Rutland on Route 4 East, pull into the parking lot of the Sugar and Spice Restaurant. Park in the far lot and look for the biggest rock in the forest that rises from the lot. Most days there's a tiny American flag flying on top. This is Mendon's *Civil War Horse Monument.* The inscription on the concave section of the rock reads THE GRAVE OF GENERAL EDWARD RIPLEY'S OLD JOHN—GALLANT WAR HORSE OF THE GREAT CIVIL WAR 1861–1865.

Just past this monument, a road goes north to East Pittsford and Chittenden, toward the Chittenden Reservoir. You will pass the *Fox Creek Inn,* a quiet retreat in the woods beside a brook. Rooms vary in size and decor, with stenciled walls, whirlpool tubs, and gas fireplaces. The inn is not opulent but is very nice indeed, and both breakfast and a candlelit dinner are included in the rates. The wine list is astonishing.

Rates are from $190 to $325 per room, rising to $410 in foliage season. Fox Creek Inn is at 49 Chittenden Dam Road, Chittenden 05737; (802) 483–6213 or (800) 707–0017; www.foxcreekinn.com.

Since this road dead-ends at the dam, you need to backtrack to the intersection and continue on to the settlement of Holden, where the road changes direction and follows Furnace Creek back to the south and into Pittsford. Here you should go north (right) on Route 7, but only briefly. The historical society museum in the center of town is open from 9:00 A.M. to 4:00 P.M. on Tuesday from March to December and the same hours on Saturdays in July and August; (802) 483–6623.

Follow signs left to Florence, on Kendall Hill Road, where you will soon see the **Hammond Covered Bridge** on your right. It is one of four in Pittsford, a 139-foot Town lattice style built in 1842. In the infamous freshet of 1927, when much of Vermont was washed away, this bridge ended up in a field about a mile downstream from its abutments. The following winter they hauled it back to its original location, which is where you now see it. A new bridge has made it redundant, but you can still walk through it.

Any of several left turns along here will take you south and back to Rutland. One goes through Proctor, where you can see the marble works, or you can follow signs to Whipple Hollow Road, for a real backroad drive past farms tucked into little hollows, meadows dotted with horses nibbling grass, and dairy farms where herds of Holsteins pasture with a backdrop of valley and mountain scenery.

At Route 4, you can turn west, instead of going back into Rutland, and head for Castleton and Castleton Corners, home of Castleton State College, Vermont's first college and the eighteenth oldest college in the nation, having been chartered in 1787. The **Christine Price Art Gallery** at Castleton State College is located in the foyer of the Fine Arts Center on campus. The display area is huge, and the exhibiting artists range from Castleton students who have created their own masks to community residents who have incorporated the avant-garde into traditional Vermont themes in line drawings and paintings, as well as more traditional Vermont pastoral landscape scenes. A showcase contains works in progress in sketchbooks, and the smell of freshly dried oil paint permeates the room. The gallery also has international art in its permanent collection, from Africa, New Guinea, and India.

The gallery and Fine Arts Center are open from 8:30 A.M. to 4:30 P.M. weekdays. Write to the Christine Price Art Gallery, Castleton Fine Arts Center, Castleton State College, Castleton 05735, or call (802) 468–5611, extension 258.

From Castleton Corners, the unnumbered East Hubbardton Road leads north about 7 miles to **Hubbardton Battlefield**. When American troops had to evacuate Mount Independence and Fort Ticonderoga on July 6, 1777, they withdrew to the east, planning to travel south again to join up with other colonists in Manchester. British advance troops, cock-sure of themselves and holding the ragtag local militia in contempt, caught up with them on July 7. At East Hubbardton the rear guard of the colonial troops turned and stood their ground on a broad hillside, firing from covered positions and showing a determination to stop the British and protect the retreat of the main force. To the chagrin of General Burgoyne, the royal troops were defeated and forced to withdraw back to Mount Independence. This victory saved the colonial army from destruction, freeing them for the Battle of Bennington and the ultimate defeat of the British northern army at Saratoga later that same year.

An interpretive center is open 9:00 A.M. to 4:00 P.M. Wednesday through Sunday Memorial Day through Columbus Day. If it's open when you visit, look at the fiber-optic map of the battle, then go out onto the battlefield to the new walking trail that leads visitors to key points in the battle. Signs tell the importance of each stop along the way. The battlefield itself is open all year. Call (802) 273–2282 for information, or write Division of Historic Preservation, State of Vermont, 135 State Street, Drawer 33, Montpelier 05633-1201; (802) 828–3051.

West of Castleton is Fair Haven, an unusual town with one large brick commercial block facing a broad common, with two fine mansions built of marble. Down the hill behind one of them is **Fair Haven Inn,** where entrees range mostly from $15.00 to $20.00, with early-bird specials at $7.00 to $10.00 Monday through Saturday from 5:00 to 6:00 P.M. The menu is Grecian/Mediterranean, and the restaurant is open daily for lunch and dinner. It is at 5 Adams Street, Fair Haven 05743; (802) 265–4907; www.fairhaveninn.com.

On the southern edge of town, shortly before Route 22A crosses the border into New York, is **Maplewood Inn.** The 1843 house is furnished in antiques and reproductions, as well as the owners' collection of antique farm and household implements. Hot drinks, with a good selection of teas, are available to guests at all times, along with complimentary cordials. Rooms and suites are priced from $89 to $150 all year, with a $20 increase for holidays. The rate includes a hearty breakfast that begins with hot oatmeal. Maplewood Inn, 1108 South Main Street (Route 22A South), Fair Haven 05743; (802) 265–8039 or (800) 253–7729; www.maplewoodinn.com.

South of Fair Haven and Castleton is the beautiful *Lake St. Catherine,* where there is a state park with trails, beaches, and a campground with boat access to the lake. Campsites are spaced well, along the shore and in the woods, some with lean-to shelters. The park is open until Columbus Day weekend, after many other parks have closed. Lake St. Catherine State Park, Poultney 05764; (802) 287–9158 in season, (802) 483–2001 in the winter.

From Poultney, Route 140 meanders its way beside the Poultney River through Middletown Springs (whose entire village center is on the National Register of Historic Places), Tinmouth, and Wallingford to East Wallingford. In this last stretch it forms the border of the Green Mountain National Forest's southern section, passing White Rocks Recreation Area with its many hiking trails. The road is an attractive and interesting way to travel through rural Vermont. At East Walling-ford, you can turn north onto Route 103 to return to the Rutland area or continue through Bowlsville (logically named for an early wooden bowl mill that provided the town's only industry) to Ludlow and Route 100 North or South.

If you choose to travel northwest on Route 103, make a detour in Shrewsbury, following signs up into the scenic hill towns to find *Meadowsweet Herb Farm.* The greenhouse is an overwhelming multitude of scents; a different one attacks you when you take a step in either direction. Kitchen windowsill herbs abound, herb tea plants cover the tables in the woodstove-heated greenhouse, and the back door of the greenhouse is open and looks out onto a pond where a few ducks swim.

Inside the main house is a gift shop offering pottery, potpourris, spices and spice mixes, books, and made-in-Vermont foods. Meadowsweet also sells seeds for spring planting; many of the varieties are antique flowers, such as heliotrope, purple coneflower, and wormwood. Everything is packed and made in-house, from the herbal vinegars and spice blends to the potpourri and spice mixes.

Meadowsweet is open from early May through the end of October, from 9:00 A.M. to 5:00 P.M. daily. If you crave balsam and pine potpourri for Christmas, Meadowsweet runs a mail-order business, whereby you can call up in the dead of winter for a dose of summer. Write Meadowsweet Herb Farm, 729 Mount Holly Road, North Shrewsbury 05738; call (802) 492–3565, or fax the farm at (802) 492–3566.

On the way to Meadowsweet you will pass one of the most comfortable, welcoming and relaxing places that we have found in Vermont: *Maple Crest Farm Bed & Breakfast,* in the tiny town of Shrewsbury. When it was built in 1808 by ancestors of the present owner, one side of the first floor was a coaching tavern and the other a general store and post office. Today these rooms are cozy places to curl up and read a book. Family antiques are used throughout the house, but you shouldn't get the idea that it's at all like a stuffy museum. Its comfy and casual atmosphere is popular with people hiking the nearby Long Trail. Rooms are $55 to $60 with shared or half baths, and two apartments rent at an astonishing $75 per night for two, with $10 per extra person. Two couples on a getaway weekend could have separate bedrooms, a living room, and a full-sized, well-equipped kitchen for $95 a night. Quilting weekends are held at the inn on four weekends during September and October each year. From Cuttingsville, head east from Route 103 toward Shrewsbury on Town Hill Road. The inn is on the right when you get to Lincoln Hill Road, in the center of the old village; 2512 Lincoln Hill Road, Shrewsbury 05738; (802) 492–3367.

At the village of Cuttingsville, near the turn for Meadowsweet, is *Vermont Industries,* where they make hand-forged wrought-iron lighting fixtures and home accessories. The shop seems small when you first enter, but each room leads to another, taking you through a large building where you'll find candleholders, fireplace tools, garden furniture, hooks and racks, hinges, and decorative items. It's open daily from 10:00 A.M. to 5:30 P.M. year-round; Route 103, Cuttingsville 05738; (802) 492–3451 or (800) 639–1715.

MORE PLACES TO STAY IN MIDDLE WEST VERMONT

(ALL AREA CODES 802)

MIDDLETOWN SPRINGS (05757)
Middletown Springs Inn, on the Green, is in a carefully restored Italianate home, serving a fixed menu dinner to overnight guests by prior reservation, which is helpful, since there is no restaurant in town; 235–2198.

For other lodgings in the area, contact Historic Lake Champlain/Middlebury Region Lodging Association, P.O. Box 711, Middlebury 05753; www.vermont-lodging.com.

MORE PLACES TO EAT IN MIDDLE WEST VERMONT

(ALL AREA CODES 802)

MIDDLEBURY (05753)
Storm Cafe, Frog Hollow, serves a great paella, laden with shrimp and mussels. Big portions, little restaurant; 388–1063.

BRISTOL (05443)
Mary's at Baldwin Creek,
Route 116, serves an
innovative menu of dishes
based on fresh local
ingredients; 453–2432.

To Learn More in Middle West Vermont

For more information on Brandon, contact
the Brandon Area Chamber of Commerce,
P.O. Box 267, Brandon 05733;
(802) 247–6401.
The information center is in the tiny white building
opposite the Civil War monument. For information on
the Middlebury area, call the
Chamber of Commerce at
(802) 388–7951;
www.midvermont.com.

Index

INDEX

Historic Sites and Museums

Inns and B&Bs

Restaurants

About the Author

Lisa Shaw is a magazine and book writer and former Vermonter who now lives in Grafton, New Hampshire, with her two cats, Margo and Squiggy. She has written for *Reader's Digest, Woman's Day, American Health, Travel & Leisure, New York* magazine, and many other publications. Her fourteen books include *The Quotable Cat* (Contemporary Books), *Time Off from Work* (Wiley), *Moving to the Country Once and For All* (Country Roads Press), *Latin for Pigs* (NAL/Dutton), and *The Cat on My Shoulder* (Avon).

About the Editors

Barbara and Stillman Rogers are New England natives who write frequently about their home states. They are the authors of *New Hampshire: Off the Beaten Path* (The Globe Pequot Press), *Natural Wonders of Vermont* and *Country Towns of Vermont* (Country Roads/NTC), *Secret Providence and Newport* (ECW Press) and *The Rhode Island Guide* (Fulcrum), as well as guides to far-flung destinations. They write regular travel columns and restaurant reviews, and their work has appeared in *Yankee, Yankee Travel Guide to New England,* and the *Los Angeles Times.* They live on a farm near the Connecticut River, and you can often find them on Saturday mornings at the Brattleboro Farmers Market.